D0560730

THE
CORPORATE
OLIGARCH

David Finn

SIMON AND SCHUSTER · NEW YORK

338.0973
F51c

FIRST PRINTING

SBN 671-20173-5
LIBRARY OF CONGRESS CATALOG CARD NUMBER: 69-14282
DESIGNED BY RICHARD C. KARWOSKI
MANUFACTURED IN THE UNITED STATES OF AMERICA
BY H. WOLFF, NEW YORK

F11

To Kathy, Dena, Peter, and Amy

Contents

THE
CORPORATE
OLIGARCH

1

The
Corporate
Oligarch

THE CORPORATE OLIGARCH IS ONE OF THE RELATIVELY SMALL GROUP of men who preside over the major corporations of our day.

That he is a major figure in the contemporary world few will deny. Contrary to popular belief, however, it is not a simple matter to identify him precisely, to define his powers, to describe his methods or to explain his motives. A massive literature exists on the subject of management, most of it published in the last fifty years. The lives of men at the top of the corporate hierarchy have been treated in novels, motion pictures, biographies and television programs. Yet the subject remains confusing and overburdened with generalizations.

The problem begins with definitions.

Underlying the most widely accepted definition is a belief that "the motive of business is pecuniary gain, the method is essentially purchase and sale. The aim and usual outcome is the accumulation of wealth. Men whose aim is not increase of possession do not go into business . . ." So wrote Thorstein Veblen. This seeking after wealth would make the corporation no more than "a legal device," as A. A. Berle and Gardner Means put it, "through which private business transactions may be carried on."

If this were the whole story, the subject of this book would be the men who have become rich through successful business ventures which are set up as corporations. Many of the top executives of the 1,323,180 corporations in existence in the United States at the beginning of the 1960s would consider this definition of their role correct. But observers of the modern corporation differ. To most of them corporations have become what Reinhold Niebuhr called "quasi sovereignties," what Earl Latham called "a rationalized system for the accumulation, control, and administration of power," what others have called plutocracies or oligarchies.

This suggests that the lives of the men who head corporations have changed in ways that have not been fully acknowledged. How much they have changed is unclear. For instance, it is generally agreed that the older type of businessman was an entrepreneur and that the new type of businessman is a professional manager. But the distinction between the two is not a sharp one. No one man is all entrepreneur, none all professional manager. Every executive of modern corporations is an entrepreneur as well as a manager, since he assumes the risks of his business very much as he would if he owned it. And some of the great fortune makers, or moguls, or robber barons, of yesteryear were conscientious managers as well as entrepreneurs, since they were extremely efficient in the way they conducted their business. The change has only been one of emphasis in this respect. Many contemporary businessmen tend to give a higher priority to running a well-organized company than to making a lot of money. And it is only to dramatize the difference in emphasis that the generalizations "entrepreneur" and "professional manager" have been useful.

The value of the phrase "corporate oligarch" is that it distinguishes a new feature in the life of modern top executives that did not exist among the old captains of industry. That feature could well be the most significant factor in the shaping of future corporate power.

To understand the nature of this new feature it is necessary to review some of the environmental changes that have taken place in the corporate world during the past one hundred years.

First, corporations have gradually become less personal, more institutionalized. The success of the company is considered to be of value to society because the company is a supplier of goods, an employer of people, an instrument of investment, a user of capital —not because it is a means of making men rich. Businessmen who looked at their business as a personal fief were willing to sell their interests and go into some other line of investment if they could make more money that way. Not so the corporate oligarch. He tends to see his responsibilities in terms of the three functions defined by Peter Drucker: the survival of the corporation, the organization of its human resources, and the orderly succession of management.

Second, the political environment of the twentieth century has led to an increased idealization of nonauthoritarian approaches to management. Capitalism is equated with democracy in an era when totalitarianism has been the declared enemy of our society. Corporate oligarchs tend to feel guilty when they run their companies as one-man operations.

Third, there has been a much-discussed separation of ownership from management. This has been a slow process that began in the early days of the corporation. The year the American colonies declared their independence, Adam Smith recognized the independence of management from stockholders in the business structure of his day.

> The trade of a joint stock company [he wrote in 1776] is always managed by a court of directors. This court, indeed, is frequently subject, in many respects, to the control of a general court of proprietors. But the greater part of those proprietors seldom pretend to understand anything of the business of the

13

company, and when the spirit of faction happens not to prevail among them, give themselves no trouble about it, but receive contentedly such half yearly or yearly dividend as the directors think proper to make to them.

In the course of the next two centuries, the proliferation of public corporations gave rise to the practice of trading stockholdings as a means of increasing one's wealth; the way to get rich, therefore, was to become a wise investor or financier. The manager of a large corporate enterprise performed his job as a company employee—highly paid, to be sure, but one who owned a relatively small part of the capital possessed by the corporation.

A little more than one hundred and fifty years after Adam Smith, A. A. Berle and Gardner Means stated that the relative independence of management from ownership had created the "quasi-public corporation." In the early 1930s they analyzed the two hundred largest corporations in the United States and found forty-four per cent of them under management control. They believed the trend would continue and affect nearly all large business enterprises. They were right. Some thirty years later *Fortune* found that the forty-four per cent had risen to seventy per cent.

Fourth, corporations have become larger and more complex, and they have spawned a host of specialists in marketing, research, investment and many other fields which an earlier businessman felt he could handle on his own. The man at the top has become more of a coordinator than a commander.

A significant gauge of this change has been the strange anonymity of chief executive officers in recent years. This is evident in the absence of top executives from encyclopedias which include sketches of painters, writers, clergymen, baseball players and movie stars. It is also evident in the relative indifference of the stock market to the retirement, death or replacement of company presidents of major corporations. Shrewd investors apparently believe that, except in rare instances when particularly colorful personalities are involved, changes at the top have little if any effect on the prospective earnings and growth of the company. The efforts of public-relations specialists to gain visibility for top management, and the thousands of speeches made by, articles written about, honors and awards given to corporate oligarchs have not helped them become more famous. The role of coordinator in a giant enterprise is simply less dynamic, less vital than that of a commander, and no amount of drumbeating can compensate for this difference. The corporate oligarch is not a captain of industry. As James Burnham and John Kenneth Galbraith have each pointed out, much of the power held by the nineteenth-century entrepreneur has passed to the technocracy; the operating managers of the technical processes of production and distribution are more responsible for what a corporation does than the top executives whose job it is to oversee the whole operation.

As a result of these changes in the corporate environment the top executive officers of the modern corporation are no longer the great individualists their predecessors were. "The boss" has been replaced by "top management." The company president is a member of an oligarchy which guides rather than directs the corporation. He is not a baronial lord. He is a servant like other servants of the corporation. His position at the top of the hierarchy does not enable or entitle him to have a markedly greater influence on the behavior of the corporation than other members of top management, such as the vice-president in charge of production or the vice-president in charge of marketing; or, even more significantly, than the engineers in the product development department. This was best stated in a recent study in which Ithiel de Sola Pool observed that no cliché can be heard more often from the head of a good-sized publicly held manufacturing firm than that he is just an employee. "He seldom sees himself as a man of great power," de Sola Pool wrote. "He seldom believes that he can do anything he wants to in the industrial world. Unlike a nineteenth-century robber baron, he sincerely believes that the union leaders and the men in Washington are more powerful than he is."

The organizational outlook of the contemporary chief executive with his nonauthoritarian power provides a sharp contrast to the classical theories of management developed in the early 1900s, when writers like Frederick Winslow Taylor in the United States and Henri Fayol in France began a long struggle to define the types of decisions made at different levels of the corporate hierarchy. As exponents of what became known as scientific management, they saw specialization in the corporation as a function of the natural order, observable both in the animal world and in human societies. The most efficient way to organize this specialization was through what Fayol called the "scalar chain," which is an order of rank ranging from the ultimate authority to the lowest ranks. At the top was a single authority. The top "organ" or "member" (the use of medical terms was inspired by the conviction that this was a scientific theory of management) of the "body corporate" was the shareholders. This collective entity was represented in a single box at the head of the organization chart. Next in line was a box representing the board of directors. A third box represented general management. Here, one felt, is where command (another favorite word, this time borrowed from the military, which also provided a model for this picture of the corporation) began in earnest. "The responsibility of general management is to conduct the enterprise toward its objective by making optimum use of available resources," wrote Fayol, and as far as he was concerned this was a function of supreme authority. All responsibilities for company operations were assigned downward in pyramid fashion from management to workmen.

The changes that have taken place in the corporate environment since those early years have made this basic diagram of command obsolete. The same three boxes representing shareholders, board of directors and management still appear at the top of the organizational charts of most companies, but this traditional pyramid has become an archaic symbol. The current literature of management is filled with references to the top executive function as a "humanist art" aimed at motivating employees to work together "as a team." To reflect this new concept some organiza-

16

tional charts now show top management at the center and other functions radiating out in a complex web of interacting forces. Those who have the clearest view of how top management works have abandoned the effort to make neat-looking charts of organizational responsibilities, with their simplistic definitions of who reports to whom. Freed from this restricting and unrealistic image, the process by which major corporate decisions are made shows the highest-ranked officers of the company as members of an informal group jockeying for status, playing politics, trading favors, forming alliances, promoting pet ideas, modifying proposals put forth by rivals, seeking credit for outstanding performances, avoiding blame for failures, and acting the part of manipulators pulling strings inside and outside the company to further their interests. A telling commentary on this complicated, unchartable interrelationship among men at the top was a *Saturday Review* cartoon which showed an executive seated at a massive desk instructing his secretary to send in a "deal" because "I feel like wheelin'."

The most consistent characteristic of modern corporations is that their approach to authority keeps changing all the time depending on the personalities involved and the circumstances in which they find themselves. There is no standard pattern which can be applied across the board. The supposedly rational approach to decision making, in which data on a wide range of alternatives are collected and analyzed by subordinates to help superiors make a wise final judgment, is rare. There is, rather, a continuous stream of operating problems which have to be dealt with by a constantly shifting power structure. At times major corporate moves are made because a particular executive has an idea which no one else in top management objects to. At other times relatively unimportant moves which the chief executive wants to make are abandoned because someone whose support he values doesn't like them. At still other times an entire top-management group can be thwarted from accomplishing an objective which all agree is important because no one person takes responsibility for seeing that the job gets done. In short, corporate top management does not deserve its reputation for marvelous efficiency and decisiveness. It gets the job done more often by mastering the "science of muddling through," as one observer put it, than by directing an orderly system of administration.

2

Although in every large corporation one man is designated as the "chief executive officer" (he is usually the president or the chairman of the board), it has long been apparent that the label does not properly identify the job. The man who holds this title may or may not be the ultimate authority in the corporate hierarchy; even if he is, it is likely that there are one or two other executives so close to him in the degree of authority they hold that it is inaccurate to consider that one man holds the top administrative position in the company.

This was not so when the captains of industry were in control of American business. Whatever title they may have held individually, there was no question about who was the boss. To identify the leading figures in the corporate world all one had to do was to list the major companies and indicate the one man in each company who held the power. Thus William Miller's study *The Business Elite,* covering the years 1901–1910, was based on a selection of 185 executives who were *either* president *or* board chairmen of their companies. But as the corporate oligarch emerged in the next several decades the picture changed. The leading figures in the corporate world became more difficult to identify. There were still some companies in which only one man held the power, but there were others in which two or three shared the authority of top management. To avoid examining the structure of each company separately, students of management began to use general directories as starting points for their investigations. The study published in 1932 by E. W. Taussig and C. S. Joslyn, entitled *American Business Leaders: A Study in Social Origins and Social*

Stratification, was based on an analysis of about 7,000 business-men listed in *Poor's 1928 Register of Directors.* Then came C. Wright Mills's *The American Business Elite: A Collective Portrait* (1945), based on an analysis of 1,464 eminent American business-men whose biographies appeared in *The Dictionary of American Biography.* In 1953, *Fortune* used a new method of identifying the corporate power group when it published its famous analysis of "the Nine Hundred." This was a round number which was ar-rived at by selecting the three highest-paid executives of each of the 250 largest industrial corporations, plus the twenty-five largest railroads and the twenty-five largest utilities. In 1955, Mabel Newcomer's classic, *The Big Business Executive,* appeared, based on a study of 765 officers of 428 corporations, and in 1964 *Scientific American* updated the Newcomer study by analyzing the backgrounds of approximately 1,000 of the top officers of the 600 largest U.S. nonfinancial corporations then in existence.

All sorts of interesting bits of information were provided by these studies. Newcomer, for instance, found that eighty-three per cent of her group of executives owned one per cent or less of the company's stock. *Scientific American* discovered that thirty-eight per cent of America's big-business executives had technical or engineering backgrounds, also that the proportion of executives with higher education had risen from less than forty per cent in 1900 to more than ninety per cent in 1964. Only 10.5 per cent of the 1964 generation of big-business executives identified them-selves as sons of wealthy families, whereas at the turn of the cen-tury the corresponding figure had been 54.6 per cent. The con-clusion drawn by *Scientific American* was that the business lead-ers of today were becoming increasingly professionalized, con-tradicting the earlier convictions of Taussig and Joslyn, as well as of C. Wright Mills, who believed either that the class of business leaders was characterized by inbreeding or that it was primarily dedicated to the goal of preserving its privileges in the corporate world.

But for the purposes of identifying the corporate oligarch the major significance of these studies is that since the 1930s it has been tacitly assumed that more than one executive was responsible for running a company. *Fortune* picked the three highest-salaried executives in its study. Newcomer picked an average of about 1.8 executives per company. And *Scientific American* selected an average of 1.6 executives per company.

Recently the term "top management" has been understood as a group consisting of as many as a dozen executives. An American Management Association study published in 1958, based on a review of practices in one hundred and forty corporations, indicated that top management should include the chairman of the board, the president, the executive vice-president and all corporate officials and executives who report directly to presidents or executive vice-presidents. This included such officers as treasurer, controller, secretary and vice-presidents in charge of research, marketing, manufacturing and public relations, and occasionally officers in charge of industrial relations, governmental relations and foreign operations. An illusion of well-defined functions was given through detailed listings of job descriptions for each executive, but the reliability of the analysis was brought into question by the admission that the functions had not been easy to identify. "It appears," the report stated, "that it is more difficult to formulate descriptions for top company officials than for middle management, or that many of the responding companies believe the duties of a president, chairman of the board, executive vice-president, or other really top post are perfectly well understood and there is no necessity to write a formal description." It is more likely that the individual executives involved could not satisfy themselves that any description could adequately describe the multitude of activities in which they were somehow involved.

Current management practices tend to limit the size of the top-management group to a smaller number of executives. It was not surprising, for instance, when in the spring of 1968 a story in the New York *Times* reported that Bache and Company had formed a top-management group consisting of four executives. Since Bache did not designate any one of the four as chief executive officer, the implication was that the head of the company was not a single man but what psychologists call a "psyche group." A few months later a similar management structure was announced by the Chase Manhattan Bank, which established "an executive office" with a new chairman, a new president and two new vice chairmen. David Rockefeller, the new chairman, explained that the executive office was formed because the bank had grown to the point that "no one or even two men can adequately handle" all areas of banking. This form of group management, in fact, exists in most corporations regardless of what the titles or job descriptions may imply. Even when there is a strong chief executive officer, a few other individuals (whose titles and jobs may vary) are generally the confidants of the head of the firm, while in companies that stress the importance of delegating responsibilities—particularly among the largest—there is something similar to what the Russians call collective leadership. In some cases the president and the chairman of the board share responsibility in an arrangement especially suited to their personalities; in diversified companies there may be several men with autonomous status functioning as heads of their division but occasionally subordinating their interests to others whose job is to formulate and work toward the goals of the total enterprise. But in every instance one can be sure to find some combination of top-executive relationships which makes it clear that ultimate responsibility is shared by a number of individuals who have learned to collaborate with each other in coordinating the affairs of the corporation.

3

The problems which the top-management psyche must deal with effectively in order to maintain its stability have to do with the interests of major stockholders, members of the board, operational departments, financial resources, customers, labor unions, government and public groups. By making their influence felt in all these areas, a few individuals in key positions leave their imprint on how corporations affect the society in which they function.

It may well be that this cumulative personal impact is the key to what top management actually contributes to the direction of corporate activity. The technocracy may have a greater influence on specific corporate moves, but the character of the company is determined by the personal style of the few men who occupy its top executive positions. It is as difficult to say precisely what this corporate character is as it is to say what individual character is, but there can be little doubt that both have to do with the distinctive quality manifested in daily behavior.

This book proposes to study the character of the men who head the major corporations of the United States. Because we are interested in the effect of their character on society rather than of how they do their job, it is not necessary here to try to resolve the question of whether there are two or four or twelve men in each company who deserve to be considered top management. We wish only to make it clear that there is an elite group which affects, if not determines, the values embodied in the life of the modern corporation, and that members of this group tend to share common motivations and subscribe to common beliefs. Since they are the highest-paid and highest-ranked members of the hierarchy which presides over the corporate wealth of the country, we describe them as corporate oligarchs.

The word "oligarch" has an emotional tone which helps to establish the direction of this book. My intention is not to give a dispassionate sociological report on the lives and work patterns of the men who head large companies. It is to present an historical study of the changing motivations of these men and an analysis of their current search for new directions. Much of what I write is based on personal observations which have convinced me that the men in the psyche group referred to as top management are facing a conflict which they don't know how to resolve. They believe that officially their job is to govern the moneymaking process of our society, but at least some of them have begun to wonder whether they should not be applying their talents for leadership toward more worthy goals.

In the Platonic and Aristotelian definitions, an oligarch is one of a small, privileged (monied) group which governs a community. Plato said an oligarchy was "a government resting on a valuation of property, in which the rich have power and the poor man is deprived of it." Many believe that the modern corporation is not an oligarchy, because the men in top management positions do not own the property belonging to the corporation; this property is owned by a large number of stockholders. Since a company is owned by *the public*, which *elects* its directors, who in turn elect officers, it is held that the corporation is a republic rather than an oligarchy. Supposedly it is the poor who have taken power away from the rich in the democratization of the corporation which has occurred in the twentieth century. However, a more realistic view of how power is exercised in the corporation indicates that top executives are not responsible to stockholders in the way that elected officers are responsible to their constituencies. The manager maintains his position on the basis of how well he handles his relationship with other key men at the top who share his interest in increasing the power of the corporation.

The problems with which this book deals arise from a struggle between this interest in corporate power and those forces in society which are directed toward noneconomic goals. The conflict is no longer a simple one between the rich and the poor; it may and often does take place in the mind of one individual who is both a stockholder anxious to increase the value of his property and a citizen who wants corporate power to be used responsibly in relation to community interests. The head of the corporation is theoretically entitled to use the cumulative economic power of the stockholder *as if it were his own*. He is supposed to be as devoted to the cause of increasing corporate property as he would be if he were its sole proprietor and *his only aim were to become as rich as possible*. At the same time, since he does not as a rule accumulate a giant fortune for himself, he identifies with the aspirations of ordinary citizens who do not want the interests of economic power to dominate their lives.

He is an oligarch because he is one of a group of men who represent the monied interests of the owners of corporate property (stockholders). But he is also an oligarch because his responsibilities have taken on the character of government and the decisions made by him and those around him have a substantial effect on the lives of the general populace. By calling him an oligarch I am in effect asking whether his rule as a representative of property ownership can be consistent with the public welfare.

I think of the corporate oligarch as any executive who plays a senior role in corporate management and who considers himself one of those who are broadly responsible for the welfare of the company. I believe the personal goals of such an executive and his judgment as to what is and what is not good for society and his ideas of what he would like his company to accomplish during his tenure, leave a marked imprint on the value structure of contemporary society. I do not exaggerate his importance in the business community or in public life. He is not a tycoon or a baron or even a capitalist in the traditional sense. He is a manager in a capitalist-democratic world.

The central question I attempt to answer in this book is whether the man I call the corporate oligarch has the necessary personal motivation and the conceptual frame of reference to enable him to identify the interests of the corporation with the interests of the community, and to relate his task as a corporate manager to his aspirations as a human being.

2

His
Genesis

WHEN WAS THE CORPORATE OLIGARCH BORN INTO AMERICAN LIFE
and how did he develop into the man he is today?

Like most lineages in America, that of the corporate oligarch
can be traced back to Europe, where corporations came into existence early in the sixteenth century. Initially the men who formed
corporations were individual businessmen who conducted their
own private business while sharing a common governing body.
Later there were joint ventures, with several shareholders investing in and profiting from a single business operation. The date of
1555 is given as the year the first joint-stock company was incorporated. The English law of corporations was clarified in 1612 by
Lord Justice Coke, whose decision in the case of Sutton Hospital
stated that corporations were a form of special privilege established by the Crown. In the next several decades the new corporate form spread all over Europe, and eventually it provided the

framework in which were conducted the overseas trading adventures which led to the colonization of the New World.

It seems appropriate in retrospect that the oldest ancestors of the corporate oligarch were the first men of vision to see the possibilities of developing the American continent, and that they, more than any others, gave our country its first start. Yet commercial corporations were markedly unsuccessful in the New World for the first two hundred years after colonization, a fact which makes the record of the nineteenth and twentieth centuries all the more remarkable.

In sixteenth-century Europe, the first corporations were formed by men of wealth who were looking for new ways to invest their money and build their fortunes. Some of these had become rich as a result of pirating adventures and were looking for legitimate enterprises to provide a relatively secure method of achieving long-term gains. The corporation was a form of doing business through which they could pool their resources. Overseas trade was the new business enterprise that offered great expectations of high return on investment. Special privileges given to the corporation by governments were supposedly justified by the high risks involved in such ventures.

The rights obtained by incorporators from governments in those early years would make a present-day corporate oligarch's mouth water. In 1578, in one of the first of the new enterprises, the famous half brothers Sir Walter Raleigh and Sir Humphrey Gilbert secured a patent from Queen Elizabeth which granted them and their heirs the right to "have, hold, occupy and enjoy" forever any lands they discovered which were "not actually possessed of any Christian prince, nor inhabited by Christian people." Furthermore, these hopeful entrepreneurs were given the power "to correct, punish, pardon, govern and rule . . . in causes capital, or criminal, or civil . . . all such our subjects as shall from time to time adventure themselves in the said journeys or voyages or that shall at any time hereafter inhabit any such lands."

Unfortunately, despite these sweeping privileges the two brothers did not succeed in their enterprise. Gilbert died at sea. Raleigh continued the corporation with John White and twelve others; they managed to found the city of Raleigh in Virginia in 1587, but it did not last long. The project suffered from a shortage of funds. Raleigh personally gave the corporation a generous sum of one hundred pounds, but this was not enough to fill the colonists' needs. By 1591 the colony was abandoned.

Companies which were formed to do business elsewhere in the world did better. The Muscovy Company, created in 1554, achieved a monopoly of all trade with Russia; the Levant Company, formed in 1581, had a similar monopoly of trade with the Near East. The East India Company, formed in 1599, gained a monopoly of trade with the Orient.

Although Sir Walter Raleigh used the corporate form for his Virginia colony, it was primarily his own money that was invested. A more ambitious enterprise, this time with funds from over one hundred stockholders, made another attempt in 1606, when the London Company was chartered for the adventure to the New World. This time the colony, also in Virginia, caught fast and held. Those pioneering investors did not make money for themselves. In the years that followed their company's first voyage, £200,000 of the investors' funds were used up without producing any return at all. Nevertheless, these unsuccessful enterprises managed to establish the foundation for a new land in which more money would one day be made than anywhere else in the world.

The colonists were employees rather than stockholders of the London Company, and they endured many hardships because of their failure to produce profits. "So lamentable was our scarcity," wrote the Virginia Council in a report to England in 1624, "that we were constrained to eat dogs, cats, rats, snakes, toadstools, horse-hides and what not. One man, out of the misery he endured, killing his wife, powdered her up to eat her, for which he was burned. Many besides fed on the corpses of dead men . . ."

The managers of these early colonizing corporations, who were as different from their twentieth-century successors as the pithecanthropus was from modern man, were neither efficient nor good businessmen. The failure to achieve profits soon caused their downfall as leaders of the colonies, and local governments—in some cases also corporate in form—took their place. In this transition, power shifted to a new class of property owners that quickly developed, not infrequently from stockholders of the original corporations now acting as individuals rather than as members of a joint enterprise. Most of the colonizing corporations were dissolved within a decade or two after they were chartered.

Among the corporations which met this fate were the Dutch West India Company, which colonized what later became New York; the Massachusetts Bay Company, which in 1629 saved our Plymouth Rock ancestors from extinction; and the Swedish West India Company, which founded Delaware. Perhaps the most successful of these, the Dutch West India Company, which had an authorized capital of six million florins (£500,000), made money by robbing Spanish treasure fleets rather than trading in the New World; but, even then, the company's monopoly was abolished in 1638, seventeen years after it had been granted.

2

When this first burst of commercial corporate activity in America exhausted itself, there followed a long period of about one hundred and fifty years in which property owners built the same kind of feudalism as that with which their fathers had been familiar. The territory that had been initially colonized with hopeful business expectations provided instead an opportunity to create a new landed aristocracy, repeating the pattern of European countries where earlier generations had carved up the countryside in family estates. The method was simple. In the Dutch territory around New York, for instance, any man who came to the colony with fifty souls became a patroon, which meant that he was given sixteen miles of land along the shore or on one side of a navigable river.

While feudalism was being exported to America, the Industrial Revolution was taking place in Europe, particularly in England. It was to the advantage of these entrepreneurs to stifle any possible competition from the colonies. As late as 1766, the Board of Trade in England asked the American governors to give their assurance that industry was not developing in the New World. Proudly the Governor of Massachusetts reported that there had been only four manufacturing enterprises in his colony (linen, bottles, stockings and potash) and *all* had failed because of mismanagement or bad luck. He was sure that this had "put a stop to efforts of this kind, and . . . disposed people to pursue those businesses which are sure to make them better returns than manufactures are like to do." Other governors gave equally heartening reports to the protectionist guardians of English industrial interests.

The repression of manufacturing in America did not mean that no business initiative was evident in the New World. The feudal landholders had developed thriving real-estate operations by the middle of the eighteenth century. Fishing and shipping had also become prosperous enterprises, and by 1765 there were four thousand seamen and twenty-eight thousand tons of shipping in the employ of American entrepreneurs. Men were beginning to get rich in the span of a single generation.

One of the earliest self-made businessmen in America was Israel Thorndike, who became wealthy after a lifetime devoted to real-estate, fishing and shipping enterprises. A more dramatic example was Robert Morris, called by some the first American captain of industry, who became rich trading in tobacco and other commodities while, at the same time, helping finance the Revolution (a conflict of interest severely criticized by Thomas Paine). He made some bad deals after the war and ended up in debtors' prison—one of the first examples of an American businessman who both made and lost his fortune in a single generation.

The charter for the first commercial corporation with a base in America was given in 1682 to William Penn. It was called "the Free Society of Traders in Pennsylvania." Nonresident stockholders were restricted to one vote, unless they owned a thousand acres of inhabited land in the provinces; all others had two votes per share. The corporation engaged in all sorts of enterprises, including a tannery, a gristmill and a glass house (factory), but it suffered so heavily from mismanagement that it was forced to stop operations five years after it began.

The next corporation to come into being in the New World was chartered in Connecticut in 1732 "for the promotion and carrying on Trade and Commerce to Great Britain and His Majesties Islands and Plantations in America, and other of His Majesties Dominions, and for encouraging the Fishery, &c." Officially it was called "the New London Society United for Trade and Commerce." It lasted only a year.

The third corporation was the Union Wharf Company of New Haven, chartered in 1760. It never paid any dividends to owners, but it did make enough money to build extensions of the wharf out of profits.

After the war, Alexander Hamilton made a concentrated effort to stimulate the development of American industry. In 1790 he issued a "Report on Manufacturers" which was designed to help transform the country from an agricultural into an industrial nation. Men with business acumen had had a chance to pool their resources during the war, with good results. There was a relatively large labor force available from soldiers returning to civilian life. A certain speculative fever was in the air. The time seemed right for industry to come into its own.

Hamilton's brainchild (at least, he is given credit for it) was the Society for Establishment of Useful Manufactures, chartered 1791 by the New Jersey legislature. This was to be a sort of national manufacturing enterprise, and the city of Paterson was founded as the seat of the ambitious plan. Unfortunately, Hamilton's efforts were premature and the company was forced by reverses to discontinue operations a few years later. The corporate shell was never actually dissolved, and it still exists today as the owner of some property in New Jersey, a living testimony to the spirit of the early days of the Republic when many Europeans were quoted as saying, "The Americans are fond of engaging in splendid projects which they could never accomplish."

The failure of the Society for Establishing Useful Manufactures did not affect what Hamilton had correctly recognized to be the country's great capacity for corporate development. By 1800 there were three hundred American corporations in existence (as compared to only twenty in Britain). Most of them were in such fields as real estate, banking, insurance, public utilities and transportation, but in 1805 the first major industrial corporation in the modern sense, and the first to be successful on a large scale, was formed. It was called the Boston Manufacturing Company, and the list of stockholders reads like a Who's Who of the old trading aristocracy (the dividend books are preserved at the Harvard Business School). Beginning with a plant in Waltham to make cotton fabric, the company started a boom which by 1834 led to the opening of nineteen other mills, four thousand looms and one hundred thousand spindles, in a community that Anthony Trollope called "the realization of a commercial utopia."

The success of the Boston Manufacturing Company was soon matched by other enterprises. In 1831 Tocqueville was in America observing that "the whole population are engaged in productive industry." He believed that as yet there were no fabulously rich men in America. (He was wrong; that same year Stephen Girard died, leaving behind a fortune of about $6,500,000, and John Jacob Astor, in partnership with his son, had an income of $500,-000 on a capital investment of $1 million.) But Tocqueville was able to see in 1831 that a new type of industrial aristocracy had emerged, headed by men who, unlike the leaders of other societies, "rarely [settle] in the midst of the manufacturing population which [they] direct; the object is not to govern that population but to use it."

3

In his *History of the Great American Fortunes,* Gustavus Myers observed that "the Revolution was a movement by the native property interests to work out their destiny without interference by the trading classes of Great Britain." Once this was accomplished, the propertied classes ran the country to suit their tastes. "At first the landholders and the shipping merchants were the dictators of laws, then from these two classes and from the tradesmen sprang a third class, the bankers. Factory owners followed. And finally, out of all this a new class of great power developed, the railroad owning class. This class ruled from 1845 to 1890, only to be superseded when the industrial trusts became even mightier, and a time came when one trust alone, the Standard Oil Company, seemed supreme."

American business fortunes, Myers was convinced, were made through bribery, chicanery, ruthlessness and an extraordinarily successful form of political manipulation. He believed that nineteenth-century America was ruled by economic dictators. Each had his own domain, in which he ruled supreme. Where power overlapped there was war. When the tyrants chose to work together they formed alliances. The corporation was not just an institution in American life, it was the structure in which the most powerful men of an era ruled and expanded their empires.

According to Myers, the first of the great exploiters was John Jacob Astor, who in 1808 was able to supply the entire $500,000 with which the newly incorporated American Fur Company was capitalized. With his entrance on the stage, Myers believed, small corporations were eclipsed by the tyrannical rule of a giant business enterprise in which the corporate form was simply a device by which a rich man could assign part of his wealth to speculative enterprises without risking his entire fortune. Wielding the kind of power which Queen Elizabeth had offered to Sir Walter Raleigh but which he had been unable to use, Astor's expeditions to the West created a *de facto* government of those regions and developed a complete monopoly of fur trading with the Indians. As in the case of the colonizing corporations, the men who supplied the basic labor suffered great hardships; but this time it was not lack of funds that caused the trouble, it was raw, capitalist exploitation. To get merchandise at the lowest possible price, for instance, Astor's men set up an organized system for getting the Indians drunk in order to take advantage of them. So bad did conditions become that in 1825 a report was received by the Secretary of War that "the neighborhood of trading houses where whiskey is sold presents a disgusting scene of drunkenness, debauchery and misery . . . the road [is] strewn with the bodies of men, women and children in the last stages of brutal intoxication."

Unlike the original corporate investors of the early 1600s, Astor was able to expand his power and wealth at a dizzying rate. By 1844 he had acquired a personal capital of $20 million in a country where the total industrial capitalization was a little over $300 million.

Myers' book was a masterpiece. Its sensational thesis that the American public was cheated by its great industrialists from Astor to Rockefeller was so well-documented that it affected the twentieth-century businessman's view of his past heritage. Believing this to be a distortion of history, the editors of *Fortune* published in 1951 a series of articles about the same period which were more consistent with their sympathies. Written by John Chamberlain, the articles were later published as a book under the title *The Enterprising Americans.* Chamberlain's text describes early-American businessmen in mid-twentieth-century terms. In effect, he wrote what a contemporary *Fortune* might have published about the men Myers found to be so vicious. Nineteenth-century businessmen were inventors and pioneers; they overcame enormous obstacles and built undreamed-of industries in a wild and

33

primitive land. It was a century of miracles which came about because the government was attuned to the virtues of an expanding industrialism.

Readers of business news as reported in the 1960s would find the Chamberlain account of nineteenth-century entrepreneurs far more convincing than Myers'. Chamberlain's report did not indulge in the excessive flattery of early-nineteenth-century apologias, such as the volume by Walter R. Houghton entitled *Kings of Fortune, or The Triumphs and Achievements of Noble, Self-Made Men Whose Brilliant Careers Have Honored Their Calling, Blessed Humanity, and Whose Lives Furnish Instruction for the Young, Entertainment for the Old and Valuable Lessons for the Aspirants of Fortune.* Chamberlain's purpose was to defend the industrial leaders of an explosive era against the charge of venality.

Nineteenth-century business leaders, he believed, were very much like their twentieth-century counterparts—executives who rose to the challenge of extending the frontiers of progress.

The attractive picture painted by Chamberlain, however, was an expression of the business community's faith in the virtue of economic growth. This history of the enterprising Americans applauded the accomplishments of men who changed the face of the nation. But Myers' history of the great American fortunes was still valid in its condemnation of their method. Their crimes against humanity, to use a modern phrase, were no less evil simply because we enjoy the goods and services they made possible. They were men who knew how to employ brains and labor to make money, and because they were such effective businessmen they built America into a first-rate industrial country; but they created a strain of ruthless self-interest in the economic nerve center of our society which unfortunately still tingles the spine of the present-day oligarch.

4

The important economic needs which the industrial tycoons of the nineteenth century filled were characteristic of a rapidly growing country.

Populations were expanding, towns were springing up all over a vast countryside, so lumber was needed, and it was abundantly available from Maine to Washington. Lumber companies proliferated from 1830 onward as the industry grew and spread over the Midwest and then to the Pacific Coast. This trend gave rise to other businesses which served the lumber companies, to supply liquor, for instance, to the outlying towns, and axes by the tens of thousands to cut down the white pine.

The mass production of weapons for warfare spurred another crop of early entrepreneurs. The first important market was created by the Mexican War of 1846–48, when the inventor Colt got his big opportunity. His early production was subcontracted to Eli Whitney, Jr., but five years later he built in Hartford the greatest mid-nineteenth-century arms plant in America. The Du Ponts enjoyed their first major expansion during the Civil War, when they made four million pounds of powder for the government.

Supplying the farmers who plowed the lands cleared by the lumberjacks led to another industry. Cyrus McCormick invented his reaper in 1830 and started his factory in Chicago shortly afterward, developing a new sales approach to fit the uncertainties of the agricultural market (time payments which could be extended if there was a bad harvest). Peter Drucker recently called McCormick (the founder of what today is International Harvester) the first to develop modern marketing methods.

Consumer products found their way into the marketplace as large urban centers grew. Benjamin Babbitt built a giant soap factory in New York City in the middle of the nineteenth century. Charles Goodyear secured a patent in 1841 for the invention of "gum elastic" (vulcanized rubber), and Akron, Ohio, became a factory town to produce it. About the same time a string of telegraph companies were formed to capitalize on Samuel F. B. Morse's invention. The sewing machine, invented in the mid-1840s, led to the development of still another industry.

The big corporate story of the mid-nineteenth century, however, was written in transportation, an inevitable consequence of the geography of the new nation. First there were highways, then toll bridges and canals, and finally railroads.

Railroading was the industry in which the great fortunes were made. Cornelius Vanderbilt, the old Commodore, died in 1877 with $105 million, and his income had been as high as $6 million in a single year. It started in a big way with Peter Cooper's first locomotive, Tom Thumb. The subsequent race to build railroads produced the biggest boom in American industry, and a few depressions as well. First there was a tremendous spurt in iron manufacturing. (One of the largest pre–Civil War integrated companies was Great Western Iron, which was started in 1839 with an investment of $500,000.) Then there were the railmakers, who built their first factories in the town of Trenton, New Jersey. Finally, with the Union Pacific Railroad Act of 1862, by which the government gave cash for mileage of track built as well as large grants of land along the right of way, the big arena of industrial expansion became the railroading companies themselves. The giant was Vanderbilt, but not far behind were Daniel Drew, James Fisk, Jr., Jay Gould, Collis P. Huntington, Leland Stanford, Mark Hopkins, Charles Crocker.

It was the railroad revolution that was primarily responsible for the development of the corporation into a sprawling structure that would one day be ruled by an oligarchy. Earlier companies tended to be dominated by one man, or one family, or a small group of men who considered themselves partners (even though technically they may have been stockholders). With the railroads there came into being corporations with broad stock ownerships. The dominant figures were those who mastered the technique of manipulating the stock market to gain control of enormous capital resources. They also devised extraordinary schemes to increase their fortunes, like the famous Crédit Mobilier of America, which enriched its already wealthy stockholders by charging the Union Pacific nearly $94 million to build a railroad that cost only $50 million.

These financial promoters for the most part did not divorce themselves from management. They didn't hire professional executives to run their companies, as a twentieth-century financier would do. The railroad tycoons kept the reins of their companies in their own hands. The major innovation introduced by them was the technique of using large sums of other people's money—as well as government funds—to increase their own power and their own wealth.

The railroad boom lasted until the panic of 1873, when Jay Cooke overreached himself in the marketing of securities for the Northern Pacific Railroad, and his bank, which had pledged to support the security, failed, setting off a string of other failures. The tapering off was gradual; twenty-five years later, sixty per cent of the securities listed on the New York Stock Exchange were still in railroads.

5

It was not until after the collapse of the speculators and their watered railroad stocks that had made millions for them overnight that the corporation began to assume its modern character. Top executives with authority began to appear at the helm of large companies. Financial control often remained with powerful financial interests, but the corporation had become more than simply a tool of their ambitions. Public companies acquired lives of their own, and managers were charged with the responsibility of running them effectively. The day of the corporate oligarch was approaching.

One of the earliest to assume responsibility for the health of the corporation as distinguished from personal enrichment was J. Edgar Thomson, who managed the affairs of the Pennsylvania Railroad in the 1860s and 1870s. Although he by no means disdained making personal investments to increase his wealth, he conducted himself like a twentieth-century top executive, rigorously maintaining that his primary interest was the economic soundness of his company. Another was Chauncey M. Depew, a lawyer-adviser to Vanderbilt who became president of the New York Central lines and whose corporate idealism received such a good press that he became a U.S. Senator in 1905 and was once boomed for President of the United States.

However, the major stimulus to the emergence of the corporate oligarch came not from these respectable executives, but from the greatest economic master in American history, John D. Rockefeller. Although the popular press of his day never gave him credit for it—so busy were his critics denouncing him for the methods he used in building his vast empire—he pointed the way to the collective leadership of the industrial community. It was this vision which led Rockefeller to expand the Standard Oil Company of Ohio, which he had formed with five partners (including his brother William) in 1870, into a giant trust that encompassed virtually every oil-refining operation in the country and most subsidiary production facilities, like cooperage plants, pipelines, and oil cars operated by railroads. He hated what he called the "idiotic, senseless, destruction" and "wasteful condition" of competition. He considered total integration as the most reasonable approach to efficiency in the industry. To accomplish this, he explained that "every refinery in the country was invited to become a member of the Standard Oil Company . . . The Standard . . . turned to them with confidence and said: 'We will take your burdens, we will utilize your ability, we will give you representation; we will all unite together and build a substantial structure on the basis of cooperation . . .'"

The desire to create this unity was, of course, motivated to a large extent by the ambition to amass personal wealth. He succeeded so well in this that he was viewed as a conqueror who would stop at nothing to satisfy his greed. Rockefeller seemed to move across the oil industry like a reincarnation of Alexander the Great. He surrounded his enemies, baited them into ingenious traps, tricked them into complacency and struck swiftly when least expected. In the best miltary tradition he believed there was no substitute for victory. To give one example, in 1875 the Titusville operators hung him in effigy and twenty-five independents joined forces to merge themselves into the Acme Oil Company, which they thought would protect them against his advances. Having sworn to resist Rockefeller to the death, they discovered to their dismay that while they were working to consolidate their forces their savior, the Acme Oil Company, secretly had become a subsidiary of the Standard Oil Company!

Yet what Rockefeller was most interested in was to find a way to pool the talents and resources of men who ran a great many small companies which had common interests. He didn't want to displace entrepreneurs; hc wanted to bring them together in a consortium which could accomplish far greater works than any individual businessman could do on his own. The trust, which was the device by which he hoped to form this oligarchy, was the brainchild of a young lawyer, Samuel Dodd, who worked for Rockefeller (of whom he had once been an outspoken critic). Dodd's belief was that if trustees could be appointed for property held for children, trustees could also be appointed for property held for companies. To create the pattern, participating companies turned over their stock certificates and voting rights to trustees and received in turn trust certificates entitling them pro rata to dividends on general earnings. The trust committee made all major policy decisions for the companies, but operational management was delegated to executives of the individual corporations.

The public outcry against the practices of Rockefeller and other trust builders who followed in his footsteps led to an historic confrontation between government and business. The Sherman Antitrust Act was passed in 1890 after a mighty battle, but it took another twenty-one years for the government to win the war. (It was the Supreme Court decision of 1911 that broke up the Standard Oil Company.) In the meanwhile, at least seven other mighty trusts continued to thrive, with capitalizations from $145 million on up. One of them, the Consolidated Tobacco Company, had one hundred and fifty plants and a capitalization of $502 million.

In retrospect, it would seem that Rockefeller was not wrong in his dream that men who presided over the destinies of many different companies could work effectively together toward goals which they shared in common. This is what takes place today in every trade association which aims to further the interests of a particular industry. He failed to see, however, that the form he used to create the unified command gave too much power to too few men. What today operates as a genuine oligarchy, with a substantial number of top executives in American industry exerting collective leadership of the business world, was in Rockefeller's time a highly centralized form of power in which the trusts and the practice of interlocking directorates placed control of American industry in the hands of a tight little group. Indeed, it was said that seven men controlled the economic affairs of the nation: J. Pierpont Morgan, John D. Rockefeller, Andrew Carnegie, Edward H. Harriman, James Stillman, George F. Baker, William Rockefeller and H. H. Rogers.

As a result of this concentration of power the coalition of corporate resources accelerated the accumulation of the industrialists' wealth. William H. Vanderbilt, son of the old Commodore, doubled his father's fortune in seven years after his father's death. With $194 million to his name in 1883, he was the richest man in the world; his only competitor was the Duke of Westminster in England, who was said to be worth $200 million but whose wealth was mostly in land and houses with only a two per cent yield ($4 million a year), while Vanderbilt's fortune produced more than a five per cent return ($10 million a year). Twenty-one years later, Rockefeller had built the biggest fortune of all, with an income estimated by the New York *Commercial* at $72 million a year.

The tide of the future, however, was making its appearance in the rapid proliferation of new corporations. This suggested that corporate life would in the long run be marked by organizational diversity rather than monolithic unity. Firms of all types increased twice as fast as the population from 1860 to 1890. By 1880 there were 750,000 business firms; by 1890 there were 1,100,000. A good portion of these were small proprietary firms, but a growing number of incorporated enterprises were also coming into being. By 1900, two thirds of the manufactured products of the country were produced by corporations.

Added to this was the growing influence of banking interests, which made the business community aware of the difference between investment and management. The giant in the banking business was J. P. Morgan; when he died in 1913 his firm held seventy-two directorships representing investment interests in forty-seven corporations. He had made it clear that the best security a large investor could obtain was to make sure that the board of directors employed competent executives to run the company.

Morgan's pivotal deal was the one he made in 1901 with Andrew Carnegie. The undisputed master of the steel industry, Carnegie had built and run his corporate empire in as thoroughly individualistic, colorful and ruthless a manner as any of the other tycoons in the latter decades of the nineteenth century. He had known little about the steel business itself, but he had known how to buy brains that did. He had suggested for his own epitaph "Here lies the man who knew how to get around him men who were cleverer than himself," a note of humility which no doubt raised the eyebrows of many top executives who found him a difficult boss to work for. One of the great nineteenth-century fortune makers, he had owned approximately fifty-nine per cent of his corporation's stock, which at the turn of the century was netting him $20 million a year. Then along came Morgan to buy him out and pass on his reign to a new type of corporate personality, Judge Elbert H. Gary. A combination of steel trusts had already been started under Gary's leadership. Carnegie had been the big fish to hook, and it had taken the great Morgan's ingenuity—and cash—to work out the deal. The amount of money required to buy Carnegie out was fantastic—$492 million in bonds and stocks of the new company called United States Steel Corporation. Approximately three hundred participants were needed to make up the syndicate that floated the issue, including several other banks and underwriters (the company was capitalized at $1.5 billion). And the complex transfer of power from Carnegie to Morgan to Gary gave birth to the modern corporation with a managing oligarchy relatively separated from investor-owners.

So monumental was the deal that put U. S. Steel together that Morgan was looked upon as the new ruler of American industry. President Arthur Twining Hadley of Yale warned that there might be "an emperor in Washington within twenty-five years." A comic character of the time impersonated Morgan saying, "James, call up the Czar an' th' Pope an' th' Sultan an' th' Impror Willum, and tell them we won't need their services afther nex' week." Others referred to him as Jupiter and Perpontifex Maximus. He was, however, more of an impresario, a financial promoter, than an emperor. The estate of $78 million he left on his death was far smaller than Carnegie's. U. S. Steel was not Morgan's private fief; it was a new type of corporation. The emperor never arrived in Washington; instead the deals made by Morgan created the framework in which, several generations later, the corporate oligarch became the key figure in the economic life of the nation.

6

Like the four-minute mile, once the billion-dollar mark in corporate capitalization had been cracked other records followed shortly after. The giant corporations which emerged in the first decades of the twentieth century included A. T. & T., which, under the careful guidance of its first president, Theodore N. Vail, managed to steer a course that kept it from being nationalized;

General Electric, which had been formed in 1892 with a merger arranged by Morgan; and Westinghouse. Ford and General Motors got off to their amazing and unprecedented growth, the latter becoming the model, under the leadership of Alfred P. Sloan, of modern management in big corporations. (During its first eleven years, General Motors, which was formed in 1910, was subjected to the shifting of control from William C. Durant, the founder, to James J. Storrow, representing bank interests, to Pierre Du Pont, back to Durant, then back to Du Pont, who supported the appointment of Sloan. In the following thirty-four years Sloan earned the title of "architect of the modern corporation" by designing and running the best-managed corporate complex in history.)

Now fully matured, the corporate oligarch played a major role in the historic developments of the twentieth century. The Great Depression, when corporate profits plummeted from a high of plus $8.2 billion in 1929 to minus $3.4 billion in 1932, demonstrated that the oligarch's performance was crucial to the welfare of the nation. World War II made it clear that his performance was crucial to the security of the nation. In the postwar years, with industrial growth achieving a spectacular record and with corporate influence making itself felt in every phase of private and communal life, it became clear that his performance was crucial to the character of the nation.

The American businessman was no longer a king of fortune, a robber baron, a mogul. He was a member of an executive elite that managed the economic system. The new era was acclaimed in a *Fortune* advertisement published in the early 1950s under the headline "The Tycoon Is Dead." He was no longer a diamond in the rough as were the seven men who were said to control American industry in 1900, none of whom had been a college graduate. The percentage of all the top executives of major corporations with college degrees rose from 28.3 per cent in 1900 to 74.3 per cent in 1964. He no longer had a free hand in the way he ran his company. He had to deal with countervailing powers of labor unions, which had grown enormously since the turn of the century; of public opinion, which had become increasingly visible through the expansion of mass-communications media; and of government, which considered the regulation of industry one of its primary concerns. He was no longer a secret-deal maker. Since the passage of the Securities and the Securities Exchange Acts of 1933–34, full and accurate disclosure of all corporate activities was mandatory.

Today the corporate oligarch has become the head of an enormous institution, perhaps the central institution in American life. He is a public personality who wants to be respected for doing an important job. He believes he has an essential purpose to fulfill and a reliable way of measuring his achievements. He thinks that he represents the highest ideals of our society—efficiency, invention, employment of capital, job opportunities, an increasing standard of living and democracy. He is convinced that those who question his usefulness to society or his ethics are misjudging the positive role which the modern corporation plays in the shaping of the American character.

3

His
Legal
Responsibilities

IN A CONSTITUTIONAL GOVERNMENT, ELECTED OFFICIALS ARE accountable to their constituents for carrying out policies in their interest. Such accountability does not exist for the corporate oligarch. There are laws prescribing practices and procedures and setting certain broad limits on corporate actions, but the major policy decisions which the oligarch makes within those laws are for the most part discretionary. A politician must compete periodically with an opponent for public support. The oligarch is usually unopposed when he seeks stockholder support for major corporate moves; only in a small percentage of the cases is there a public battle in which conflicting views are put to the test. And even these battles are waged more like a party caucus in which large power blocs decide the issue than like a public election in which the vote of each citizen counts.

This absence of accountability is not fully understood by the oligarch. He thinks that he is paying as much attention to his stockholders' interests as any elected official does to his votes. His appointment by a board of directors elected by stockholders is his idea of a legitimate democratic process. He believes that the price of his stock on the market reflects to some degree his stockholders' confidence—or lack of confidence—in his management, and that this is an effective way for them to make their sentiments felt about his policies. He is also subjected regularly to differing opinions from stockholders, through letters, personal interviews, speeches at annual stockholders' meetings, and he knows that he must treat each complaint with care and respect. He recognizes that every time some criticism of his company appears in the press it will be read by his stockholders and may provide ammunition for future attacks on his management. And he is constantly on the alert for threats from other company managements or financial interests who may try to wrest control from him by quietly acquiring large blocks of stock. His position, therefore, does not seem at all secure. He is convinced that anyone who talks about his tyrannical control over the corporation simply does not know the facts.

The conviction is reinforced by the amount of legal activity which is involved in practically every major move he makes. Lawyers are consulted regularly on matters concerning stockholders, employees, suppliers, customers, banks, government agencies; and their judgment is so important that every major instrument in these areas of corporate activity bears their imprint. Indeed, the presence of lawyers in top-management circles is so widely felt that a mystique has grown up around them which gives them an air of omniscience. Their advice is sought on a whole range of matters that have nothing to do with the law, and when the oligarch follows their advice, which he most often does, he believes that his policies have been sanctioned by qualified guardians of the democratic process.

All this, however, is an illusion. The threats to the corporate oligarch's power come essentially from other centers of power, not from the people. He maintains his position on the board of directors by controlling the nomination of directors; the board in turn maintains its position through control of major blocks of stock; stock market prices reflect the opinions and strategies of professionals on Wall Street, not those of the individual stockholders; and the lawyer's activities are so extensive (and his fees so high) because of the tremendous amount of regulatory legislation that has been passed in recent years, and also because the strategic skills developed by his legal training make him an often masterful adviser on all kinds of corporate maneuvers, but not because his credentials are so authoritative.

To be sure, the sense of propriety associated with the practice of law does introduce a sense of responsibility in the oligarch's mind as he consults his lawyers, but this is hardly a substitute for true accountability. Indeed, sound legal counsel may well be in conflict with what many would consider the public responsibilities of management. "Do what the law requires" can have as its companion injunction "Do not do what the law does not require," and this can be taken to mean that the oligarch should be careful not to go overboard in the information he gives to the public about his future plans or in the degree to which he gets involved in community affairs. Both of these can get him into unnecessary trouble. A conservative lawyer prefers secrecy to exposure, timidity to courage, and profit to public service. It is because of these tendencies that lawyers are not generally considered the best advisers to management on matters of public relations, and the fact that their advice is heeded so frequently is not an insignificant factor in the poor record of so many major corporations in responding to public criticism.

2

The freedom from accountability enjoyed by the corporate oligarch is the product of a long evolutionary process. Contrary to the popular impression that business has changed over the years from what was once an almost lawless institution to one that is being increasingly brought into line with democratic processes, the degree of accountability on the part of management has actually been declining.

In sixteenth- and seventeenth-century England, when it was first stated that men did not have the inherent right to create corporations, special privileges were granted by the Crown through "letters of patent" or charters in exchange for certain clearly stated obligations. "None but the King alone can create or make a corporation," was the famous ruling of Justice Coke, and it meant that each corporation had to be erected by an act of government or it would not stand up as a legal entity. The government granted such privileges only when it was convinced that some good would thereby accrue to the whole country. What that good was can be seen from some of the documents of the time.

When Sir Walter Raleigh organized his first commercial corporation to colonize the New World—a corporation which was to be operated at a profit—his lawyer, Richard Hakluyt, presented to Queen Elizabeth a discourse setting forth the purposes of the expedition. The first purpose was "the glory of God by planting of religion among those infidels." Then there was "the possibility of enlarging the dominions of the Queen's Most Excellent Majesty." Next came "an ample vent in time to come of the woolen cloths of England, especially those of the coarsest sorts, to the maintenance of our poor, that else starve or become burdensome to the realm." There were many more purposes listed to prove how productive this enterprise would be for the country. Significantly, Hakluyt didn't mention a return on investments as a purpose of the enterprise. This self-interest was apparently not a consideration which would justify the privileges given in a corporate charter.

Few will deny that the privileges granted early corporations were excessive, particularly when they were tools of the wealthy aristocracy, not of the common man. But at least a mechanism existed to deny requests for a charter or to revoke a grant if the government decided that its interests were not being served. This was true also when the corporate form was used for enterprises which had no commercial purpose at all. It was a legal entity which was entitled to own property and conduct specified activities for the community. Thus towns were incorporated to create a legal basis for public property owned by all the residents of the neighborhood as distinguished from private property which an individual resident owned by himself. Universities, churches, charities and houses of correction were incorporated for the same purpose. Even those corporations which were organized for profit operated in areas which are today recognized as functions of government. By far the largest number of such corporations built and operated highways, inland waterways, toll bridges and turnpikes. There were also water-supply and fire companies. The only corporations which operated in fields that are now considered part of the private sector were those in banking and insurance, plus a tiny number in mining, agriculture, land and manufacturing, all of which had a clear-cut public purpose.

The same requirement to perform a public good was made when the first major manufacturing corporation, the Society for the Establishment of Useful Manufactures, was organized in the United States. Its prospectus began with the following declaration of public benefits:

> The establishment of manufactures in the United States when maturely considered, will be found to be of the highest importance to their prosperity. It seems an almost self evident proposition that communities which can most completely supply their own wants are in a state of the highest political perfection. And both Theory and Experience conspire to prove that a nation . . . cannot possess much active wealth but as a result of extensive manufactures.

The democratic spirit of the new Constitution prompted some observers to attack the corporation as a vehicle which could be used by the rich to exploit the poor. In public debate at the time, many critics insisted that corporations only pretended public good as their purpose and were in reality profit-seeking ventures. An anonymous critic who called himself "Anti-Monopolist" wrote:

> The present prevailing propensity for corporations and exclusive privileges is a system of politics well calculated to aggrandize and increase the influence of the few at the expense of the many. Wealthy speculators of all denominations are incorporated and vested with exclusive privileges, partial laws are made in their favor, the benefit of which others do not enjoy; and they are exempted from the common burthens imposed on the rest of society. This propensity for corporations is very dangerous to the liberties of a people . . .

Under the influence of Hamilton (who is thought to have drafted the bill which was submitted to the New Jersey state legislature for the granting of the society's charter), the first industrial corporation in the United States was clearly dedicated to public purposes rather than private profit, and commercial benefits were strictly limited to what was considered a fair return on investments. The privileges to be given by the state were extensive. The charter made "all artificers or manufacturers in the immediate Service of the said Society [corporation] free from Poll and Capitation Taxes and Taxes on their respective Faculties or Occupations . . . and other taxes specified . . . and exempt from Military duty except invasion or imminent danger . . ." But to insure that the public would receive something in return, it was provided in the charter that in case the net profits from canals (to be built by the company to transport merchandise) in any three-year period exceeded fifteen per cent on cost, the excess was to be paid to the New Jersey state legislature "to be applied in their Discretion to the Encouragement of Literature, Arts and Sciences within this State." And the state legislature actually bought $10,000 worth of company stock.

The clearly defined connection between corporate and public interests was the basis on which the government created the "immortal but fictitious person" to have a more favored position in society than mortal and real persons. In giving it life, the state was assuming almost supernatural powers. The corporation was to be as real as a human being, with a name of its own, a face (its common seal), the right to own property, and the right to have privileges under the law, including the right to sue and be sued as a legal entity. The corporation was not simply a collective entity made up of the people who owned its shares; it was a new person which could receive investments from its stockholders and pay dividends, but which had a life of its own. Through perpetual succession it could go on forever, while its members changed. But the purpose of this enviable existence was to benefit the society which gave it life. Any rewards which private investors could gain in the process were incidental.

The purpose of each corporation was spelled out in its letter of patent. It was made clear that it was only because this purpose was related to some vital public good that the corporation was given privileges which would not have been given to any natural-born individual. These privileges varied according to the purpose of the corporation, but they might include the acquisition of land at no cost, freedom from taxes, monopolistic rights for trade and traffic, the right in certain circumstances not to pay its debts, and freedom from military service.

With such privileges, it is not surprising that men who wanted to pool their resources to accomplish ambitious economic tasks would prefer to do so in a corporate framework rather than as self-employed entrepreneurs. Often it would have been impossible for them to have even considered such enterprises under any other circumstances. The corporation thus helped to accelerate the economic development of the nation; without it the unprecedented advances made by the effective organization of capital and labor in the last two centuries would not have been possible. Those who managed the corporation, however, knew that unless the welfare of the community spelled out in the corporate charter was served its charter could be revoked.

3

Community welfare was not the only obligation which the corporation had to fulfill in its early days. The original charters were considered contracts between three parties: the state, the combined associates considered as a single entity, and the individuals who were associated as stockholders. In making the contract, the government sought to protect the interests of the general public, corporate creditors and corporate stockholders.

The general public would be served by the careful limitation of the scope of the business to a purpose that would benefit all. This limitation also protected the community against the assumption of too much power by one corporate group.

The shareholders were protected by the stipulation that their money was not to be used for any other than the stated purpose of the corporation. Their financial interests were protected in the charter by a rigid capital structure which meant that the entire system of preferred and common stock had to be laid out in the beginning and that the stock could not be diluted. No change in the nature of the enterprise or capital structure could be made without the *unanimous* approval of the stockholders.

The creditors were protected by the requirement that a certain number of shares had to be paid for before business operations began, and by the provision that dividends were to be paid only out of surplus profits. Thus capital was preserved as something of a guarantee of prompt payment of corporate debts.

It was always understood that a corporation had an obligation to produce a return on investment for the shareholders, but what was a fair return was never made clear. Furthermore, it was up to management and the board of directors to decide how profits should be returned to stockholders; the decision to reinvest the profits for expanding the business or for some special enterprise consistent with the corporation's charter was considered a valid method of fulfilling the contract.

The obligation to make money for stockholders which today has become paramount in the mind of the corporate oligarch was not then the primary objective. An increase in stockholder equity was incidental to the purpose of the corporation. The only specific financial obligations on the part of management were those of propriety. The managers were not allowed to make money for themselves at the expense of stockholders. If one man became rich through the success of his corporation it was only because he owned most of the stock and received his proportionate share of the returns. This was the meaning of the common-law assumption that management was to act as trustee for the shareholders. This meant only that a manager had to be guided by three rules of conduct: (1) a decent amount of time had to be devoted to the affairs of the business; (2) fidelity had to be shown to the interest of the corporation; and (3) at least reasonable business prudence had to be exercised. The most important of these was the second, and it is still a major rule in corporate conduct, continuously upheld by the courts, that the controlling group of a corporation may not use its power for private advantage. Thus, a manager could not sell his own property to the corporation at an inflated price. Nor could he use his inside information to buy shares of the corporation, thereby putting him at an advantage over other stockholders.

It was not until the middle of the nineteenth century that a profit-making commitment to stockholders was formulated as the major corporate goal. In the process, what was once management's obligation to contribute to the public good became a matter of personal taste.

4

The basis for this transformation was a change in the method of granting charters for corporations. In the sixteenth century, charters were granted exclusively and directly by the Crown. Then as the colonies developed it was assumed that this power was delegated from the Crown to governors and assemblies. The procedure was for a legislature to pass an act for each corporation, for the governor to approve it, and then as a formality for this to be approved by the Crown. To establish their legality, acts of incorporation often began with a tribute to the Crown "praying his most sacred Majesty that it may be enacted." After the Revolution, the right to grant corporate charters was retained by the states, since there appeared to be no reason to transfer it to the federal government.

The prodecure remained the same until 1811, when the legislature of New York State passed the first general act of incorporation; and in 1837 a broader statute was passed by Connecticut which became the basis for similar acts passed subsequently by all other states of the Union. These new acts meant that it was no longer necessary to write a special bill in connection with each corporate charter. What was described as "any lawful business" could be incorporated by simply filing a document with a state official, usually the secretary of state, and he would accept such a document so long as it complied with the laws of the state.

The passage of general acts of incorporation brought to an end the practice of conducting public debates as to whether a particular corporate charter was in the interests of the general community. The change in procedure made it possible for corporations to be formed for any purpose the incorporators wanted at the time of incorporation or at any time thereafter. Since the legislatures relinquished their powers to approve each individual charter, the public had no way of being informed about the intentions of the corporation, and no way of protecting its own interests. The practice of posting notices in newspapers about proposed charters was eliminated; no effort was made to examine the public consequences of a new corporate enterprise; there was not even a public record made of the contents of the charter. Attorneys merely drafted a certificate according to a standard form, had it notarized, and then filed it with the office of the secretary of state in the state of incorporation, where, for all practical purposes, it was buried.

Curiously, the certificate of incorporation retained its traditional pattern, and lawyers continued to go through the motions of describing the business in which the corporation was supposed to engage even though this was of no legal consequence. It has remained a practice to this day for attorneys and the incorporating group to take considerable pains in drafting this section so that it will have some resemblance to what the corporation is being set up to do. But this serves a communications function more than a legal one, for it tells the stockholders and other interested persons what type of business activity the founder-managers plan to engage in, without preventing management from changing its mind later on. To assure this latter freedom the lawyers see to it that the language gives the corporation freedom to engage in the broadest possible range of activity should management wish to change the character of the business.

Thus, for instance, the General Motors certificate of incorporation which was filed in the state of Delaware on October 13, 1916, listed nine purposes for the corporation. The first was to "manufacture, buy, sell and deal in automobiles, trucks, cars, boats, flying machines and other vehicles, their parts and accessories, and kindred articles, and generally to conduct an automobile business in all its branches." The other purposes had to do with purchasing leases, mortgages, trademarks, patents, buying and selling stock, acquiring businesses, borrowing money. But so that none of these should be considered limitations, the charter also listed as one of its powers to "engage in any other manufacturing or mercantile business of any kind or character whatsoever, and to that end to acquire, hold, own and dispose of any and all property, assets, stocks, bonds, and rights of any and every kind." And lest there still be any doubt, the final purpose was:

To carry on any business whatsoever which the Corporation may deem proper or convenient in connection with any of the foregoing purposes or otherwise, or which may be calculated, directly or indirectly, to promote the interests of the Corporation or to enhance the value of its property; to conduct its business in this State, in other States, in the District of Columbia, in the Territories and Colonies of the United States, and in foreign countries; and to hold, purchase, mortgage and convey real and personal property, either in or out of the State of Delaware, and to have and to exercise all the powers conferred by the laws of Delaware upon corporations formed under the act pursuant to and under which this Corporation is formed.

The significance of this new type of charter, insofar as it affected the attitude of the men who controlled the destiny of corporations in the nineteenth century, and eventually of the corporate oligarch as he emerged in the twentieth century, is that public benefit was at best considered discretionary. Citizens no longer had any right to judge the activity of any particular corporation; it was free to engage in any kind of business activity it wanted. The only criterion which remained as a measure of the manager's performance, and this was a criterion of his own choosing, was how much money he made for his stockholders.

True, a whole series of other laws then came into being regulating the performance of industry as a whole. Berle and Means compared studies of the legal development of corporations in fifteen states and found the material voluminous enough to fill six hundred pages of text. As a result there is today a legal aspect to almost every corporate move management wants to make. Indeed, the 1964 *Scientific American* study showed that since the turn of the century approximately ten per cent of the top executives of major corporations have been lawyers.

But these laws are primarily concerned with the regulation of business practices to protect the public from specific forms of exploitation rather than to establish a method by which management would be held generally accountable for its policies. These have increasingly had an effect on the procedures employed by corporations without creating a basis on which the performance of management can be judged. Regulatory legislation states what corporations may not do; it does not specify the positive acts which corporations must perform in order to satisfy public responsibilities. And, by omitting such specifications, the law leaves the oligarch free to set his own standards in this respect.

With the abandonment of the old charter procedures, regulatory legislation became increasingly extensive. Commissions set up by the states have regulated banking since 1838, railroads since 1844, insurance companies since 1854, public utilities since 1907. The enactment of state laws requiring safe and sanitary conditions of employment dates back to 1877, laws forbidding the misrepresentation of securities to 1911, laws insuring workers against industrial accidents also to 1911. The Sherman Antitrust Act was enacted under Benjamin Harrison in 1890, the Pure Food and Drug Law under Theodore Roosevelt in 1906, the Clayton Antitrust Act under Wilson in 1914 and the Federal Trade Commission Act the same year. A host of new regulatory agencies were set up under Franklin D. Roosevelt in the early days of the New Deal. Under Dwight D. Eisenhower, federal control was extended to the labeling of furs, textiles and hazardous substances, to the sale of flammable fabrics and to the pricing of natural gas at the wellhead.

So widespread has regulation of American business activity become that George Champion, chairman of the Chase Manhattan Bank, said recently, "It used to be fashionable to talk about the triad of banking, insurance and public utilities as 'regulated industries,' meaning industries requiring government permission before they could undertake certain activities. Today that term is redundant. If anyone can find such a thing now as an 'unregulated industry' he can sell it at a profit to the Smithsonian!"

There is no doubt that at least in some instances the extent of government regulation is so great that the capacity of a corporation to make a profit is seriously jeopardized. Thus ocean shipping lines are so burdened by controls and regulations that a government subsidy is required to save the companies from operating at a loss. An analysis of this issue by the Transportation Center of Northwestern University indicated that policies imposed by trade-union and government regulations are more responsible than any other factor for the way the shipping business is conducted.

All these restrictions and controls have been made on the basis of a tacit assumption that the purpose of business is to make a profit. What Alexander Hamilton deemphasized in his state-sponsored attempt to promote new industries and utilities for the country has now become the stated purpose of engaging in any business enterprise. Because investors who think they can make more money by selling stock in one company and buying stock in another are free to do so, the corporate oligarch believes that by expanding the company's profit-making potential he is living up to his primary legal responsibilities.

5

What the oligarch tends to describe as a "legal obligation" to produce profits for his stockholders appears to be, however, no more than a practical strategy by which new sources of capital can be attracted to increase the scope of his operation. With the elimination of specific responsibilities from his charter, he is no longer bound by legal obligations to make a specified contribution of any sort to any public group, including stockholders. Regulatory legislation has not replaced the public purposes of early corporate charters. It has protected the public against abuses without providing the basis for any specific, legally binding corporate contribution to the stockholders or the public.

Even if a return on investment were the legal requirement for corporations there is no way it could be enforced. The development of the proxy as a means of representing stockholder votes means that management cannot realistically be held accountable for such a performance. The right to remove directors at will has been taken away from shareholders, and even the right to board representation for holders of large blocks of stock is limited. The right to issue stock without the right to vote, the advent of nonpar stock and warrants and of noncumulative preferred and participating preferred stock—these and other developments have created a complex network of stockholder relationships which help to free management's hand even further to engage in a wide variety of corporate maneuvers which happen for one reason or another to serve its interests.

Since a return on investment is no more obligatory on the part of the oligarch, nor more enforceable by stockholders, than any other purpose, the function of management can best be understood as a struggle for power in a giant, nonconstitutional enterprise. The dangers of this condition were highlighted in a conference sponsored by the Center for the Study of Democratic Institutions in 1959. Scott Buchanan suggested that the problem of excessive concentration of power could be solved only by giving the corporation a constitution and a rule of law within its own body, or by changing the federal constitution or the state constitutions to provide greater control over corporations. A. A. Berle, Jr., pointed out that the corporation as presently constituted is prohibited from stealing from its stockholders, exploiting its customers, exploiting its labor, discriminating in buying and selling, creating a monopoly, contributing excessively to political campaigns; but as to its form of government, Berle said, "The traditional democratic process that we know about in politics does not work very well within a corporation for practical purposes, so there are oligarchies." He believed that since a corporation has the power to affect a great many lives, "it should be subject to the same restraints under the federal Constitution that apply to an agency of the federal or state government." In another context, Earl Latham suggested that the "crude corporate power" which makes a corporation a "satrapy" instead of a "commonwealth" should be curbed through a variety of techniques including a revision of laws of incorporation, which would require that charters be written by public agencies rather than by the managers themselves, and that these agencies be empowered to restrict corporate operations within clearly defined purposes.

It is difficult for the corporate oligarch to recognize himself as a satrap, so embroiled is he in negotiation with agencies and organized groups which also have great influence on corporate policies. He does not realize that the array of competing forces with which he has to deal are manifestations of the looseness of the corporate structure and commitment. The fact is, however, that so long as this commitment is not precisely defined he has enormous latitude in choosing the goals toward which he directs the resources of the corporation.

The variations in what are grandiosely called corporate philosophies by heads of large companies show how extensive is the freedom of the oligarch to decide how he wants to manage his company. He may be concerned with community activities at the expense of corporate profits or vice versa. He may provide many employee benefits or none. He may attempt to raid other companies or fight to maintain his company's freedom from raids by others. He may ignore sales and devote himself to increasing profits, or ignore profits in the interests of building sales. He may be interested in "glamour" products or in "staple" products. He may devote considerable funds to research and development or concentrate exclusively on existing business. He is free to spend extraordinary sums of money on advertising, public relations or plant architecture if he chooses to. He may, if he wishes, spend personal time on public affairs or serve on a large number of corporate and community boards and act as an adviser to many government projects. Or he may do just the opposite: spend practically no money on promotion, avoid the public spotlight completely for himself and his company. There are no binding rules which guide him to make these decisions, no criteria on the basis of which the validity of his policies can be objectively proven. So long as he can make a reasonably good case to his directors and stockholders that his policies are for "the good of the company" (a criterion which is sufficiently vague to justify almost anything a powerful chief executive thinks is proper) he is on safe ground.

This point interested a group of students at the University of Chicago Law School with whom I once held a discussion about the motives of top corporate executives. We were talking about executives who sought to gain prestige in the community by engaging in activities that would gain public recognition. I was convinced that top executives tend to rationalize those ambitions in terms of eventual economic benefits to the corporation just to keep their consciences clear. They try to give legitimacy to their participation in public affairs by claiming that this will help build customer loyalty, enhance stockholder equity, prevent government legislation and build a positive image for their company, and they are delighted when public-relations advisers assure them that this is so. Public-relations advisers obligingly give this assurance not because they have any proof to support the thesis but because they know management wants an excuse to spend time on community work, and they believe part of their job is to encourage management to do what it considers worthwhile. I thought public-relations specialists—myself included—should try to stop playing this game and persuade management that it has a right to do good things because they are good to do, and not because they may provide some ulterior benefit to the company. If a top executive wants to play a role in public life, he shouldn't try to dream up any excuses; he should frankly state his belief that heading a great corporation involves other considerations than making money for stockholders. He should insist that contributing to public welfare, whether or not it adds to corporate profits, is a legitimate aspiration for a large-scale organization that utilizes such important economic and social resources of the community.

The students wondered about the legality of such a position. Corporate management is not permitted, they contended, to spend company funds on activities which will not contribute to profit. If funds were used for purposes which could not be rationalized in terms of company benefits there would be stockholder suits. Management, they said, is simply a caretaker of stockholders' funds and as such is responsible for conducting business affairs for the sole purpose of producing a maximum return on investment.

I found their comments unsettling, for, although they expressed a narrow academic point of view, they reflected the attitudes so often taken by corporate lawyers. As Eugene V. Rostow once put it, "The law books have always said that the board of directors owes a single-minded duty of unswerving loyalty to the stockholders and only to the stockholders." I realized for the first time that this point of view was to blame for the fiction which haunts public-relations specialists, that the major purpose of community activities is to improve the corporate image.

As I shall explain later, no one really knows what a corporate image is. If the corporate image is seriously considered to be the only legal basis for management's concern about the welfare of society, the structure is very shaky indeed. Corporate images have no more substance than shadows on the wall; the more one tries to illuminate them the more difficult it is to see them. Fully lit they vanish altogether. The real issue is whether the oligarch will choose timidity or leadership as his basic management policy. Only if he is willing to risk corporate security in the interests of public good will he be taken seriously as a man dedicated to the good of humanity, and this is the important decision he has to make.

It is therefore not true that the oligarch has a single-minded duty to adopt policies which are aimed exclusively at producing a return on investment for stockholders. If he acts as if he has such a duty it is only because this is part of the folklore of the corporate world. But a courageous corporate manager is entitled to try to persuade his stockholders that under his leadership they too must assume certain responsibilities for the betterment of society. As

Theodore Sorenson pointed out in a recent article in *The Saturday Review*, the Federal Banking Act, the Internal Revenue Act and most new corporate charters provide management with a legal basis for assuming such leadership. In business it is only safer, not better—and certainly not more legally correct—to concentrate on making money and to ignore the broader needs of mankind.

The degree of latitude within which the corporate oligarch is legally permitted to formulate his policies is illustrated to some extent by the operations of the so-called conglomerate corporations. Some use this approach to corporate expansion as a vehicle "for building the fortunes of the old industrial entrepreneur wearing a new hat," to quote Ralph E. Ablon, president and chairman of the Ogden Corporation. He was not an admirer of this approach; his interest in building a diversified company was to extend the scope of an effective system of management rather than to amass a giant personal fortune. Others, like Litton Industries, seem intrigued with the idea of using their management and financial resources to solve important economic and social problems of the world. Still others, like the major automobile companies, prefer to keep their diversified interests restricted to fewer industries, building a sense of pride in the company's product.

All take pains to describe their policies as profit-oriented because management is interested primarily in protecting itself, and a good profit record will help keep management in power. But it is obvious that corporations can take vastly different shapes and still be made to fit this same description. The oligarch has a pragmatic need to cater to many interests in order to maintain control, but his accountability is very flexible indeed. He must live by rules set by government agencies, labor unions and the courts, but there is no legal requirement which specifies the return of investment he owes his stockholders, the rate of growth his company must maintain, the nature of the contribution it should make to society or even the type of business it should be in. Thus, whatever style the corporate oligarch employs, and whatever the character of the corporation he heads may be, his legal responsibilities do not define his goals. Under present laws the essential question is not what the corporation was created to do, but what the oligarch wants to accomplish and is capable of achieving with the corporation he heads.

4

His Personal Wealth

As the man who heads the system by which the majority of his fellow citizens make a living and through which a good portion of them invest their savings, the corporate oligarch naturally tends to feel that one of his most important personal goals is to make a handsome living for himself.

To the outside world his monumental earnings make him the latest example of a long succession of wealth seekers who had what Robert L. Heilbroner has called "the acquisitive itch." If he is not the wealthiest man in history, he is nevertheless a multimillionaire, he draws the highest salary in the country, and he has at his disposal the greatest economic resources the world has ever known.

One cannot help taking his measure, therefore, against the background of other wealthy men in the past who embellished their lives with whatever money could buy—even if it was to show the world that they had achieved that degree of success in

65

which money no longer counted, or they no longer counted their money. Homer wrote of kings whose palaces were so vast that visitors "opened their eyes in wonder" at surroundings which seemed "lit by something of the sun's splendor or the moon's." Nero's famous palace was so large, according to Roman commentators, that it had a complete lake inside it with tilled fields, vineyards, pastures, woods and wild animals decorating its shores. The ninth-century caliphs of Bagdad built palaces laid with twenty-two thousand carpets, hung with thirty-eight thousand tapestries, equipped with nine thousand horses, camels and mules and trees fashioned of silver and gold and adorned with mechanical birds. The famed Taj Mahal was built in India as a tomb for a shah's wife at a cost of $230 million.

In eighteenth-century France this same enjoyment of expensive luxuries found expression in fabulous dinners consisting of as many as one hundred and sixty courses and served in special rooms, constructed at least on one occasion by two thousand men working for five days. It caused the mistress of Samuel Bernard, the richest man of his time, to eat a bill worth 500,000 francs as a feat of extravagance. It prompted the American rich of the 1890s to arrange dinners that were eaten on horseback, to smoke cigarettes that were wrapped in hundred-dollar bills, to entertain monkeys as guests at fantastic parties, to serve pearls in oysters at elegant meals, to set diamonds in teeth, to have pet dogs driven in chauffeured cars for airings in the park.

Despite the obvious relationship between the corporate oligarch and the rich men of other eras, he doesn't believe that his interest in making money is the same as that of Homeric kings, Roman emperors, Indian shahs, French aristocrats and American socialites of the Gilded Age. No matter how much money he makes, he feels that he is still primarily a working man. He identifies with those nineteenth-century captains of industry who considered the making of money, rather than its spending, the great virtue. His heroes are the fabled businessmen who worked themselves up from poverty to found the great industrial empires of

an earlier era—men like Collis P. Huntington, who began life as a
farmboy; E. H. Harriman, who began as an office boy; John D.
Rockefeller, who began as a bookkeeper; Andrew Carnegie, who
began as a factory hand. When these men became rich they lived
well; but their luxury was taken as the reward of industry. The
enterprises they created were more valued and respected than the
trappings of wealth.

2

To be sure, becoming rich has been considered the natural goal
of the American industrialist since the early days of the Republic.
He has taken for granted that the desire to acquire wealth is the
most reasonable of human aspirations. When Stephen Girard died
in 1831, his career was memorialized in a pamphlet which stated:
"Whatever relates to the acquisition of wealth . . . must be considered of the utmost importance to mankind, as it implies the
practice of all the virtues that make men happy, and countries
prosperous. The history of wealth is, in other words, the history of
virtue." When Jay Cooke, one of the first to build a post–Civil
War fortune, was a young man he wrote, "I shall be rich, [and
shall live] in palaces and castles which kings might own." When
many of his fellow tycoons became rich, that is precisely how they
lived. Charles Crocker's house on San Francisco's Nob Hill was
said to have cost $1,250,000 and featured a seventy-six-foot obser-
vation tower to give him a proper view of the harbor. Potter
Palmer built a similar castle on Lake Shore Drive in Chicago. William H. Vanderbilt built a massive home in New York that was
supposed to have cost $3 million. These successful industrialists
were delighted to live according to their station and to demonstrate to their fellow men that money was something worth working for.

Some tycoons had reservations about spending the money they
had worked so hard to acquire. Girard, who was an early apostle
of wealth, lived like a miser. Carnegie, who headed one of the

largest corporations in the country, once wrote that it is a "duty of the men of wealth to set an example of modest, unostentatious living, shunning display or extravagance." Rockefeller subscribed to the same theory, and none of his three homes, according to Ida M. Tarbell, could "claim to rank among the notable houses of the country." These more prudent nineteenth-century captains of industry made a point of appreciating the value of a dollar. Although they often felt justified in enjoying luxury as the reward of their financial genius, they were wary of being extravagant in their personal spending when it had been an ability to buy cheap and sell dear that had produced their fortunes in the first place.

Yet there was a degree of self-deception among these supposedly modest millionaires which showed that they enjoyed the pleasures and privileges of wealth more than they cared to admit. Some undoubtedly valued their humble beginnings and didn't want to betray their ancestry, but when they saw something they liked they bought it no matter how much it cost. Although Carnegie was opposed to extravagance, he didn't hesitate to buy a thirty-two-thousand-acre estate in Scotland. When Henry Ford started to build a home in Dearborn, Michigan, in 1913, he insisted that the house would not be anything like the pretentious structures that many rich men in Detroit were then erecting. He didn't want an army of servants. "I still like boiled potatoes with the skins on," he said, "and I do not want a man standing back of my chair at the table laughing up his sleeve at me while I'm taking the potato jackets off." When a local newspaper predicted that Ford was going to build a marble mansion which would cost $2 million, he exclaimed, "What on earth would I do with a place like that?" He was going to build a simple modern house of Indiana limestone which he was sure would not cost more than $100,000. Somehow, however, he miscalculated. The home he finally erected took three years to complete and involved damming the river, building a powerhouse to furnish lighting, heat, refrigeration, water softening and a dial-telephone system for the house, installing a swimming pool and planting elaborate landscaped areas. In the end he made the local journalist a prophet by spending the $2 million he had originally thought outlandish.

An even more amusing story, which showed how ludicrous the bargain-minded entrepreneur could look when he came across something that cost far more than it was worth, was told of William Randolph Hearst. In the 1920s Hearst built a house in Santa Monica, California, which turned out to be one of his seven fabulous castles. Seventy-five wood-carvers worked for a year on the balustrade alone. To complete the estate Hearst decided that he wanted a strip of land next to his property for a tennis court. Unfortunately, the land was owned by Will Rogers. Hearst sent a real-estate man to see Rogers and arrange to buy the property. Under the circumstances, the identity of the purchaser could hardly be disguised, and Rogers saw an opportunity to exercise his famed sense of humor. At first he asked an outrageous $25,000 for the small strip of land. Hearst was willing to pay that much, but his business instincts made him feel uncomfortable about agreeing to such a preposterous price. He tried to satisfy his conscience by offering Rogers $20,000. To Hearst's astonishment, Rogers responded by raising his asking price to $35,000. Hearst sent the real-estate man back with a compromise of $30,000, whereupon Rogers raised his asking price again, this time to $45,000. On and on the unprecedented negotiations went, until finally Hearst gave up and agreed to buy the property for Rogers' price, which by then had reached $105,000! When it was all over, Hearst told his bewildered realtor, "Pleasure is worth what you can afford to pay for it."

3

One of the primary benefits of wealth which the nineteenth- and twentieth-century American businessman has rarely taken advantage of is leisure. Henry Adams scornfully observed that in his day "America contained scores of men worth $5 million or upwards whose lives were no more worth living than those of their cooks." The successful businessman tends to believe that he is undeserving of such acrimony because he is the antithesis of both idleness and servility; as the boss of a giant organization he is happiest when he can prove that he works harder and longer than anyone else in the company.

The virtue of industry as compared to indolence was an article of faith among the founders of American industry. Benjamin Franklin's Poor Richard insisted that "God helps them that help themselves," and that "diligence is the mother of good luck and God gives all things to industry." To him idleness was sin. "Remember that time is money," was his message to eighteenth-century America. More than a century later, Charles Elliott Perkins, president of the Burlington Railroad, pointed out that industry was the key to progress. He wrote: "Have not great merchants, great manufacturers, great inventors done more for the world than preachers or philanthopists?"

It was not the simple fact of hard labor which was revered by the captains of industry; it was working hard at the business of business. One of the great convictions of the American industrialist was (and still is) that an hour of his time was worth far more than that of anyone else. The wealth he acquired was a measure of his unique contribution to the advancement of civilization. "The old nations of the earth creep on at a snail's pace," began Carnegie's *Triumphant Democracy;* "the Republic thunders past with the rush of the express."

In time others came to agree with the industrialist's self-adulation. In 1900 Professor Oscar Lovell Triggs of the English department of the University of Chicago compared Shakespeare and Rockefeller in their value to humanity and found the latter superior. As a result of the spectacular success of industry, "sound business thinking" came to be accepted as the best method of dealing with any problem, whether in government, education, art or religion. If something was a "moneymaking proposition" it had the respect of the whole community. The successful businessman was looked on as the wisest, most experienced, most practical man of his time, and his active participation in practically every phase of community affairs became a major force in the shaping of American society.

This appreciation for business skill was part of the religious heritage of a Protestant country. Wesley, the founder of Methodism, had exhorted all Christians to work hard, to gain all they could and to save all they could—that is, in effect, to follow the business ideal with such devotion that one had to become rich. In 1890, at the high point of American fortune making, the Baptist minister Reverend Russell Herman Conwell hailed the fruits of success in business as proof of its virtue. He said, "To secure wealth is an honorable ambition and is one great test of a person's usefulness to others. Money is power. Every good man and woman ought to strive for power, to do good with it when obtained. I say, 'get rich, get rich!'" Horatio Alger popularized this new faith, and Andrew Carnegie proposed an authorized businessman's version in his *Gospel of Wealth*.

4

The captains of industry believed that working hard at business prevented them from being corrupted by their wealth. As Edward Chase Kirkland of Bowdoin College observed in his *Dream and Thought in the Business Community, 1860–1900*, the masters of capital thought that the essence of virtue was to maintain a killing pace. He wrote:

> The executive had his lunch sent in to his place of business and carried his unfinished work home or on vacation. The House of Morgan gained a reputation as a man-killer, and by 1900 all the partners who had aided Morgan to greatness were dead, many of them at a premature age. From Stephen Girard, who said, "When death comes for me, he will find me busy," to Charles C. Scaife, who confided to his diary in 1876, "I cannot be idle; to me idleness is the most terrible

punishment," diligence in business was characteristic and excessive.

At the turn of the century the sociologist Max Weber diagnosed the executive's work compulsion as a peculiar malady caused by the Protestant ethic. "Man does not *by nature* wish to earn more and more money," he wrote in 1904–5. He gave as an example the hypothetical case of a laborer who works on the basis of piece rates, but who consciously decides not to earn more money when the rates go up. Instead, he prefers to work less so that he can have more time to himself while earning the same amount of money. This, Weber thought, was man's natural approach to labor. But the businessman is different. He accumulates wealth and works harder the more he makes. This is because, Weber believed, the Protestant ethic has left its mark on the capitalist ethic, which since the time of Franklin had lost its religious content. "The idea of duty in one's calling," he wrote, "prowls about in our lives like the ghost of dead religious beliefs." He predicted that the compulsion to work would always be an iron cage from which the businessman would find it impossible to escape.

This devotion to work was, according to Weber, the businessman's curse, not his blessing. Far from being a noble service to mankind, it was the heritage of an illusion and a futile attempt to expiate a sense of guilt.

Some wealthy businessmen had made an effort to be more rational in their way of life. When Andrew Carnegie was thirty-three years old he wrote in his diary:

> By this time two years, I can arrange all my business so as to secure at least $50,000 per annum. Beyond this never earn—make no effort to increase fortune, but spend the surplus each year for benevolent purposes. Cast aside business forever, except for others.
>
> Settle in Oxford and get a thorough education, making the acquaintance of literary men—this will take three years' active

work—pay special attention to speaking in public. Settle then in London and purchase a controlling interest in some newspaper or live review and give the general management of it attention, taking part in public matters especially those connected with education and improvement of the poorer classes.

Man must have an idol—the amassing of wealth is one of the worst species of idolatry—no idol more debasing than the worship of money. Whatever I engage in I must push inordinately; therefore should I be careful to choose that life which will be the most elevating in its character. To continue much longer overwhelmed by business cares and with most of my thoughts wholly upon the way to make more money in the shortest time must degrade me beyond hope of permanent recovery. I will resign business at thirty-five, but during the ensuing two years I wish to spend the afternoons in receiving instruction and reading systematically.

Carnegie later justified his failure to carry out this sensible plan by channeling a large part of his wealth into philanthropy. He became one of the richest men in America, but he gave away more than half his fortune before he died. He believed that as an entrepreneur and a philanthropist he helped to make America one of the greatest nations on earth. John D. Rockefeller, who also became a philanthropist, found an additional rationale for his continued labors by devoting himself to improving the efficiency of American industry. He thought that his accomplishment in life was not that he had become the richest man in the world, but that he had erected the largest corporate structure the world had ever known. This, he believed, was "the origin of the whole system of modern economic administration."

Undoubtedly there was some validity to both concepts, and men like Carnegie and Rockefeller could derive legitimate satisfactions from their accomplishments in life. They probably made a far greater contribution to society than they would have made if they had retired at an early age and lived on their capital. Yet in both instances their motivations were formulated after the fact; they were the result, not the cause, of a compulsion to continue to work hard as their fortunes mounted. The inner drives which made it impossible for them to stop were undoubtedly closer to Weber's blind "sense of duty" than they would have been willing to admit.

5

This same "sense of duty" is still operative in the later twentieth-century corporate oligarch's attitude toward his work. But the jus-tification for his compulsion to put in long hours and maintain a hectic pace has changed. Since it is unlikely that he will amass anything like the giant fortunes of his predecessors, he doesn't feel obliged to rationalize his wealth in quite the same way. Basically he feels he is like everyone else who works for the company; he receives the highest pay package only because he is at the top of the hierarchy. He claims that his work motivations are closer to those of most other executives who are employed by the company than to those of the old captains of industry. He must put in long hours to meet the demands of a responsible job, not because he wants to make more money or become a greater philanthropist or manage a larger organization—although he might do all those things as well.

The most important new factor in the corporate oligarch's atti-tudes toward work and wealth is the split that has taken place between the economic performance of the company and his own financial reward. He can work hard to improve the former be-cause that's his job. It is what he believes he is being paid to accomplish. But it doesn't follow that as the company grows in size he will become a man of great wealth. In 1966 General Mo-tors had sales of over $20 billion and assets of approximately $13 billion, while the net worth of the company chairman, Frederic G. Donner, was only a few million dollars. (He owned $3,917,000 of

General Motors stock, which in all probability was his major personal asset.)

John Calhoun Baker of Harvard in his book *Executive Salaries and Bonus Plans* analyzed the pay of one thousand officers and directors in one hundred large industrial companies and found little or no relationship between executive pay and corporate profit. An even larger study conducted by David R. Roberts of Carnegie Tech concluded that the statistics of nine hundred companies "do not lend themselves to facile generalizations" about the relationship between top executives' pay and corporate profit.

A look at the 1966 figures of the ten largest companies shows typical inconsistencies between executive compensation and corporate performance. General Motors was the number-one company in sales and earnings. Its chairman, Donner, received the highest pay package of any executive of the giant companies. The figure was $926,978. However, although Donner's salary plus incentive compensation (excluding 1966 contingent credit) rose by twenty per cent over the previous year, company earnings fell that year by sixteen per cent. At Standard Oil (New Jersey), the salary of John E. Swearingen, chairman of the board, rose by nine per cent from 1965 to 1966, while profits rose by 6.5 per cent. Although the company was number three of the top ten in sales and number two in earnings, Swearingen's compensation was the lowest of the top ten, at only $206,000.

The corporate oligarch therefore satisfies his desire to make more money by getting a raise each year. A study by Leonard Randolph Burgess of North Texas State University showed that the average yearly income of the most highly paid executives of the twenty-five largest corporations listed on the New York Stock Exchange rose from $166,000 in 1929 to $268,000 in 1958. This increase is more in line with the pay rise of other company employees than it is with the growth of the corporations they worked for.

This is not to say that it is no longer possible to make large sums of money in business. It is true that the $70-odd million untaxable annual income which John D. Rockefeller was making in the early 1900s was a fantastic sum when compared to top-executive salaries of the 1960s; but in 1966 Howard Hughes received $566 million for his seventy-eight per cent holding in Trans World Airlines, and *Fortune* believed this to be the largest sum ever to come into the hands of one man at one time. Each year the Internal Revenue Service reports quite a number of spectacular incomes, and not infrequently the beneficiary manages to take advantage of a variety of tax benefits to achieve sizable after-tax incomes. In 1959 there were five men who made $5 million without paying any taxes at all.

The attitudes of the oligarchy as a whole toward money are not determined by these special situations. Most top executive officers do not generally identify themselves with the ultrarich of their time. An analysis made by Robert L. Heilbroner indicates that their estimate is generally correct. Analyzing the 1955 Statistics of Income of the Internal Revenue Service, he showed that among those whose income was over $1 million a year only 1.5 per cent of their income came from salaries and bonuses. This meant that the very rich were not working for a living. Among those with incomes from $500,000 to $1 million, the percentage rose to 6.9 per cent (including income from business, profession or partnership). Among those with incomes from $100,000 to $500,000 it rose to 40.4 per cent. Among those with incomes from $50,000 to $100,000 it was 62.8 per cent. The corporate oligarch fitted into one of the latter two categories. He was one of the poorest rich men in America.

No doubt the opportunity to acquire large sums of money would give the corporate oligarch considerable pleasure. He would not mind being a rich rich man rather than a poor rich man, but he prefers to think that the object of doing a good job of management is not simply to amass a great fortune. He agrees with Henry Ford, who said that money is simply what the businessman uses to keep tally of his accomplishments, and with

Crawford H. Greenewalt, who observed that money is only a top executive's Nobel Prize for making an important contribution to society by being a good manager. Elmo Roper made an analysis of top-executive motivations and found the first two to be recognition of achievement and dignity of position; money wasn't listed at all. *Fortune* pointed out in its study "How Hard Do Executives Work?" that the head of a corporation "feels himself one of a band of men engaged in great adventure, and when he speaks of making more jobs, of helping people find more satisfaction in their work, the new frontiers in the industry, of better things for better living, he is not simply rationalizing. Unlike the European businessman, he believes it."

What appears to the corporate oligarch to be a credible explanation for his long work hours is, of course, not necessarily credible to others. A *Fortune* study of two hundred and twenty-one management men, including fifty-two company presidents, showed that an average work week consisted of forty-five to forty-eight hours of daytime work, one night working late at the office, two nights working at home, one night entertaining—all in all some fifty-seven to sixty hours. According to the study, wives, doctors, friends could not understand why arriving at the top of the ladder should not bring the privilege of taking things easy and enjoying life.

Writers of biographical profiles of modern executives frequently emphasize the long hours of a top executive as if there were something irrational about this devotion to work. These writers obviously continue to be skeptical about the motivations of a man who, despite his claims to selfless dedication, makes more money than most other people. They don't as a rule question his right to a substantial income, they merely wonder why he doesn't take advantage of it. Fletcher Jones, the head of Computer Science Company, told a *Time* magazine reporter, "Money allows me to do some of the things I want to do. Still, I don't have time to do most of them—travel, for example—so really the money doesn't count that much." The logical rejoinder would be:

"Why don't you rearrange your life to do the things you both want and can afford to do? Why indeed do you apply yourself to your work with a greater passion than men who are devoted to the great causes of society?" As a young clergyman in Detroit, speaking of the top executives in the automobile industry, observed, "These men are monks—monks who have traded in their prayer books for a production line. From the way they work, I sometimes think they want to overwhelm God with their cars. It may seem odd for me to say this, but I don't give as much of myself to my church as many of them do to General Motors and Ford and the rest."

6

The element of incredulity in regard to the oligarch's devotion to his job (after all, the clergyman would not have been surprised about the work habits of doctors) arises from a natural skepticism and suspicion about the motives of men who make a lot of money. And regardless of what the corporate oligarch says about his non-economic incentives for working so hard, no one can accuse him of ignoring the lure of money in his attitude toward his job. In that respect he is far from monastic in his outlook.

It is a fact, as we have already pointed out, that the men who head large corporations are extraordinarily well paid. Indeed, they are so eager to make money that all sorts of compensation schemes have been worked out to augment their income. Seventy per cent of the companies surveyed by *Business Week* in 1967 had fringe-benefit schemes for top executives. Among the many varieties of bonus plans that have been developed are short-term deferred, long-term deferred (extending to post-retirement, when taxes will be lower) and, since the Revenue Act of 1950, stock option plans which provide an opportunity for long-term capital gains if the price of the stock rises. Burgess found in his study that bonuses have been as high as four hundred and twenty per cent of salary. Richard C. Smyth suggested in a *Harvard Business Review* article that a bonus is no incentive if it is less than twenty per cent, and that it should be as high as forty to sixty per cent in good years to be effective. The receipt of such a bonus does not mean that the top executive shares in the corporate profits, but it does give him an opportunity to achieve some personal financial gain if he turns in a good performance for the company.

Because the top executive is in such a high tax bracket, he is especially concerned about his after-tax income. Lesser executives, according to a *Fortune* study, tend to be more interested in their gross figures, since these provide a better index of status. The chief executive wants as much money as possible to take home. To provide tax savings, some companies have given top executives an opportunity to buy treasury stock or debentures at a favorable price. Chrysler experimented with management trusts for its top executives (the company lent money to the trust at one-and-a-half per cent interest to buy company stock, and the dividends were income to the executives which could eventually be taken out on a favorable tax basis). Other well-publicized benefits include the payment of life insurance premiums, expense accounts, country club membership, and company-paid yacht cruises and hunting trips.

The keen interest which the corporate obligarch has in the size of his pay package contradicts his contention that money is not one of his major goals. Why, then, do so many top executives claim, as Elmo Roper's survey showed, that their real motivations lie elsewhere? Why did Crawford Greenewalt state that money is only like a Nobel Prize for making a contribution to society? Why does the corporate oligarch want to believe that he does not worship the idol of great wealth which Carnegie warned against, while at the same time he makes it clear to his board of directors that if he is not paid well enough he will lose his incentive for work?

A contradictory attitude toward money is not unique to the corporate oligarch. In a society that is both affluent and well-educated there are many who are troubled by such conflicting values. All thoughtful men know that money is an illusory goal in life and that there are other far more serious purposes to which they should devote their energies. At the same time, any person who is constantly exposed to the lure of greater pleasure, comfort and status which comes with increased earnings feels that he is foolish not to want to make as much money as possible. Most people try to resolve this paradox by striking a balance between these two impulses and making sure not to go so far in pursuing one goal as to totally sacrifice the other. The corporate oligarch, however, seems to have unusual difficulty in achieving this balance. He is the head of the system which creates the lure for making money, and, as we pointed out earlier, he is inclined to believe that he has a legal obligation to maximize profit for the stockholders. He knows that he is the supreme symbol of the desire to make money, and it would be illogical for him to damp down in any way his passion for making money. At the same time he has an equally natural aspiration to direct the enormous human resources under his management toward the achievement of a common objective. This too is difficult to suppress. He is therefore persuaded that each of these is his most important motivation, even if this creates in his mind an all but irreconcilable dilemma.

7

During the past several years I have queried several score top executives about their double motivations and found that most of them try to escape this dilemma by insisting that they are interested in making money only because of their financial obligations to their families. They insist that it is not a question of avarice but of dealing with the high cost of living and taking care of one's children properly. The company, of course, comes first, they say, but one has to live. And besides, it is only fair that each employee receive an income commensurate with his responsibilities, and this should include the president of the company as well as the office boy.

Unfortunately, this is convincing only to the oligarch himself.

Others recognize it as the same type of self-deception which led Henry Ford to believe that he was a man of modest appetites. The only difference is that the corporate oligarch carries the charade to an unprecedented extreme by convincing himself that he needs his enormous earnings in order to live. He does not see himself as one who indulges in the lavish excesses described in Thorstein Veblen's theory of conspicuous consumption, which, like Max Weber's theory of the Protestant ethic, was a revolutionary doctrine at the turn of the century. (Veblen's *The Theory of the Leisure Class* was published in 1899.) The corporate oligarch believes that he is more interested in convenience than in conspicuous consumption. He claims that he likes chauffeurs because they help him move around efficiently and save time, not because they show off his wealth. Yet he rides around in cars that are far more expensive than he needs, travels about the country in costly private airplanes, spends a fortune on company conventions held at luxury hotels. He doesn't want to be met at the door of his house by a valet who hangs up his coat and hat, but he has two or three secretaries trained to take care of his slightest wish in the office. He would vigorously deny that he indulges in "wasteful expensiveness" to establish "the signature of one's pecuniary strength" or to enjoy the "uplifting spirit" of extravagance, to quote some of Veblen's phrases. But the difference between him and the men Veblen described is one of epoch rather than attitude; conspicuous consumption simply takes different forms today than it did sixty years ago.

In some cases, it is true, the oligarch appears to live so frugally that one is hard put to find signs of wealth. Royal Little of Textron, who lived in a three-bedroom rented home in Providence, Rhode Island, and spent his summers in a similarly modest house in Narragansett, once complained to a reporter about the fancy homes in Newport near his own summer home. "It burns me up," he said, "that people were allowed to sink good working capital into piles of masonry." Ralph B. Schneider of the Diners Club once tried being extravagant: he bought an $11,000 Cadillac limousine and hired a chauffeur to drive him around town; but after six months he sold the car because it made him feel pretentious. Benjamin Fairless of U.S. Steel was a man of relatively simple tastes who liked nickel cigars. The extent of his luxury was a ten-room apartment in Pittsburgh and a suite at the Biltmore Hotel in Manhattan. McGregor Smith of the Florida Power and Light Company, whose office was a small, unglamorous affair, rarely wore a necktie and often pulled out a cheap harmonica to play a few bars of "Dixie." Chauncey William Wallace "Tex" Cook, president of General Foods, lived in a ranch house on a three-quarter-acre plot in Larchmont, New York. Mrs. Cook prepared most of their meals at home without the help of a housekeeper.

But even with these exceptions there is no doubt that evidence of extravagance can be found. One is reminded of Lincoln Steffens' famous challenge to any American town which considered itself free of corruption: given the opportunity, he promised to prove the claim false. It is equally unlikely that any corporate oligarch lives frugally in every respect. His appreciation for what money can buy inevitably leads him to some extravagance.

In general, corporate oligarchs enjoy extremely comfortable surroundings in their homes. They are not inclined to live in anything like the palatial estates of previous eras primarily because their fortunes are smaller. In Bloomfield Hills, a suburb of Detroit, sixty out of the one hundred top executives in the automobile companies (including all four presidents) live on plots which are an average of only two acres. Some of the homes are big and expensive, but the highest recorded price in the neighborhood is said to have been $300,000. "The way things are here," one of the executives said, "I have all the privacy I want, and at the same time a hundred yards away there are neighbors I can talk to if I want." Buckhead is the Atlanta counterpart to Bloomfield Hills, and although Coca-Cola's Robert Winship Woodruff lives in a grand Georgian mansion, this onetime estate region is now filled by newer, less costly houses in the $75,000-to-$100,000 range. But none of these homes can be considered Spartan by any measure.

On the contrary, they prove that the corporate oligarch is used to spending far more than he needs to on family real estate.

The same pattern of spending can be found in connection with trusts for his children. The corporate oligarch has a strange notion that however many millions he will leave behind for his heirs, he is not providing adequately for their security. He complains that too much of his income is devoted to upkeep, and that he doesn't have enough funds to meet his long-term obligations. "Believe me," one top executive told a *Fortune* reporter, "you can't get to first base on a salary, even if it is $180,000. It's hardly enough to maintain a reasonable standard of living." He described what had happened to the $180,000 he had made the previous year: $57,000 deferred payment for retirement; $74,000 income tax; $14,000 to the support of his aged mother and mother-in-law; $25,000 to maintain himself and to pay for the maintenance of his house, his housekeeper's salary, his daughter's college tuition, clothes, etc. All that was left was $10,000 for improvements on the house, a new car and savings.

This supposedly constant drain on their resources is considered a hardship by corporate oligarchs who worry endlessly about how much money they will be able to put aside for the future. Yet an executive making over $150,000 is likely to have accumulated net assets of at least $2 million to $3 million, which should take care of his children handsomely by any standards. They may not have as great an annual income as he does, but this will hardly evoke sympathy from others. Obviously the necessity to acquire additional funds for his children's security is as unreal as the need to finance more comfortable living quarters.

Some oligarch fathers are aware of the folly of trying to make life too easy for their children. Royal Little, who didn't appreciate the idea of spending extravagant sums on fancy homes, was equally concerned about leaving too much money for his children. He was wary, for instance, of setting up trusts which would deprive his children of initiative while guaranteeing them security. This is a problem which has occurred to quite a few wealthy men;

as Franklin D. Roosevelt once said, "Creative enterprise is not stimulated by vast inheritances. They bless neither those who bequeath them nor those who receive them." (Curiously, F.D.R.'s cousin Theodore Roosevelt felt differently. "I have known plenty of men," he once said, "who are only able to do their work because they have inherited means.")

But these are exceptions. The number of corporate oligarchs who are eager to make their heirs wealthy can be inferred from a Brookings Institution study which found that half of those with incomes over $300,000 believed that bequests were an important stimulus for further accumulation of wealth. Perhaps more than any other stated goal, this idea of establishing sizable bequests gives the oligarch the comfortable feeling that he is enduring the great pressures and long hours on his job for an admirable purpose. If he deprives his children of a father while they are growing up, he thinks he will be doing them a favor in the long run by making sure they will be taken care of after he is gone.

8

If the financial requirements to maintain the comforts of home and secure economic independence are greatly exaggerated by the corporate oligarch, the desire to maintain his status within the company is a consideration which is not easy to ignore. It is necessary, he feels, to keep the record straight; since he is the top man in the hierarchy, he should make the most money. Even David Rockefeller, chairman of the Chase Manhattan Bank, will not relinquish his salary, although he has stated that he uses this money only for philanthropic purposes.

But this is not a rational purpose for making money, either. It is a matter of pride rather than economics. A survey by the American Management Association of 1953–54 executive salaries showed an average differential of thirty per cent between the number-one and number-two men in large corporations. A study by Ralph W. Ells, chief economist of the Allen-Bradley Company, found that presidents of companies employing over one thousand men are often paid approximately twice as much as the number-two men. Both of these reports suggest that even though the corporate oligarch has a practical interest in his after-tax income he still pays close attention to the relative size of his pay package and those of lesser executives. If others lower down in the hierarchy are constantly seeking higher incomes, then his must rise as well, whether or not he can find any sensible purpose for making more money. Not surprisingly, one of the reasons the men below want to increase their incomes is that they want to catch up to him; the result is a never-ending inflationary spiral.

Thus the system itself is a factor in the corporate oligarch's compulsion to increase his personal wealth. If he didn't want a high income he would be an outcast in his culture rather than its hero. There would be no way not to want money even if his reason told him it was useless. He is trapped by the machinery of business, which makes it a matter of pride to feel that no matter how much money one makes or is worth it is never enough.

None of these popular excuses for seeking a perpetually rising income can be considered rational solutions, therefore, of the dilemma with which the oligarch is faced.

Indeed the only oligarchs I have ever known who appear to have satisfactorily answered the question of why they want to make money do not rely on the standard rationalizations of security, children and status. They say they want to make money because they like it, that the only purpose of being in business is to make as much money as possible, and that any businessman who claims otherwise is deceiving himself and the public. It is not impossible for such men to have nonpecuniary ideals in their private lives; but they insist on leaving these ideals home when they go to the office. Untroubled by the lack of a reasonable motive for making money, they can be and usually are ruthless in their single-minded ambition to make as good a score as possible in the corporate game.

But I do not believe such men are typical of the corporate

oligarch. For the more sensitive and thoughtful executive, the picture is far more complex. It is hard to dismiss his oft-stated desire for recognition of achievement and dignity of position—his "psychic income," as he likes to call it—as window dressing. His concern is too persistent and too pervasive. And his attempts to rationalize his interest in money as a function of need rather than greed are too compulsive to be an act. There are, I believe, deeper psychological factors at work.

The connection between man's attitude toward money and his unconscious drives and fears has long been a subject of speculation by psychoanalysts. Particularly interesting in regard to the corporate oligarch are those studies of anxiety among emotionally disturbed persons who suffer from similar combinations of excessive claims to nobility of purpose and irrational fears about financial security. Theodore Reik once told about such a case in which a wealthy businessman had an emotional breakdown while his wife was dying of cancer. The husband was considered a model of devotion in the way he handled himself during this difficult period, but after several weeks he felt he needed psychiatric help to keep him going. The only symptom he had of inner turmoil was a strange fear of financial insecurity. There was no history of such an anxiety in his past and no possible justification for it now, since he was an extraordinarily wealthy man. Eventually, Reik helped him admit to himself that he really wanted his wife to die, even though this emotion was unacceptable to his conscious sense of nobility. His fear of financial insecurity was a manifestation of his guilt feelings. Once he recognized the true nature of his emotions and understood that they were natural under the circumstances, he was able to regain his balance.

Reik felt that this connection between an irrational fear of financial insecurity and an unwillingness to acknowledge destructive or hateful impulses is quite common. It may well be that the corporate oligarch who experiences the conflicting fantasies of selfless devotion to his business and fear for the security of his family suffers from a similar sense of guilt. Consciously he may think he loves his business and will do anything he can for it. Unconsciously he may hate it, resent the great burdens it places on his personal life, yearn to free himself of the slavery of his job. Consciously he may be convinced that he is making a contribution to society in the work he does. Unconsciously he may feel that the work he is doing is as useless to a strife-torn society as the efforts made by the husband in Reik's classic case were to his dying wife. Consciously he may believe that the need to satisfy the financial demands made by his family justifies his personally unrewarding labors. Unconsciously he may know that such demands are imaginary and that his family's greatest wish is that he free himself from the obsessive relationship he has with his company. The strange combination of quixotic heroism and irrational financial anxiety which the oligarch so often manifests could well be the result of these conflicts between his "sense of duty" to his company, his family and society and his repressed emotional wish to throw off the yoke.

If this analysis has any validity, the picture of himself which lurks in the deeper regions of his mind is appalling. The self-destructive pattern of his business life is fruitless. His job is as senseless as throwing stones into the water. He is working to make money which he doesn't need, which his family doesn't want and which may even bring harm to those he loves most, his children. To believe that money is the greatest incentive and the greatest reward for his labor is insane; the more money one makes the more useless it becomes; dedicating himself with great passion to the business of making a fortune is lunacy.

Could a man who feels this way about his life not be troubled by anxiety? Would it be any wonder for him to be struggling to find some way to convert his business from a moneymaking proposition into a social cause to which he could sensibly dedicate himself? Would it not be clear that if he were ever to banish the ghosts of dead beliefs which prowl around in his life he could recognize at long last that it is not a mark of success to die a wealthy man?

These are questions which the corporate oligarch has not yet been able to answer. Indeed, they are questions which many top executives have not even begun to ask. This perhaps is the most serious commentary on the oligarch's prospects for resolving his money dilemma in this generation. The mystery cannot be penetrated if it is not fully recognized. It is virtually inevitable, therefore, that the corporate oligarch will continue his present course until he admits his real feelings to himself, and that he will suffer the consequences of the system or of his neurosis, if that is what it is, until he develops a more meaningful purpose for his corporate life.

5

His Family Relationships

NEXT TO MAKING MONEY, THE MOST IMPORTANT PERSONAL CON-
sideration in the job held by the corporate oligarch is whether he
will—or even wants to—bring his children into his business.

To put in perspective the oligarch's attitude toward his children, one must recall the ambition of the old industrial magnate
to found a new aristocracy of wealth that would go on for generations. This was his wish even in the early days of the Republic,
when a major economic revolution took place, eliminating the
legal privileges of the old royalists. No sooner had this been accomplished than a new type of aristocracy arose—not by royal decree this time, but by entrepreneurial achievement. These economic dynasties, however, had no fixed political system to sustain
them, and as the industrialist became a more dominant figure in
American society it became increasingly difficult to bequeath his
power to his descendants.

Until the eighteenth century, the practice of passing to one's heirs the privileges of one's position as a means of insuring for them the pleasures of wealth was based on property ownership. This was the foundation on which feudal aristocracy was built. "The transmission of this property from generation to generation in the same name," wrote Thomas Jefferson in his *Autobiography*, "raised up a distinct set of families who, being privileged in law by the perpetuation of their wealth, were thus formed into a Patrician order, distinguished by the splendor and luxury of their establishment."

The American colonies took the lead in bringing an end to this tradition. In 1776 the General Convention assembled in Philadelphia to draft a constitution for Pennsylvania and, in Section Thirty-seven of the document, provided for the regulation of entail (which kept an estate intact from generation to generation) "in such a manner as to prevent perpetuities." Georgia followed in 1777, abolishing both entail and primogeniture (which granted the eldest son the possession of his father's landed estate, to the absolute exclusion of the younger sons and daughters). North Carolina and Massachusetts passed similar laws in 1784, Virginia (under the leadership of Thomas Jefferson) in 1785, New York, Connecticut and Maryland in 1786, and the rest of the states in short order, with South Carolina as the last in 1791. Thus the United States anticipated even France, whose National Assembly abolished hereditary rights in 1790. Curiously, it wasn't until 1925 that the British Parliament finally abolished entail and primogeniture. Germany did not abolish them until 1939, when Hitler issued a decree to that effect.

The early businessman in America was both the leader and the beneficiary of this advance in democracy. With the breaking up of the big estates, it became possible for him to acquire property for roads, canals and real-estate investments. He may well have been an estate holder himself, but he was no longer frozen into the size of the property granted to his ancestors. The ending of a rigid system for keeping property intact provided an opportunity for him to acquire the means to improve his position on the basis of entrepreneurial skill rather than birth. The rise of the industrial tycoon was therefore made possible through the political as well as the industrial revolution that took place in the early days of the Republic. "The mild and moderate, judicious and republican government of the United States," wrote Pierre-Samuel du Pont, the French Physiocrat who argued for the end of landed estates and who was the father of one of the few successful corporate dynasties in America, "offers almost the only asylum where the prosecuted may find repose, where fortunes may set aside a reserve, a last storehouse to ensure his children's sustenance."

As industrial wealth and power emerged in the rapidly prospering country, the desire to provide for children's sustenance gave way to the ambition to create a new privileged class based on the ownership of business enterprises rather than of land. This new class was not born in frontier log cabins, despite the legends which grew up around those industrial giants who rose from poverty to riches in nineteenth-century America. The industrial aristocracy of the nineteenth century was, with few exceptions, a direct descendant of the landed aristocracy of the eighteenth century. The men who directed the proliferating business enterprises of the young nation felt at home in the higher social and economic levels of their day. But the structure had changed from one defined by rigid property boundaries staked out by previous generations to one defined by newly created business enterprises which could be expanded through the exercise of entrepreneurial skill.

The essential characteristic of the new business-oriented aristocracy was that in the course of a single lifetime entrepreneurs were able to acquire wealth which dwarfed the holdings of the landed aristocracy from which they had sprung. The economic power which accompanied this personal wealth was intoxicating to men who were discovering that there was virtually no limit to the expansion of their enterprises. Presumably the next generation could begin where the last left off, and the process could go on as far as the mind could foresee. It was understood that American society would always have to keep the door open for new entrepreneurs to rise up and compete with those who were established, but it also seemed logical that the business empire which would span several generations would have advantages over competitive ventures which lacked such continuity. The best way to consolidate the gains of one generation was to pass them on to the next and to keep corporate control in family hands.

2

After a century of industrial evolution the emerging oligarchy therefore found itself attacked for being the beneficiary of a system of inheritance that had become almost as much an obstacle to private initiative and free competition as the old tradition of entail. In 1915 a report by the U.S. Commission on Industrial Relations stated that "they [the corporate heirs] are frequently styled by our newspapers as 'monarchs of industry,' and indeed occupy within our Republic a position almost exactly analogous to that of feudal lords. These heirs, owners only by virtue of accident of birth, control the livelihood and have the power to dictate the happiness of more human beings than populated England in the Middle Ages."

One year later, in 1916, the Congress passed the first federal inheritance-tax law, at least partially aimed at curbing the accumulation of great wealth in America and, by indirection, the economic power of the families which controlled the great corporations.

The results, at least for the next decade or two, did not seem to be impressive. By the time the Great Depression occurred, the families still appeared to be in control of American industry, and Franklin D. Roosevelt spoke out sharply against the "economic royalists" of the country. In 1936 Anna Rochester's *Rulers of America* was published, and in 1937 Ferdinand Lundberg's *America's Sixty Families*. Both books attempted to document the charge that the centralization of corporate power in the hands of wealthy families was increasing. Lundberg cited a report from the

Internal Revenue Bureau supporting his thesis. "It is often asserted," the report stated, "that large wealth is dissipated in three generations. . . . [It] was doubtless once true that all a grandfather saved from the fruits of his labor could be spent by a grandson. It is probably true today of very moderate fortunes. It is not true of large invested fortunes under present conditions. They not only perpetuate themselves, they grow."

An extraordinary number of intermarriages between the families involved in ownership and management of major corporations was making matters worse, according to Lundberg. Some of these combinations were Rockefeller-Aldrich, Rockefeller-Dodge, Rockefeller-Carnegie, Kuhn-Loeb-Schiff-Warburg, Hutton-Post-Woolworth-McCann-Donahue. Lundberg did a masterful job of untangling many of these interrelationships to estimate the total worth of family clusters, separating out, for instance, the holdings of seventeen Lehmans (Lehman Brothers), sixteen Phippses (Carnegie Steel), twenty-two Vanderbilts (New York Central Railroad), eight McCormicks (International Harvester and the Chicago *Tribune*), six Guggenheims (American Smelting & Refining Company), and twenty-eight members of the Standard Oil group, including Archibalds, Rogerses, Bedfords, Cutlers, Flaglers, Pratts and Benjamins. His findings seem to confirm a report made twelve years earlier by Pitirim Sorokin, who analyzed two generations of millionaires to demonstrate that more than half of those then alive (52.7 per cent) inherited their wealth, while less than a third (29.7 per cent) of the previous generation inherited theirs. "Modern capitalism," Lundberg concluded, "has become, like feudalism before it, a family affair."

Not surprisingly, the families which were under attack did not recognize any conflict between the establishment of corporate dynasties and the American Dream. Capitalism was supposed to guarantee the retention of capital as well as the opportunity to acquire it. And corporate power was the instrument by which control of capital was maintained. Ownership was not a privilege of class, but a reward for entrepreneurial success. The country had become great because of what the great corporate families had been able to accomplish. It would become greater still, the argument concluded, if the dynasties could continue their traditions and build their corporations even larger, stronger and richer.

The outstanding example which was—and still is—most commonly cited to demonstrate the economic contribution to the nation made by a corporate dynasty is E. I. du Pont de Nemours and Company. Here success was due not to the mere ownership of stock but to the development of a tradition of skilled family management. Since the corporation was founded in 1803, there have been twelve successions of management. The founder, Éleuthère-Irénée (son of the Physiocrat Pierre-Samuel), ruled for thirty-one years, from 1803 to 1834. His son-in-law, Antoine Biderman, ruled as regent for the oldest son for three years, from 1834 to 1837. Then the oldest son, Alfred Victor, took over for thirteen years, to 1850. Next came the founder's second son, Henry ("the General"), who ruled for thirty-nine years, to 1889. The youngest son of the founder died before he could get his chance to run the company, but his oldest son, Eugene, represented the third generation of Du Ponts to come to power. Eugene ruled for thirteen years, from 1889 to 1902. On his death the family had its greatest difficulty in agreeing on a successor. The company was about to be sold when three members of the fourth generation worked out a plan for a triumvirate consisting of three grandsons of Alfred Victor, the oldest son of the founder. By their agreement, one of them, Thomas Coleman, was president for thirteen years, from 1902 to 1915. Pierre S., the second member of the triumvirate, was president for four years, from 1915 to 1919. Next came Pierre's younger brother, Irénée, who was president for seven years, to 1926. Then Irénée's youngest brother, Lammot, took over, and he was president for fourteen years, to 1940. Next came a fifth-generation member of the family, Walter S. Carpenter, Jr., a grandson-in-law of Eugene's (the fifth president's) younger brother. (Carpenter's older brother was also married to the sister of Pierre S.) He ruled for eight years, from 1940 to 1948.

Then there was Crawford Greenewalt, a shift back to the Alfred Victor branch of the family (he was the son-in-law of Irénée); he ruled for fourteen years, from 1948 to 1962. Finally there came the current president, Lammot Du Pont Copeland, who is the son of the older sister of Pierre S.

What took place at Du Pont, therefore, was a sort of family stewardship in which the best-qualified executive of the current generation was selected for the post. This was in part due to the heritage of the communal capitalism established by the founder's three sons, who formed something of a socialist phalanstery in which they shared all their property. But it became, in the course of more than a century and a half, the model corporate dynasty to which many executive-fathers pointed with pride—the supposedly best demonstration in the corporate world that nepotism was consistent with the healthy economic growth of the country.

3

The history of other family dynasties in the nineteenth and twentieth centuries revealed, however, a number of forces which threatened the stability of hereditary control of corporations. Although Du Pont was considered the ideal corporate dynasty, it was hardly typical of how power in the great corporations was handed down through the generations.

Many heirs of corporate power followed a different pattern. While family succession from a father to a son has been characteristic of a large number of corporations for the past one hundred and fifty years, the social and psychological environment has been increasingly unfriendly to the establishment of stable dynasties. What the social critics of the 1930s recognized as a ruling class held together by blood ties was at least partly made up of unstable family relationships hovering around the center of power rather than a fixed system of maintaining hereditary control.

The most serious threat to the establishment of formal dynasties in corporate America was the failure to inspire a sense of *noblesse oblige* among succeeding generations. The tradition of skilled family management ability that was established at Du Pont did not take root in many other companies, because the children of financial magnates were not raised in the atmosphere which surrounds a reigning aristocracy. Frequently they were not born to rule; they were born to be rich, and hopefully to get richer as they grew older. And since they lived in an economy which enabled them to make money by investing their wealth as easily as or more easily than by retaining control over the vast enterprises built by their ancestors, power was relinquished by succeeding generations without any feeling of deprivation. Often an interest in the corporation was maintained only to provide a source of jobs for descendants who didn't have the imagination or the ability to make better use of the privileges of wealth. Thus Lundberg was right when he wrote, "Scratch any big corporation and the chances are even that one will find an in-law of the wealthiest families." But the picture was incomplete, because he didn't specify that many of these were family retainers. These were at least partially offset by a growing number of new oligarchs who were being selected to guide the destinies of corporations because they were career men with management talent rather than descendants of royal blood.

Typical of the families which achieved corporate power in the nineteenth century and abandoned it to outsiders in the twentieth century were the descendants of Cornelius Vanderbilt. The history of the family was succinctly summarized by a biographer who wrote: "In one generation a Vanderbilt had created the great fortune. In two generations the family had become the richest in the world. In three generations the Vanderbilts had become the first family of the land. But at the end of four generations, power had slipped from their hands—and while the Vanderbilts did not suffer poverty, the family had lost its place of leadership in the affairs of America."

The old Commodore, founder of the dynasty, was more interested in his later years in preserving his name than in building his fortune. He wanted to be sure that his sons would retain control of his business (and that, for instance, it would not fall into the hands of his sons-in-law, who were not his name descendants). He didn't care how much money he would leave his heirs or how much they would make. "A million or two is as much as anyone ought to have," he once told an acquaintance, and when the suggestion was made that there would be no problem in taking a few millions off Vanderbilt's hands, he explained that "what you have is not worth anything unless you have the power. And if you give away the surplus, you give away the control."

But early in life Vanderbilt had been contemptuous of his sons' ability and expected little more from them than carrying out his orders. To escape from his father's domineering personality, one of his sons, Cornelius Jeremiah (a friend of Horace Greeley), lived in a world of fantasy. He was constantly getting involved in unsound ventures, borrowing money, using bad checks, which his father had to make good, and being a general source of embarrassment to his family. He once had to be committed to an insane asylum to escape criminal charges. Another time, his financial commitments were so heavy he was forced into personal bankruptcy. The old Commodore grew so disgusted that he once said he would give a million dollars if his son was not named Vanderbilt. Eventually Cornelius Jeremiah solved his father's problem by committing suicide.

The most successful son of the old Commodore was William Henry. (There were three sons in all; the youngest, George Washington Vanderbilt, chose a military career.) Initially William Henry and his father had little to do with each other. The Commodore gave his son a piece of property and an allowance to live on; but the father became furious some years later when he learned that his son had taken out a mortgage on the property (the old man hated mortgages) to pay expenses for the upkeep of his growing family. Eventually there was a reconciliation, and William Henry came into the business. Even then his father always treated him like a boy, and when William Henry was close to fifty years old and had nine children of his own he made sure to ask his father's permission before making a policy move.

After his father died, William Henry proved to be a chip off the old block, and in a few short years he doubled his father's fortune, to become the richest man in the world. He also shared his father's feeling about the importance of keeping control of the business in the hands of his sons. His will left the bulk of his estate to the two sons who were in the business and whom he trusted most to carry on; they were Cornelius Vanderbilt II and Willie K., both of whom had started in the business under their grandfather's tutelage. They each received over $60 million, while the other sons and daughters received $10 million each. Also, the two sons divided up the presidencies of the major corporations owned by the family. But neither of them had the same sense of dedication to these corporations that their father and grandfather had had. Cornelius became interested in religion and concentrated an increasing amount of his time and money on philanthropy. Willie K. was a playboy and became a socialite. In time, nonfamily management was allowed to take over, as, for instance, when Chauncey Depew became president of New York Central. The next generation lost interest completely in the family corporations. The heirs of the great fortune became engaged in a great variety of activities, including translating contemporary works into ancient Greek, sailing yachts and racing motorcars.

The dynasty was thus fragmented into scores of diverse personalities, and the chain of succession which the old Commodore dreamed of perpetuating in the family name was broken.

4

Another cause of instability in family succession has been the personal incompatability of well-educated sons with the crude methods of the business world. Sometimes sons were just not cut out to be managers; at other times sensitive young men couldn't adjust to the demands of an executive career. Many sons who had intellectual, artistic or social interests took over the reins of the family company from their fathers or grandfathers because that was what was expected, not because they believed it was a useful or satisfying way to spend their lives. The result was that they ran the company—and sometimes themselves—into the ground.

One of the finest persons I ever met in the corporate world was such a man. He was the grandson of a nineteenth-century captain of industry, Milton Prince Higgins, the founder of what became one of the largest abrasives companies in the world, the Norton Company. Two of Milton Higgins' sons went into the business; one, Aldus Higgins, became president of the Norton Company, the other, John Higgins, became president of the Worcester Pressed Steel division of the company. My friend, and one-time client, was Carter Higgins, the son of John Higgins. When I became acquainted with the company it had severed its connection with Norton and was independently owned by this offshoot of the family.

I remember vividly my first trip to the Worcester Pressed Steel plant. A typical nineteenth-century New England factory, it was strangely out of tune with modern times. Inside, the halls and offices were so old-fashioned they seemed to be a caricature of what things were like in the old days. But there were aspects more strange than that to the place. One entire floor of the building was devoted to a collection of armor put together by Carter's father, John Higgins. I met the old man once, but by that time he had nothing to do with the business. His lifelong interest had been his collection of armor, which, I was once told, was one of the largest private collections in the world. John Higgins was still interested in his museum, but others in the company considered him an eccentric. The son, Carter, a tall, gawky gentleman, had another interest, World Federalism, and there were several signs around his office and in the halls with messages about the importance of creating world order.

The corporation itself was small and somewhat stagnant, with sales of only a few million dollars. Obviously, John had been far more interested in his armor than in building sales and profits. Carter had an intellectual interest in the corporation, and he enjoyed working with members of our staff on thoughtful articles for *The Harvard Business Review* and other publications analyzing theoretical aspects of the business he was in; but he was never able to get the company on the move. It plodded along from year to year, a misfit in a corporate world peopled with Jack-and-the-Beanstalk climbers. He and his wife were active in World Federalism, and his gentle, patient, considerate presence was a regular feature of many local and national meetings of the organization.

Years after I first met Carter, his son took a summer job with us. Like his father, he was idealistic about world affairs and not particularly responsive to what is so widely called the challenge of business. None of his distant cousins in the Higgins fourth generation was heading into the family's business, the Norton Company, and apparently he wasn't heading into the Worcester Pressed Steel Company. But he never had a chance to find out. When he was in his early twenties he went to Africa with the Peace Corps and was killed in a sudden local flare-up. The loss of his son proved to be a great blow to Carter, and shortly afterward he died, at the age of forty-nine. Some months later I received a note from his wife saying that she had moved to New York and taken a job in an art gallery just a few blocks from our office. I replied, promising to drop in and say hello. Somehow I didn't get to it for several weeks. When I did, I missed her by just a few days; she had committed suicide.

This tragic story has its counterpart in many family-managed corporations where sons are misfits in their fathers' shoes. It is awkward, for obvious reasons, to give examples from personal experience, but everybody in the corporate world is familiar with the problem.

One example given in a *Wall Street Journal* story entitled "The Son Also Rises" is the Sharon Steel Corporation, which employed as president two sons of its long-time head, Henry A. Roemer. One son, Henry, served from 1950 to 1955 and then resigned and left the company. The other, James A. Roemer, served from 1957 to 1962, and afterward moved down to vice-president for public relations. The succeeding president, Don W. Frease, openly confessed to stockholders that the company's poor performance during the years of the son's reign was due to a lack of foresight on the part of management and its failure to keep up with the times. The father also publicly conceded that his company's experience made it clear that father-son successions in business often do not work out.

Another company cited by the *Wall Street Journal* as an example of a questionable, or at least a controversial father-son succession is Douglas Aircraft Company. Donald Douglas Jr., took over from his father in 1957, and under his management the company experienced many lean years. Some observers believed that the son should not be blamed for this record, but others insisted that a better choice could have been found for the Douglas presidency. One of the latter, a Los Angeles management consultant, was quoted as saying, "Douglas Junior doesn't dig deep enough into problems and doesn't investigate the second and third layers of management. He doesn't know how the nuts and bolts are made." According to a former long-time Douglas official, the son just "doesn't have his father's financial acumen."

5

Differences in ability and personal outlook have caused many heirs of industrial tycoons to make a conscious effort to escape the family business. This was the case among several generations of descendants of Marshall Field. His fortune, variously estimated at between $90 million and $150 million (it was difficult to arrive at an accurate figure, because he habitually undervalued his property in order to reduce taxes), was made in dry-goods department stores, railroads, real estate, banking and manufacturing. Although his success led many of his contemporaries to consider him as "a businessman of the best type," his hard-driving determination to make money led others to accuse him of paying near-starvation wages to his thousands of workers. He was described in later years as a man "wholly and irreclaimably obsessed by money mania." His ambitions were enormous, and his corporate interests extended to England, Ireland, Scotland, France, Spain, Italy, Germany, Austria, Russia, China, Japan and Brazil. He would have liked his son, Marshall Field II, to go into his business, but the latter showed no inclination to do so. Instead he attempted to concentrate on scholarly studies, first at Harvard, then in England, where he spent much of his time in later years. He didn't even want to be physically near his father's Chicago-based empire. Ultimately he was unable to adjust to the problems of his life, and he committed suicide at the age of thirty-six.

The father, who died only two months later, left a will which has been called one of the most complicated ever drawn. It contained iron-clad stipulations which tied up and solidified the mass of his property for decades. An attorney for one of the heirs who contested the will was astonished "at the amazing complications of the scheme by which the testator sought to tie up his property." The lawyer for the estate contended that Field's purpose had been to protect his descendants from "leading useless lives of luxury and idleness." The result was also that none of his heirs became interested in taking over the management of his farflung corporate interests. One grandson, Henry Field, died at an early age. The other, Marshall Field III, shared his father's distaste for the family business. When he launched the Chicago *Sun* in 1941, he felt impelled to place advertisements declaring that the newspaper was not connected with the department store. Also, his way of life would no doubt have appalled his grandfather. A clause in the old man's will withheld the bulk of his estate until his second-generation heir was fifty, perhaps in the hope that by that time he would be mature enough not to squander his inherited wealth. However, Marshall Field III spent his money on many liberal causes which his grandfather would not have approved of, on extensive traveling, expensive hobbies and many extravagances in his personal life. The fourth generation, in the person of Marshall Field IV, followed suit. With the fifth-generation Marshall Field, however, there was a revival of family business interests, and his publishing enterprises became bigger and more successful than his grandfather's.

6

Not to be overlooked as a source of difficulty in the transference of corporate control from one generation to another is the tendency for the child of a successful father to experience self-doubts about his ability to match his father's accomplishments. It is to be expected that the progeny of many eminent men fail to live up to the successes of their fathers, while others exceed their fathers' achievements. But when a young man is brought up to feel that his father has accomplished something so marvelous that no son can hope to equal his record, his chances of doing something worthwhile in his life are limited. In this respect, the sons of industrial giants have had a particularly hard time. Ever since the era when business entrepreneurs emerged from the landed aristocracy, the hero of American industry has been the self-made man. Thus the son of a successful businessman is denied the opportunity to accomplish that one feat which he knows will be most admired by his peers. As the son of one successful entrepreneur told a psychologist, "Any fool can wind a watch and keep it running. The question is, who made the watch in the first place?"

I have known personally many men who have become presidents of companies started by their fathers or grandfathers and who are jealous of men who started businesses completely on their own. Those who have inherited their position feel cheated because they can't claim to have started from scratch. There is something almost paranoid about their fear that everybody secretly accuses them of having been born overprivileged. This anxiety often stays with them as long as they live.

The authoritarian makeup of a successful businessman, whether he was an old-time captain of industry or is a modern corporate oligarch, is a major cause of the psychological difficulties suffered by his sons. Such a man seldom allows competition from his wife or children any more than from his employees. This may be because he is used to giving orders and having them followed or because, as some psychologists have suggested, he feels threatened by the expression of other people's ideas. If he marries a woman who is unwilling to stand up to him at home, his children will be burdened by an ineffective maternal figure as well as a domineering father. As a result, children may have to endure constant humiliation by a father who delights in exhibiting his superiority. One executive-son told a psychiatrist that his father often took him fishing when he was a boy. The father would always bait the hook, and when the youngster got a bite the father would take over and reel it in. Eventually the son developed a dislike for fishing and wouldn't go any more. As a result of many such experiences, the son grew up with a chronic depression and a conviction that he could never work competently at a job. During the course of treatment the young man complained that his father constantly humiliated him at work and had no faith in him whatsoever. He said that this had been the pattern of his whole life. This is undoubtedly typical of many stories told by sons who have never adjusted to going into their fathers' business.

The family pattern created by the compulsively hard-working top executive is all too familiar: he feels he is far too busy to spend time with the family, too important to waste his time on the trivial jobs his wife asks him to do at home, too absorbed in the intricacies of his work to discuss his business with his children, too satisfied with the financial privilege he has given his family and too proud of the legacy he intends to leave his heirs to feel he is in any way short-changing those who are his beneficiaries. These attitudes are a natural product of the total personal commitment to the company made by dedicated executives who give only the scraps and leftovers to their families. The result is that too often they are a great success as executives but "mere shells at home," as a *Wall Street Journal* story put it, "unable to function effectively as husbands and fathers."

Published comments by many leading figures in the corporate world show how widespread these failures are. The occasional reference in business circles to the "little woman at home" who is not supposed to be forgotten while executives devote themselves to their careers makes it clear that the corporate oligarch considers his role as a husband and a father secondary to that of an executive. It is not easy to be a devoted member of the family when, like Benjamin F. Fairless of U.S. Steel, he spends an estimated one third of his time on the road visiting subsidiary offices, or, like Lewis S. Rosenstiel of Schenley Industries, travels more than fifty thousand miles a year on company business. "Business dominates your whole life," stated E. J. Thomas, chairman of Goodyear Tire & Rubber; "time with the family suffers terribly." David Sarnoff confessed that one of his big mistakes as a parent was "that I did not find sufficient time to spend with my children when I was young. It is perhaps the common mistake with men in my position." A survey of family attitudes toward top-executive husbands reported that most wives advise their daughters to marry "some kid with less ambition."

It is significant that when a top executive's children have been able to develop their personalities and achieve a position of eminence of their own, it has often been because the executive's wife was a strong person and was able to maintain a sense of family priorities in the face of the father's business interests. This suggests that, because of the nature of his emotional involvements, the most important contribution a corporate oligarch can make to the welfare of his children is to marry a woman who is capable of asserting herself effectively at home.

The difficulty which sons have in dealing with their executive fathers has led many of the former to seek academic or professional careers in order to get as far away as possible from their fathers' orbits. If they are lucky, the change in atmosphere enables them to realize their full potentialities. As James C. Hormel, whose father was head of the George A. Hormel meat-packing firm, put it, "The kind of challenge my father saw in a young and growing industry I have found in the law and the academic life." At the tender age of twenty-eight he was appointed dean of students at the University of Chicago Law School.

Those who fail to escape but are not capable of assuming management responsibilities sometimes become charges of the oligarchy and are given jobs to keep them busy either in their fathers' businesses or in companies run by friends of their fathers. Rumors are often circulated about suppliers to large corporations, particularly in service businesses such as insurance, advertising, public relations and management consulting, to the effect that they hire unqualified sons of top executives as a way of cementing relations with important clients. In these cases the implication is that the sons are incompetent and must be cared for as if they were mentally deprived persons. A recent article in *Life* suggested that Parsons College in Fairfield, Iowa, had been organized principally to take care of wealthy businessmen's sons who lacked the capacity or the desire to engage in serious studies but who wanted to have a degree. Much of this is hard to document, but the variety of measures taken for the care and feeding of top executives' sons who are considered incapable of doing anything on their own is common knowledge. It is unlikely that such emotionally pulverized offspring could be effective managers if and when they take over the reins of corporations from their fathers.

7

Not infrequently, the alienation between the businessman-father and the son who does manage to follow in his father's footsteps leads to great personal inhibition, as with Edsel Ford, who apparently suffered considerable frustration before his early death at the age of forty-nine. A biographer, Roger Burlingame, wrote that "Henry Ford's shadow so obscured Edsel that no adequate estimate of him by writers or public has emerged. He has been sketched as a 'nice fellow' with gentle manners, unfortunate as the son of a giant whose stature he could not have approached even had he been permitted to grow to the full measure of his ideals."

Even when a top-executive father has tempered his natural inclination to either dominate or desert his family, his sons have testified to the difficulty of proving their worth to themselves. When John D. Rockefeller, Jr., first reported to work at his father's office, he confessed that he felt himself ill-equipped and poorly qualified. It is interesting that he never did take over his father's position in the company; Rockefeller Senior was followed at Standard Oil by John D. Archbold. Rockefeller Junior primarily took over his father's interest in philanthropy, although he continued to represent many of his father's financial interests. From the beginning of his working career he complained that because he did not have the opportunity to earn his living on the basis of merit he had no external standards by which he could measure his performance. Later he told Raymond Fosdick, who was president of the Rockefeller Foundation and who wrote the official biography of J.D.R., Jr., "I never had the satisfaction of earning my way. The secretaries in the office here have an advantage I never had. They can prove to themselves their commercial worth. I envy anybody who can do that. I never had that kind of reassuring experience." Another time, when his father increased his annual salary by $1,000, he said, "I have always wished, simply as a matter of satisfaction to myself, that my salary might represent the real value of my services to the office, while as it is, and has been in the past, it represents rather your generosity."

A similiar anxiety was reported by Thomas J. Watson, Jr. In his youth, he explained, the company was "in the family unconscious." He grew up with the idea that he must inevitably dedicate himself to following in his father's footsteps, but he wondered if he had the necessary qualities within him to do so. He feared that as the boss's son he would never have a chance to find out. He was thrilled when he discovered that the family owned only three per cent of the stock, because this meant that the presidency of IBM would not come to him as a matter of inheritance; he would have to earn it. But the deep concern he felt about whether or not he would measure up is reflected in these words written to his father: "For many years I've been pointing consciously and subconsciously to one day be able to qualify with IBM. If the job paid nothing, even if I had to pay to keep the job, I would still want it. All my hopes, fears and ambitions are pointed in this direction. Without IBM I would be lost. . . . Frankly, I can hardly wait to begin. . . . I feel that I am now [after the war] at least seventy-five per cent better equipped mentally to follow in your footsteps and I intend to do so."

A more pointed expression of self-doubt was a statement made by Robert Sarnoff early in life when he thought he had clearly decided not to go into his father's business. "After all, my father had had tremendous success in the radio industry," he said. "It was a one-of-a-kind success, you might say. I felt there was little chance of anyone else duplicating it. His intellectual capacity, his position of authority in the field of radio and communications, a position he'd made for himself when he was young—all this appeared to make it almost futile for me to try to catch up with him. So when I went to Harvard, I thought of breaking out into new paths." Robert, of course, changed his mind. But his brother Edward, who felt the same way, stuck to his guns and never went into his father's business. His attitude was, "It's easier to do something on my own working away from my father than if I were working with him in the same business where, whether we [the sons] did a good job or not, there would always be a few who thought maybe we were pushed along because we were David Sarnoff's sons." Donald Hall, the son of Joyce C. Hall, said much the same, although he, like Robert Sarnoff, did go into his father's business. "No matter what you do," he confessed, "some people will think that being the son of the boss is why you got there."

Apparently this is true even when the son far outdistances his father's accomplishments. Jean Paul Getty, one of the great business tycoons of the twentieth century, never got over being sheepish about having inherited a large sum of money from his father. In his autobiography he wrote:

> Many fanciful—and entirely erroneous—accounts of the business relationship between us, my father and me, have appeared in print. Contrary to some published reports, my father did not set me up in business by giving me any outright cash gifts. George F. Getty rejected any ideas that a successful man's son should be pampered or spoiled or given money as a gift after he was old enough to earn his own living. My father *did* finance some of my early operations—but solely on the seventy/thirty basis [the father owned seventy per cent because he put up the money, the son owned thirty per cent because he conducted the business] . . . Incidentally, there is another popular misconception I'd like to correct once and for all. It has been said that my father bequeathed me a huge fortune when he passed away in 1930. Actually he left me $500,000 in his will—a considerable sum, I'll admit, but nonetheless a very small part of his fortune. It was a token bequest. My father was well aware that I had already made several million dollars on my own, and he left the bulk of his estate to my mother.

Many sons of corporate oligarchs reveal their anxiety about being born overprivileged by pointedly keeping their fathers out of their affairs as much as possible. A New York *Times* profile of William Wishnick told how he took over active direction of Witco Chemical Company from his father in 1964 and, in 1966 (when company sales were $146 million and earnings $6.35 million, the climax of nine consecutive years of rapid growth), made what was described as one of the biggest deals in the company's history. He decided to buy the Kendall Refining Company of Bradford, Pennsylvania, for $21.7 million. The *Times* reporter devoted the first three paragraphs of his story to a description of how the forty-one-year-old chairman negotiated all the details of the acquisition himself. Not only was no credit given to the father (who was then chairman of the finance and executive committees), but a special point was made that young Wishnick did not even consult members of his board, one of whom was Gustave Levy, senior partner of Goldman, Sachs and Company, considered to be a man of vast financial astuteness. The subhead for the story was "Computing of Terms for Take-Over Was a One-Man Job," as if to dispel any doubts that the son had taken over the helm and was steering the corporation completely on his own.

8

As these problems have become more apparent the argument against a policy of inherited corporate power has become increasingly persuasive. But the greatest support for the argument has been provided by the spread of public ownership in the course of the twentieth century. This has created an appearance of democracy in the corporate world and a philosophical repugnance to the idea of family dynasties.

When top management owns a small fraction of company stock —as with chairman Frederic G. Donner, who owned only 0.017 per cent of General Motors' outstanding stock, or chairman Lynn A. Townsend, who owned 0.117 per cent of Chrysler—the succession of a father by his son in a top executive position seems to be an anachronistic form of privilege. This is even true in connection with sons of important stockholders of the company, and at General Motors it was a source of pride in the recent past that none of the five members of the board who owned three per cent of the stock—Sloan, Kettering, Mott, Pratt and Brown—had any progeny connected with the company.

Companies selling stock to the public for the first time have had to recognize that one of the problems they will have to deal with is Wall Street's general opposition to nepotism. This is a cause of some concern to owner-managers who would like to maintain their option to bring the family into the business if they should want to, but they usually decide to take the risk because of the substantial financial benefits which they gain in a public sale. In a sense it is a sign of the growing hostility to nepotism in corporations that the owner-manager is willing to sacrifice the long-term probabilities of maintaining family control for the opportunity to gain immediate financial rewards.

The current trend toward the public sale of stock dates back to the enactment of the federal inheritance tax in 1916. It was then that the multimillionaire owner-managers of corporations began to worry about the liquidity of their estates at the time of their death. If their fortunes were tied up in corporate assets, their heirs would have a difficult time finding the cash to pay the government. If the owner-manager sold part of his stock during his lifetime and at a good market price, his sons would be far better off than if they had to sell their stock on his death (and possibly at a depressed price) in order to pay taxes. It was this problem which eventually forced the largest privately held corporation in America, the Ford Motor Company, to sell stock to the public, giving the family the opportunity to obtain a substantial amount of liquid capital which it could invest in securities that could be bought and sold at will. The Ford family was able to retain voting control of the company in spite of its public-stock issue and thereby continue the possibility of maintaining the dynasty. This pattern has been followed by many other family-owned companies that have gone public.

Many owner-managers have decided to sell their stock to the public with the express idea of bringing new blood into management and hence strengthening company operations. Here concern about maintaining a competitive position has taken precedence over family pride. The owner-manager is willing to give up the promise (though not necessarily the possibility) of a continuing family dynasty because he feels he can thereby enable the company to grow more rapidly and securely. These were the goals which prompted Peter Grace, the grandson of the founder of W. R. Grace and Company, to end the family control of that corporation a few years ago. Initially there were a large number of brothers and cousins of the founder, William Russell Grace, in the business. Voting control lay in a preferred stock which was almost totally family-held. When the family sold its stock, common shares made up over seventy-five per cent of the voting stock and Peter Grace owned only two per cent himself. Each of the Grace families had a representative on the board of directors, but the once family-dominated board was supplanted by one with an outside majority. The company was therefore considered to be in a much stronger position in terms of future growth.

Still other owner-managers want their companies to go public because they are intrigued by the idea of becoming public-corporation managers as distinguished from private owner-managers. To be the head of a privately held company which one's son can one day take over is held to be a provincial aim in modern management circles. To be the head of a public company carries far greater prestige. It is also more challenging. An executive may well have to take a reduction in his salary and expense account by making this change (compensated, to be sure, by capital-gains income from the sale of his stock); but he acquires new corporate status because he now has an opportunity to become a public figure. Although the owner-manager is on the same hierarchical level as public-corporation managers, and although he is personally richer than many of them, there is a psychological limitation to the respect he can gain from his peers if his family owns all the stock of his company. He is not a full-fledged member of the oligarchy until he has proven his ability to manage the public's money. Only then will his public reputation be measured in terms of company performance, for his record will show how well he can do with the vast economic resources available through stock issues, mergers and other financial schemes. His corporate power becomes a function of his skill and ingenuity as an executive, and he gains the opportunity to extend his influence far beyond the comparatively limited resources of his private fortune.

Once a company has become publicly owned, the sentiment against family succession in management positions may lead to a formal corporate policy against nepotism. U.S. Steel Corporation, Aluminum Company of America, Westinghouse Electric Corporation, Gulf Oil Corporation, Standard Oil Company (Ohio) and International Harvester Company have rules that no one can work under a relative's supervision. The First National Bank of Atlanta has a rule against hiring any relatives closer than third cousins.

Such policies have become increasingly common in recent years. In 1955 the American Institute of Management found that twenty-eight of the three hundred and seventy-nine companies which were rated as "excellently managed" had written policies banning or restricting the hiring of relatives. This was approximately seven per cent. Ten years later, on a larger sample of five hundred and thirty "excellently managed" companies, the figure had risen to twenty-eight per cent, with another thirty-six stating that their firms had unwritten policies to the same effect.

An officer of one investment house told the *Wall Street Journal* that whenever his concern underwrites a stock offering for a family-owned company going public it tries to persuade the company to take outsiders into its board of directors. "If a company's management is completely in family control and these people don't represent a cross section of business," he said, "you can't expect them to do as well as a board of broader experience."

Policies against nepotism are encouraged by financial analysts who fear that relatives may "bleed" company profits by putting short-term family interests over long-term stockholder benefits. One Wall Street brokerage firm cited the experience of a Detroit executive working under a chief executive who was a son-in-law of the founder and who ignored investment for the future in order to gain high profits and pay high dividends to please the family. "He wanted to drain out the last dollar so the family would say he was tremendous," said his ex-associate. "I would go to discuss future spending plans, and he would say, 'I don't give a damn about the next five years. What will it do to us now?'"

The conviction that it is a bad idea for relatives to be brought into the business is fostered by nonfamily executives who rebel against the unfairness of special privilege in corporate promotions. Typical was the experience of William L. McKnight, who in the early 1900s lost a promotion in the Minnesota Mining & Manufacturing Company to a son of the company's founder. McKnight tried to quit, but couldn't find another job, so he promised himself he would change things if he ever became an important executive in the company. Eventually he became chairman of the board, and the promise was kept. The company instituted a no-relative rule, which is adhered to so firmly that a former president, Richard P. Carlton, fired an employee who became a prospective son-in-law. Carlton's daughter became engaged to Thomas Hartzl, a 3M engineer; Carlton called Hartzl into his office and told him, "One of us is going to have to leave"; Hartzl left.

In other cases, the injunction against nepotism comes from the unhappy experiences of members of the family who are personally embarrassed by a policy of favoritism. Roscoe Cook once worked for a bank in which his family had an interest, but quit after three months. "Things were made too easy," he said, "and it would have caused trouble later on. I would have gotten too good a job too soon, and it would have created resentment on the part of the others; they would have assumed there was favoritism, and they probably would have been right." Cook took a job in the San Francisco–headquartered Wells Fargo Bank, where he rose to president—and instituted a tough no-relative rule.

The very definition of nepotism explains why it is frowned upon by public-corporation managers. According to *Webster's New International Dictionary*, nepotism is "favoritism shown to nephews and other relatives (as by giving them positions because of their relationship rather than on their merits)." Such a practice invites mismanagement. As Roger W. Babson, publisher of business reports, once put it, "I do not see why the control of ten or twenty thousand men should descend by inheritance through the death of some manufacturer any more than the control of a city or a state should pass to the son of a mayor or governor."

9

Despite these widespread sentiments, family dynasties are still playing a role in American corporations, and the compulsion to bring one's son into the business has not been eliminated as a factor in the corporate oligarch's emotional makeup. Even when executives have made a concentrated effort to keep relatives out of lower levels of management, succession has sometimes continued at the top. One of these is Johnson & Johnson, which has long enforced an unwritten but strict rule that relatives may not be employed at the management level. Yet in 1961 Robert W. Johnson, Jr., took office as president under his father, General Robert Wood Johnson, who was then chairman of the board. It may have been an interesting commentary on the prospects of such dynasties in the present climate that although this exception was made the son did not remain long in his job.

The rationalization most commonly made to justify the continuation of a dynasty in a public corporation is that the son just happens to be the most talented young manager working for the company. Supposedly the succession is not a function of blood relationship but of legitimate qualifications. When Willard Rockwell, Jr., was named president and chief executive officer of Rockwell Manufacturing Company by his father, who preceded him in that position, the elder Rockwell said, "I knew he deserved it. But from the beginning if I hadn't thought he would do the job, I'd have given him a bundle of money, sent him off to be a playboy and hired somebody who could." After Robert Sarnoff became president of NBC, his father counseled other fathers in his position not to try "to save yourself from possible criticism by some uninformed person who refuses to recognize that your son's ability had better be used for your company's benefit than that of a competitor. . . . I suggest that fathers have no more right to stand in the way of their sons' progress than the sons have to stand in the way of their fathers'." Even when Edsel Ford became president of the Ford Motor Company (which was then still a privately held corporation), his father told reporters that the "real story" was that a youngster just out of his teens should show such ability that he was placed in charge of a billion-dollar enterprise.

There is no doubt that in some instances management talent does run, or can be nurtured, in several generations of a single family. The history of Du Pont may not be typical of American corporations, but neither is it unique. Fourth-generation Ralph Lazarus, president of the Cincinnati-based Federated Department Stores, was given credit for the first $1-billion-sales year in Federated's history. Fifth-generation Amory Houghton, Jr., chairman and chief executive officer of Corning Glass, was described by *Fortune* as "living proof, if further is needed, that to be born with a silver spoon in your mouth is not necessarily a handicap in business." Walter Haas, Jr., tripled the business of Levi Strauss and Company after he took over from his father. Edward B. Rust succeeded his father as president of State Farm Mutual Insurance, then brought in three million new policyholders and raised premium income by well over one hundred per cent. Robert W. Galvin succeeded his father at Motorola and increased sales by close to fifty per cent.

The Maryland Cup Corporation has been managed by three generations of the Shapiro family, and nepotism is so extensive that twelve top officers and thirteen out of fifteen board members are Shapiros or Shapiros-in-law. The family claims that nepotism helps develop a close relationship among all top officers, gives them an ability to move fast and provides a strongly felt common goal. *Business Week* published a story about the company entitled "At Maryland Cup It's Nepotism All the Way" and lauded the family (which today owns approximately sixty-seven per cent of the stock) for the company's excellent performance. *Time* published a similar story on Maryland Cup under the headline "Neat Feat for Nepotism." The feat was to quadruple sales in ten years, from $25 million to $100 million, and still keep so many relatives in the business.

The best evidence that an interest in management can be developed as a family tradition is that periodically descendants of business pioneers direct their talents into a variety of corporate enterprises. This was the case with the descendants of Ferdinand Cullman, who emigrated to this country in the middle of the nineteenth century and started in the business of selling wine and cigars. Ferdinand's two sons, Joseph and Jacob, became merchants of domestic tobacco leaf and importers of Havana, Sumatra and Java tobaccos. The next generation consisted of Joseph Junior and Howard, who expanded the business into growing tobacco and buying stocks of major tobacco companies. The fourth generation consisted of the two brothers' seven sons, of whom three are today carrying on the family tradition. One of them is president of General Cigar Company; another is chairman of Philip Morris. Philip Morris, like other contemporary cigarette companies, has diversified into a variety of other industries with the acquisition of Clark Chewing Gum, American Safety Razor and Burma Shave. It is no longer the family tobacco business; it is a large public company with broad ownership of its stock and a management that is interested in expansion in many directions.

Sometimes a skilled manager who is descended from a business-oriented family rises to the top of a company with which his family had little if any connection. In early 1967 John B. Bunker was appointed president of Holly Sugar Company, the nation's second-largest beet-sugar-producing company. His official company biography showed that he was a fourth-generation sugar man. His father, Ellsworth Bunker, formerly chairman of the National Sugar Refining Company, had served the administrations of four Presidents: Truman, Eisenhower, Kennedy and Johnson. But the son John was carrying on the family tradition of management by developing a successful business career on his own.

To cite another example, the July 1967 issue of *Fortune* carried an intriguing article entitled "The Face of the Future at General Motors." It contained the biographies of six top executives who were considered prime candidates for the Presidency. One of them was Semon E. Knudsen, executive vice-president in charge of General Motors' nonautomotive and foreign operations. His father was William S. Knudsen, who was president of the company in the late 1930s. The son was not chosen for the job, but, in one of the most curious executive switches in corporate history, he was subsequently appointed president of Ford, a convincing indication that it was ability, not nepotism, which enabled him to rise to the top.

Many oligarch sons of oligarch fathers claim that they have never suffered from the psychological burdens which are commonly associated with nepotism, and that a good filial relationship not only is possible to establish but can be a great asset. Edgar Kaiser, who was called a "furious-paced son of a fabled father," claimed that he suffered little from the problems of growing up in the shadow of his successful father. "I'm the lucky one," he once said. "Dad built a lot of bridges, and he built one for me too." Some claim that a constructive partnership can be developed between the generations—fulfilling the dream which has so long excited the hope of industrial fathers. As Thomas J. Watson expressed himself to his son, "The thing that I am looking forward to with so much pleasure is having you to counsel with and help me plan my future programs along various lines. Ever since my father passed away, while I have had many very good friends to counsel with, I never felt that I had anyone with whom I could get the satisfaction that I received from my father. . . . I suddenly realized that now I have someone in my life to whom I can look with confidence."

But these examples of successful father-son relationships are exceptional and do not explain the widespread persistence of nepotism in a time when it has been officially condemned in management circles. It is perfectly natural to find some instances of management talent running in the family; after all, the same phenomenon has occurred in such fields as music, medicine, politics, law. The difference is that a son who follows his father in these other occupations rarely succeeds to his father's position. He may show even greater skill than his father, but his position will be more a function of his own ability and interests than his family heritage. Whereas in corporate life the father has the power to steer his son's career into the top spot whether or not the son is deserving of, or interested in, such responsibility. And judging from the number of companies in which family successions are continuing, it is obvious that this power is still being exercised extensively.

Many oligarchs maintain a controlling interest in a corporation in order to keep open the possibility of placing relatives in top management positions. Sometimes the purpose of such representation is supposed to be protection of the family investment, but more often it seems that the investment is kept in order to give business-minded members of the family an opportunity to jump to the top.

Significantly, the rate of family succession in medium-sized companies appears to be as high as it ever was. This can be seen from an analysis made in 1960 of the Young Presidents Organization, the members of which had been presidents of companies with sales of $1 million or more before they were forty years old. Forty-four per cent of these men were the heads of family corporations, three per cent married the boss's daughter, twenty-eight per cent started on their own, and twenty-five per cent got control through purchase or merger or were spotted as comers by management. Thus almost one out of two presidents of medium-sized corporations was still passing the scepter to members of the family.

Among larger companies there has been some reduction in family succession to top positions, but even here trained observers have been surprised to see how extensive family control still is. In an analysis of the 1966 facts and figures of the five hundred largest corporations in America, the editors of *Fortune* were startled to discover that controlling ownership in thirty per cent of these corporations rested in the hands of an individual or of the members of a single family. This is considerably lower than the fifty-six per cent which Berle and Means discovered in 1932, but it is far higher than most observers of the modern corporate scene would have guessed. By "control" the editors meant that the largest individual stockholder or members of a single family owned ten per cent or more of the voting stock; they did not include certain industrial companies in which the Mellons had a powerful influence but less than ten per cent ownership of voting stock. Richard K. Mellon alone was the largest stockholder in Alcoa (2.98 per cent) and in Gulf Oil (1.78 per cent), and he also owned .084 per cent of General Motors and ranked as the second-largest stockholder on the General Motors board of directors; however, the only Mellon entry among the one hundred and fifty corporations was Carborundum Company, in which Paul Mellon directly owned eleven per cent of the shares.

Among the many substantial public companies in which family control has made it possible for sons to follow in their fathers' footsteps are A. O. Smith Corporation, Joseph Schlitz Brewing Company, Campbell Soup, Jonathan Logan, H. J. Heinz, Anheuser-Busch, Douglas Aircraft, General Tire, Hotel Corporation of America, Sheraton Hotels, Howard Johnson's, Johnson's Wax, International Business Machines and Radio Corporation of America.

Family control, it should be pointed out, is not necessarily accompanied by the succession of a son to his father's position. Nepotism takes many forms and is often difficult to trace. It is interesting to note, in this respect, that father-son successions in large companies have declined in recent years. In 1928, F. W. Taussig and C. S. Joslyn discovered that fourteen per cent of the top leaders of the American business system were sons of the men who had held those positions in the same companies before them. Twenty-four years later, in 1952, W. Lloyd Warner and James Abegglen found that the figure had dropped to nine per cent. In addition, the number of industrial leaders whose fathers were businessmen of any sort (as distinguished from those who held the reins of the same companies the sons later took over) declined. In 1928, fifty-one per cent of the top business leaders were sons of businessmen; in 1952, only forty-one per cent were sons of businessmen. The professions (with law as the distinct leader), white-collar jobs and manual labor had all shown increases as occupations of fathers of corporate top executives. By 1964, the *Scientific American* survey showed that only ten per cent of top corporate executives said their fathers were wealthy, which is a different but relevant statistic. Of the ten largest companies in the country (measured in terms of 1967 sales figures)—including three automobile companies, four oil companies, and General Electric, U.S. Steel and IBM—only two, IBM and Ford, were headed by a son of a president-father.

Thus the record is somewhat uneven. One out of two corporate oligarchs in medium-sized companies is part of a continuing family succession. Four out of ten oligarchs of large companies are sons of businessmen. Two out of the ten largest companies are headed by sons of fathers who held the same positions, and with the rise of Semon Knudsen a third came close to joining that figure. In a larger sample of big corporations, approximately one out of ten sons follows his father as president, but three out of ten of these companies are still under family control.

It would be a mistake to generalize from this that all corporate oligarchs are still bent on creating dynasties. The dynasties in existence today among large companies are in the minority, which was not the case thirty-five years ago. However, this decline is taking place at an extremely slow pace, and in medium-sized companies there hardly seems to be any movement at all. It is probable, therefore, that most corporate oligarchs are still giving a considerable amount of thought as to whether or not their sons or sons-in-law or nephews or cousins should go into their business, and that the emotional pulls leading the oligarch to keep his family involved are still very much alive.

10

In summary, it can be said that in the second half of the twentieth century a theory of management has been accepted which says that nepotism is bad. This is supported by a long history of dynasties that have petered out for good and understandable reasons. But alongside this theory and this history there is a stubborn and persistent inclination to continue the practice.

The corporate oligarch of today feels under some pressure to make excuses when he passes the reins to a member of his family. Sometimes the excuse is valid and the son who takes over is genuinely deserving of the post. More often, the son is pushed into the position because the oligarch father retains a vestigial wish to create or continue a dynasty, and both the son and the company suffer the consequences.

One may speculate that the same emotional tensions which are responsible for the corporate oligarch's compulsions about money are also a contributing factor in his desire to have his children or his relatives follow him in business. If he feels guilty about the obsessive relationship he has to his job and disturbed about the triviality of a life devoted to turning out a satisfactory financial performance, and if this guilt results in anxiety about the comfort and security of his family, it is natural for him to be nervous about his children's careers. Also he may be subject to pressures from his wife; besides wanting to provide money for her children in order to gain some benefit from her husband's apparent success in life, she wants to help them gain career opportunities by taking advantage of his position. Unconsciously, both husband and wife may fear that their overprotected children will prove to be inadequate to the rigors of life; and in an effort to prove their fears groundless, they feel driven not only to bring their children into his business but to see to it that one of them rises to the top. By insisting that his child has earned the right to become a member of the oligarchy on his own, the father attempts to satisfy the demands of professional-management theory and at the same time tries to overcome his fears about his son's inadequacy—as well as his own as a father.

This trait obviously does not manifest itself in the same way among all chief executives of contemporary corporations. The attempt to perpetuate a family dynasty is far less common among corporate oligarchs than the attempt to become a wealthy man. But I believe that most oligarchs are in conflict to some extent about their relationship with their families and are, at best, uncertain as to how to guide their children in regard to their careers.

Even when an executive goes out of his way to keep his children from his business, the rejection is a form of confession that something is wrong. Not a few top executives have told me that they have actively discouraged their sons from going into business because the pressure would be too great for them, or because there would be too great a sense of competition with their fathers, or because it would be difficult for them to develop their own natural abilities in a business environment. One wonders whether such executives take this firm position in order to repress their own fears and anxieties or to help their sons fulfill their potentialities. The chances are that they would be delighted if their sons could go into the business, but as fathers they are horrified by the prospect of their sons' failure. Some top executives have said that they want their sons to go into a more rewarding field of endeavor than business, contradicting their own frequent claim that business is a noble undertaking. These strange antidynastic positions are in themselves reflections of the same anxiety which prompts other executives to encourage their sons to stay in the business. Both approaches are rooted in the father's concern about his own self-respect and his reputation both as a parent and as a modern manager, rather than in his sensitivity to his children's desires. Neither approach gives the proper consideration to the innate abilities and interests which the sons could and should be developing on their own.

The point is not that corporate oligarchs make bad fathers, although for the most part they probably do. I am dealing here with the motivations of top executives in an attempt to understand their behavior. I conclude that the corporate oligarch is inclined to be tense about his offspring for complicated emotional reasons and that this is a major concern in his life. Its effect on his working outlook is reflected in his vacillating attitude toward nepotism. He is sometimes opposed to it because his reason tells him it is bad for both his children and his company, or because his emotions tell him it could betray his personal failures as a husband and a father. He sometimes favors it because the old psychological pressures to create a dynasty are still present. But whatever policy he follows, the chances are that the emotional overtones of the relationship between his business and his children adds to the confusion in his mind about what the personal motivations of his job should be.

6

His Corporate Ideology

THE OFFICIAL DOCTRINE OF MODERN MANAGEMENT IS SUPPOSED TO resolve the problem of personal motivation by calling for devotion to the welfare of the corporation instead of to the creation of a family dynasty or a personal fortune. But, as we indicated earlier, this theory arises out of a misstatement of the corporate oligarch's legal responsibilities which gives the impression that he is accountable to his stockholders, and that by working "for the good of the company" he is meeting his obligations.

Whatever similarity there is between making money for oneself and earning a profit for the corporation, and between perpetuating the family name and maintaining the continuity of the corporation, enables the oligarch to feel that he is part of both an old and a new tradition. The modern executive likes to see himself as an entrepreneur cast in the heroic mold of the towering business figures of the last century, and at the same time he likes to believe that he has become the master of a new system of management which has emerged in this century. In this mixture of entrepreneur and manager, the oligarch wants both to remain a businessman who has an eye for making money and to become a professional capable of developing management methods to deal with new production, marketing and organizational problems.

This official doctrine however, does not fit the facts of corporate life. As we have seen in the last two chapters, the corporate oligarch, in regard to building an estate and establishing a dynasty, resembles his predecessors more closely than he likes to admit; we shall now see that in his formulation of management policies he is influenced by a desire for personal power to a far greater degree than his official doctrine pretends. This chapter will examine the latter point and will begin by reviewing briefly his formal theories about profit, growth, corporate continuity and social progress.

2

The first imperative of the official doctrine of modern management is profit maximization. "Profitability," wrote Charles G. Mortimer, chief executive officer of General Foods for eleven years, "is the name of the game." According to a spokesman for the 1963 annual convention of the National Association of Manufacturers, "profit should rank right alongside such hallowed concepts as home and mother and the American flag." The conscientious manager hunts for profit as eagerly and persistently as Diogenes searched for an honest man. Minnesota Mining & Manufacturing uses the word "scrounging" in its profit-seeking programs, colorfully describing how intently its executives concentrate on digging in unlikely places to uncover internal savings. Du Pont's measure of profits is what it calls ROCE (return on capital employed). George J. Stigler wrote that profit maximization is "the strongest, the most universal and the most persistent of the forces governing entrepreneurial behavior."

In this widely proclaimed passion for profits the oligarch feels he is carrying on the most admirable traditions of the great industrial magnates of the past. For instance, 3M's practice of "scrounging" had its counterpart in John D. Rockefeller's attention to the details of manufacturing. Typical is the story of Rockefeller's inspection in the early 1870s of a building in which refined oil was being packed for shipment abroad. One employee described the following incident:

> He watched a machine for filling the tin cans. One dozen cans stood on a wooden platform beneath a dozen pipes. A man pulled a lever, and each pipe discharged exactly five gallons of kerosene into a can. Still on a wooden carrier, the dozen cans were pushed along to another machine, wherein twelve tops were swiftly clamped fast on the cans. Thence they were pushed to the last machine, in which just enough solder to fasten and seal the lid was dropped on each can.
>
> Mr. Rockefeller listened in silence while an expert told all about the various machines used to save labor and time and expense in the process. At last Mr. Rockefeller asked:
> "How many drops of solder do you use on each can?"
> "Forty."
> "Have you ever tried thirty-eight? No? Would you mind having some sealed with thirty-eight and let me know?"
> Six or seven per cent of these cans leaked. Then thirty-nine drops were used. None leaked. It was tried with one hundred, five hundred, a thousand cans. None leaked. Thereafter, every can was sealed with thirty-nine drops.

The reverence for reducing costs and increasing earnings is natural to the American businessman, whether he be entrepreneur or oligarch. But, ideologically speaking, the latter believes he has an advantage the former never had. Since only a fraction of the earnings of a large public corporation goes into his own pocket, the oligarch does not feel miserly or grasping about this love of money. He simply believes that the profit motive is the stimulus for work invented by our society. He therefore thinks he can talk about company earnings as something which does not serve his selfish interests but which serves the interests of the whole community. Achieving company profits is supposed to fulfill his responsibility to stockholders and establish him as a good public servant. Producing an adequate return on financial investments is, at least in part, the cause that justifies the emotional investments he makes to build the company.

3

The second imperative of the oligarch's theory of management is corporate growth. Mortimer believed the chief executive needs bifocal glasses (prophetically, he wrote, invented by Benjamin Franklin) to see profit as the short-range benefit for the company and growth as its long-range goal.

The idea of corporate growth as a crusade is taken to be a natural product of the entrepreneur's ambitions. The competition among the old magnates was often warlike, but it was not until the corporation acquired its somewhat communal character in the twentieth century that a moral tone was introduced into the battles. Take, for instance, the following excerpts from an address by the president of the Paint and Wallpaper Association of America.

> . . . the energy to defeat our enemies and attain our rightful victory. . . . Our strongest, most powerful allies in our drive to progress are each other. . . . Every time one of us prospers we strike a blow for our cause. Each time one takes a loss, we all suffer a defeat and retreat. . . . Together we have shaped and established a mighty force for good in the industry. . . . We should set our sights on the stars while waging our battles for victory. . . . Our ideals and our noble intent must be implemented . . . The Cold War in our industry can be won and shall be won by us if we truly dedicate ourselves . . . with a firm determination to progress—and with deep conviction we will succeed . . . The heights to which this industry

can rise are bounded only by the breadth of our vision and the depth of our courage.

The analogy between a holy war and a sales campaign can be seen in grand strategies aimed at conquering new territories, new-product programs which look like battle plans, and direct confrontations with competitors which are described as price wars. Business publications are filled with articles describing top executives as if they were generals mapping a grand strategy. Thus, for instance, when Italy's anti-American oil czar died recently, Monroe Jackson Rathbone of Standard Oil (New Jersey) was quoted in *Fortune* as telling his associates that a "power struggle" would soon ensue. "Lots of people probably want to get that plum," he told them. "But no matter who gets it, there may be some change in the authority that goes with the job. Mattei's empire may shrink. A.G.I.P.'s invasion of England may end." And then in an aside he added, "But let's be careful not to give the impression that we are dancing on anybody's grave."

The spirit of adventure generated by these campaigns gives the oligarch a feeling of being engaged in an undertaking of great significance. As *Fortune* once put it, "The chief executive who leads his company through these engagements sees himself as the protagonist of an exciting drama, one in which he has triumphed over powerful forces bent on crushing him, or buying him off by tenders of comfortable security. Other people, he feels, may act out the hero in Walter Mitty daydreams, but he has played the hero in real life." He must move forward as a gallant and courageous warrior, never looking backward in cowardice. "He bristles at the faintest suggestion," the same magazine wrote elsewhere about the head of a large company, "that he . . . may ever be expected to plan for or preside over a [company] retreat, and he compares such thinking to the reported Pentagon study of surrender plans that made Mr. Eisenhower so furious a while back."

This forward movement is considered to be an inexorable law of nature. The oligarch believes today, as Carnegie and Rockefeller believed before him, that he is an agent of the greatest force in society, the force for progress. He is confident about the cosmic importance of this function. At Du Pont it has been a tradition that each president should double the size of the business during his term of office. Crawford H. Greenewalt was proud that he was able to almost treble the sales volume during his tenure. "A nation as well as a business that does not grow," exclaimed Robert W. Johnson, chairman of Johnson & Johnson, "will go back to the Dark Ages. The price of lethargy is slavery." Charles G. Mortimer said that "growth is a law of nature. To try to controvert this law is unnatural . . . For, in trying to circumvent nature's law, we could wind up stifling the great force for good which bigness has proved itself to be in our economy and in improving our standard of living." "To stand still," said an advertisement for *Look* magazine, "is to surrender and be swallowed up."

To quote Mortimer again, he once said at a management meeting, "You have heard of the seven-year itch. Well, I have a bad case of seven-year itch—an itch to develop this business to the full extent I believe it *can* be developed before I turn in my uniform. The key to progress in a great cooperative program of development can be summed up in a two-word question: *How soon?*" After that he came to be known affectionately as "How-Soon Charlie."

Because the products sold by corporations are believed to be essential to an advanced society with a high standard of living, corporate growth is viewed as a great social good. Like profit, it is part of the cause which justifies the oligarch's devotion to his work and makes him a dedicated public servant. When the product is essential to life, as are foodstuffs, the oligarch may feel that increased sales are more important than profit. "I would rather sell two pounds of butter at a profit of one cent," said John Hartford of the A & P, "than one pound at two cents profit." The price increase that would inhibit sales, Stephen W. Shea, executive vice-president of the company, pointed out, would lead to deprivation of millions of families who have trouble making ends meet. "I sincerely believe," said Shea, "that we in this business have a responsibility to do something about the cost and the standard of living." The value of the product to society was stressed by Mortimer when he declared that General Foods aimed at "growth not based on size, volume, expansion or diversification, per se, but on customer satisfaction created by the application of imagination, enterprise and skill with more and more products essential to their everyday needs, wants and convenience at prices that will provide reasonable and dependable profits on the funds, facilities, manpower and skills employed."

Customer orientation, manifested in increased sales, is as basic to the businessman's heritage as profits. According to a 1967 advertisement by the Magazine Publishers Association, it dates back at least to Benjamin Franklin's Poor Richard, who put his finger on the simple key to an expanding economy in the following anecdote:

> The skipper of a shallop, employed between Cape May and Philadelphia, had done us some small service, for which he refused to be paid. My wife, understanding that he had a daughter, sent her a present of a new-fashioned cap.
>
> Three years after, this skipper being at my house with an old farmer of Cape May, his passenger, he mentioned the cap and how much his daughter had been pleased with it.
>
> "But" (said he) "it proved a dear cap to our congregation."
>
> "How so?"
>
> "When my daughter appeared with it at meeting, it was so much admired, that all the girls resolved to get such caps from Philadelphia, and my wife and I computed that the whole could not have cost less than a hundred pounds."
>
> "True," (said the farmer) "but you do not tell all the story. I think the cap was nevertheless an advantage to us; for it was the first thing that put our girls upon knitting worsted mittens for sale at Philadelphia, that they might have wherewithal to buy caps and ribbons there; and you know that the industry

has continued, and is likely to continue and increase to a much greater value, and answer better purposes.

"Upon the whole, I was more reconciled to this little piece of luxury, since not only the girls were made happier by having fine caps, but the Philadelphians by the supply of warm mittens."

4

This sense of mission has made the corporation itself an object of great loyalty, and this is the third imperative of modern management theory. The oligarch does not consider himself merely a broker who invests money in machines that make goods that are sold at a profit which is invested anew in more machines, etc.; he sees himself as the head of an enterprise which is part of a great civilizing force. As such he is willing to give his all to the company. He believes that previous generations of businessmen felt precisely the same way and that one of his jobs is to see to it that future generations will carry on the tradition. Thus, Maurice J. Warnock of Armstrong Cork recalled his early training at the feet of his predecessor, "a great teacher [who] instilled in us the will to live and die for Armstrong." When George L. Hartford of the A & P was on his deathbed he whispered a plea to the next chief executive, Ralph W. Burger, to "take care of the organization." When John Jay Hopkins of General Dynamics knew he was dying of cancer he worked feverishly on a detailed long-range plan which he hoped would assure the continued growth of the corporation.

The notion that industrial corporations have the potential capacity—if not an actual destiny—to live forever had its origins in corporate law. It will be recalled that the corporation was conceived as an "immortal but fictitious person" established by the state for the purpose of creating a receptacle for certain rights and privileges which were to be given to an enterprise rather than to the people who were running it. The original idea was to facilitate ventures which were of interest to the government but were too risky for individuals to try on their own. In the course of the four hundred years since the corporate idea emerged and during which the legal framework of the modern corporation evolved, the idea of corporate immortality grew from a legal definition to an article of faith. What started out as an ingenious new approach to collective financing and property ownership led to the spawning of thousands of organizations which, if the hopes of their leaders were to be fulfilled, would be eternal. When a corporation becomes old it is not supposed to die—or even fade away like an old soldier; it is supposed to go on getting bigger and stronger.

The relationship of the idea of progress and corporate growth has also become an increasingly favorite theme during these four hundred years. Appropriately, the notion that progress was the underlying movement in history became popular in the sixteenth century, when the concept of the corporation came into being. By the eighteenth century, when the Industrial Revolution came to Europe, there were men who felt with Voltaire that life in Paris, London or Rome of that era was infinitely preferable to life in the Garden of Eden. Looking into the future, the French Physiocrats and the Encyclopedists described the object of society in terms of economic progress in which industry was the prime mover. One of them, Lemercier de la Rivière, said that "humanly speaking, the greatest happiness possible for us consists in the greatest possible abundance of objects suitable to our enjoyment and in the greatest liberty to profit by them." The ideas of Darwin and Spencer helped man to turn his attention forward and to believe that there were greater expectations ahead than there were glories behind.

In the nineteenth century, during America's great economic expansion, Emerson's phrase "the land of opportunity" became a popular watchword. And by 1930 the city of Chicago organized a centennial to celebrate what it called a "Century of Progress," proclaiming that progress was the special feature of our industrial society, a contention loudly echoed by General Electric's phrase "Progress is our most important product."

The corporation is thus looked on by the contemporary oligarchy as the primary instrument for the advancement of civilization. Its central feature is thought to be the ecological development of a social organization which John W. Gardner, former Secretary of Health, Education and Welfare, once likened to "a total garden . . . [where] some things are being born, other things are flourishing, still other things are dying—but the system lives on." The oligarchy does its best to manage the system with the degree of wisdom and vigor required to perpetuate its existence.

A sense of fulfillment stirs the oligarch who looks back at the origins of his company and takes pride in how much has been accomplished since it came into being. The contemporary oligarch feels that an identity has run through the line of succession from the beginnings of the corporation until the present time. For example, the 1965 annual report of the Worthington Corporation was entitled "A Report to Henry" and was addressed to Henry R. Worthington, whose invention in 1840 of the world's first direct-acting steam pump led him to open a small manufacturing business in Brooklyn, New York. One hundred and twenty-five years later the company was enjoying sales of $383 million a year and providing jobs for 19,629 people all over the world. In his "Letter to Henry" which opened the annual report, the then president, Frank J. Nunlist, wrote:

> I only wish, Mr. Worthington, that you were alive to read this report. It is addressed to you because we still admire and respect you, and because the company that carries on your name is very much alive today. You would be proud to know how much the people of your company contribute to the economy and society of our nation today. Some of your inventions, such as the steam pump and the water meter, are still made, little changed since your time. On the other hand, most of our products, our production methods, the economy and social environment of our nation have all changed drastically since your day.

The letter then went on to describe some of those changes and to outline the grand scope of the company as it stood in 1965. It concluded with the observation that

> while Worthington is just one company, our contribution to the economy and the great society in which we live is typical of the thousands of companies that make up our free enterprise system. American business is so completely interwoven with the fabric of the American dream that all too frequently its contribution to our society goes unnoticed. Indeed, our society profits as companies earn. You might say, Mr. Worthington, that this is your company's Social Balance of Payments report for 1965.

The larger the corporation, the greater the sense of nationhood felt by those who preside over its destiny. Recognizing this characteristic, *Fortune* once called Standard Oil of New Jersey a kind of Roman Empire of the modern business world. "An affiliate may importune from the heat of competitive struggle or the environment of a foreign country," the writer stated, "but (as with the Roman Empire) Jersey can never accede to a major request from a family member without considering what the reverberations through the provinces will mean to the larger interest—that of the Jersey company itself." In another article, *Fortune* called General Motors "a Darwinian force." It is taken for granted that not only personal concerns but the special interests of individual departments or subsidiaries must be subordinated to the good of the company as a whole. It is the responsibility of the oligarch to determine what that good is and to see to it that all levels and segments of management rigorously—and, if necessary, ruthlessly—pursue over-all company goals with all the resources at his command.

5

Here, then, are the official rules which supposedly guide the corporate oligarch in the formulation of his policies: He is profit-oriented. He is growth-minded. He is devoted to the welfare of the corporation and feels that by helping it fill the common needs of society he is serving the cause of progress.

Respect for these rules of conduct is theoretically what distinguishes the modern corporate oligarch from his admired but less sophisticated, and often less responsible, predecessors. The significant change in outlook marked by these principles is thought to be a function of the institutionalization of the corporation. For the nineteenth-century captains of industry, corporations were primarily instruments by which private ambitions could be realized. Today an executive who becomes the head of an already giant corporation strives to make it even larger because, he says, he is commited to help achieve its destiny as an institution. In the lexicon of modern management the former ambition is held to be a function of self-interest, while the latter is defined as public service. By producing a profit for the old industrial empires the tycoons were enriching themselves. By producing a profit for stockholders the oligarch is making sure that the capital resources of society are being utilized to their full capacity. By increasing the output of the corporation the oligarch is helping to raise the Gross National Product and hence the standard of living in the country. By contributing to the long life of the corporation the oligarch is strengthening the basic fiber of society and furthering the progress of civilization.

There is no doubt that this theory has at least intellectually persuaded the corporate oligarch that his role in society has been firmly established. He believes that he has worked out a set of principles that are consistent with his basic legal responsibilities, and that his commitments are both clear and worthy. Whatever uneasiness he may feel about the meaning of his life he attributes to the uncertainty of the human condition rather than to any question as to the validity of his imperatives.

6

It has been said that a businessman is not a good philosopher. His uncritical acceptance of the foregoing glib, overgeneralized, unrealistic description of his corporate vision would seem to confirm such a judgment. In his formulation of responsibilities and aspirations he likes to choose those words which cast him in the role of a noble leader dedicated to a great cause, regardless of how trite and hackneyed the ideas may be. This weakness may well be a result of his preoccupation with the slogans of advertising aimed at creating still other stereotypes; but whatever its cause, the corporate oligarch's penchant for platitudes in describing his corporate purposes has produced a fuzzy, and in many respects inaccurate, picture of his approach to management.

When his various imperatives are scrutinized critically, their superficiality quickly becomes apparent. It is not difficult to discover the drive for power behind the unconvincing claims to public service, and to understand why the failure to establish a true ideal to which the exercise of his power can be dedicated has prevented the oligarch from developing a meaningful purpose for the corporate undertaking.

To begin with, it is unrealistic to regard stockholders as the permanent constituency of the corporation. Although a public corporation always has stockholders, their interest, at least as matters stand today, is not to see the company prosper but to make as much money as possible. Notwithstanding the claims made in the name of "people's capitalism," stockholders do not feel they have bought a piece of a company; they feel they have bought a ticket in a game of chance. They do well at the game if earnings rise or show prospects of rising, because this will produce an increase in the value of their holdings. As transient owners, they can eventually sell their stock and thereby take their share of the profits. Even if they have what Norton Simon calls an "ownership complex," which means that while they hold their stock they imagine themselves to be the permanent owners of the company, they are not likely to identify with the long-range goals of the corporation.

As a result, there is a marked difference in the approaches taken by the corporate oligarch and by his stockholders toward the company. The corporate oligarch's fate and future depend on the increasing influence of his company in the corporate world; the stockholder's future depends on how wisely he buys and sells stock during a particular period of a corporation's history. This difference is reflected in conflicting views which the two parties have toward company profits. The stockholder wants as much profit as possible now in order to receive maximum return on his investment or to sell his stock at an elevated price and make another investment elsewhere. The corporate oligarch needs profits to protect his financial stability and to finance the growth of his company. The former calls for profit maximization. The latter calls for a shrewd balance between, on the one hand, investing in new ventures that expand the scope of the corporation and, on the other, sufficiently increasing profits to maintain and, if possible, improve the market position of the stock.

Galbraith calls the balancing act that management performs to achieve its purposes a policy of profit minimization rather than profit maximization. This means that the bolder a management becomes in its effort to expand corporate power the less likely it is to produce maximum profits on a current basis. The ambitious corporate oligarch is always thinking of the future, when his investments will pay off, but when the future comes he will again make investments for another future. Only by ceasing to try to expand his power can a corporate oligarch truly maximize current earnings, as Sewell Avery did when, fearful of the onset of a new depression in the 1940s and 1950s, Montgomery Ward made so much money that it was called "a bank with a store front." The result was a stagnating company which eventually was taken over by a more forward-looking management.

The tangential nature of profits in management policies was observed as long ago as 1954 by Peter Drucker, who wrote in *The Practice of Management* that "profitability is not the purpose of business enterprise and business activity, but a limiting factor on it. Profit is not the explanation, cause or rationale of business behavior and business decisions, but the test of their validity." He suggested that the purpose of business is to "create a customer," which is a way of saying that its purpose is to extend its power. "A business enterprise," he wrote, "can exist only in an expanding economy, or at least in one which considers change both natural and desirable. And business is the specific organ of growth, expansion and change."

Making decisions to spend company monies on projects that are aimed at creating new customers but must for the present restrict company profits is the principal method by which the corporate oligarch exercises his power. These are the most important decisions in the chief executive's hands, and his judgment in this respect determines the fate of the corporation.

That this is truly a function of power is clear if power is understood as "the production of intended effects." This is Bertrand Russell's definition of power, and as such he believes it to be the fundamental concept in social science in the same sense that energy is the fundamental concept in physics. The drive for power is characterized by a continuous attempt to increase the range of one's influence on external events. It also means keeping a tight hold on the management processes by which crucial decisions are made. "Since men love power," wrote Russell, "and since, on the average, those who achieve power love it more than most, the men who control the State may be expected, in normal circumstances, to desire an increase of its internal activities just as much as an increase of its territory."

It is precisely this desire to increase control of internal activities as well as expand the scope of external territory which makes the corporate oligarch reluctant to delegate major money decisions to his subordinates. It is not because he considers himself responsible for profit but because he wants to pull all the strings that make the company work that he constantly keeps his eye on the profit implications of all company moves.

A typical example of how the corporate oligarch uses the profit measure as a means of exercising power over corporate resources can be seen in the following summary of an executive-committee meeting at the Standard Oil Company (New Jersey) as described by *Fortune*. A report was given on a proposed refinery to be built at Marseilles. It was the job of the staff members to present all the facts; it was chairman Monroe Jackson Rathbone's job to evaluate its impact on the company's balance sheet. Was the marketing projection sound enough to justify the new refinery investment? How good were the estimates of costs? He didn't like the idea that a ten per cent latitude for emergencies or unforeseen situations (usually allowed by the company) might result in an additional $3 million or $4 million expenditure. The project was too big for that kind of thinking. Then he made his decision: the project was approved, but the budget was limited to $35 million; if the costs came to more, the responsible executives were to come back to the executive committee. This was a measured decision, carefully balancing the drain on capital resources against the prospects of extending the reach of the corporation and creating a new profit center.

It is this kind of decision making which makes it clear that power, not profits, is the first motivation of the corporate oligarch.

7

If one could believe that corporate growth did indeed produce some tangible good for society, the oligarch would be justified in giving such a high priority to expansion. But the credibility of the claim that businessmen are seriously concerned about the social value of their products has never been very high. Benjamin Franklin's delightful story about the young ladies of Cape May reflects the traditional attitude of the American businessman toward the art of stimulating new appetites, even when they have no readily apparent relationship to real needs. In many established corporations this has long been the basis for well-organized marketing strategies. Thus, Robert T. Stevens, head of J. P. Stevens, a textile company founded by his grandfather, once explained that his company has always been interested in finding out what people will buy, which is different from what people need. "We go to the marketplace," he once said, "and attempt to find out what the public wants. If the public wants straw, we'll weave straw. We're not wedded to any particular product." The management of American Can expressed the same point of view when its 1966 annual report stated that the company goal was "to be the acknowledged and accepted leader in the packaging field and all other fields of operation in which we are now engaged or may enter in the future." To this end the company would "be market oriented rather than product oriented and make certain that our organization and planning in all areas of our business reflects this fact."

The ability to modify or change the product to take advantage of new marketing opportunities rather than serve clearly defined public needs (which can be but are not necessarily the same) has shaped the development of Du Pont for more than one hundred and fifty years. Since its inception, the company has gone through four distinct phases in its growth. Each phase was brought to an end by government or competitive action limiting growth in a particular direction, and each new phase began by developing a new kind of marketing opportunity. The earliest phase covered the company's first century of existence, when it became a monolithic producer of gunpowder and explosives. The second phase began in 1912, when the historic antitrust decrees broke up the company into three separate entities, Du Pont, Hercules Powder and Atlas Powder. The next twenty years was a period of diversification through acquisition and merger, and the company spread its operations into paints and finishes, dyes and pigments, acids and heavy chemicals, cellulose plastics and coated textiles, and rayon and cellophane. The company also bought $50 million worth of General Motors stock. The third phase began in the late Twenties, when acquisition became more difficult and growth was made possible through basic research and internal development. The result was the development of the first U.S. commercial synthetic rubber, of nylon and of many other products invented through a study of the internal molecular structure of matter. The fourth phase began in 1961, with the antitrust ruling by the courts which forced the company to start divesting itself of its $3 billion worth of General Motors stock. Basic research was no longer so promising an area of major corporate investment; Chemstrand, Union Carbide and other competitors could keep pace with Du Pont scientists. Now emphasis had to be put on intensive consolidation of operations and strong marketing programs.

The argument that what the public wants and is willing to pay for is invariably good for society has not been supported by history, as we shall see in the next chapter. Progress cannot be equated with the proliferation of goods. Although modern man is continuously confronted with scientific discoveries which "endow human life," as Francis Bacon put it, "with new inventions and riches," every new invention does not automatically contribute to the advance of civilization. The insistent determination to improve the physical condition of man well beyond basic comforts has little to do with the deeper values of human life.

In measuring progress, one must define the values which are being advanced. A corporation that grows is making progress in its own development, but a society which is inundated by a flood of commercial products may not be making progress toward a more meaningful or rewarding life for its citizens. If an oligarch is serious about relating his corporate ambition to social progress, he must be respectful of critical evaluations of his product not only in terms of its marketability but in terms of its effect on the lives of people who buy it.

It is this concern which the most sophisticated oligarchs find the least relevant to their ambitions. They would rather not concern themselves with the problem of finding an equation between corporate growth and social progress. For them the basic question is "What is good business?" A choice illustration of this can be found in the creation of newspaper chains. The field of journalism is one which traditionally has been the home of men who feel deeply about the role of news media in society. Publishers in the past have been men who wanted to help shape society according to their personal vision. Many of them were extremely powerful in relation to the development of national policy. In this respect they were more like pamphleteers and pundits than like corporate oligarchs. Samuel I. Newhouse, however, built a vast publishing empire by acquiring newspapers that others had developed. He was a newspaper collector rather than a publisher. His power rested in the properties he owned, not in the public policies he formulated. As his collection grew, he became less interested in what was published in his newspapers, which he rarely read. Often their editorial policies did not agree with his views. He was an integrationist, but he permitted his Birmingham, Alabama, paper, *The News,* to be rabidly racist. He was a registered Democrat, but many of his newspapers supported Republican candidates. The newspaper world was appalled and felt that he was doing great damage to the cause of good journalism, while the corporate world was filled with admiration.

The suggestion that the expansion of corporate power may be in conflict with progress has been raised increasingly by critics outside the corporate world. This was the view which led to the breaking up of the giant trusts in the early 1900s. It is now being discussed again in connection with the proliferation of conglomerate corporate empires. The legal question aside, what is at issue is management's responsibility to the public. The oligarch thinks his primary responsibility has to do with maximum utilization of management talent, financial resources, product capacities and marketing tools. It has scarcely entered his mind that he should find a way to assess his activity in relation to the highest values of society.

8

The only remaining justification for growth as a noble corporate aim is that it contributes to the increase of the Gross National Product, one of the country's most talked-about goals. But even if this were to be acknowledged as a worthy aim, clearly it is the *result* of corporate growth, not its conscious aim.

It is far more realistic to state that the tremendous pressure which impels the corporate oligarch continuously upward is his fear that if he doesn't keep pushing he may fall down. "Nothing is so compelling [in the corporate world]," wrote John Kenneth Galbraith, "as the need to survive."

The grandiose sentiments expressed by top executives about the virtues of growth should be understood as promotional jargon intended to persuade employees that if ever the company should begin to lose ground the forces of destruction may be unleashed. "A company must grow or it must die"—that is the oligarch's real first principle. Because the fear of death is the deeper motivation underlying the desire for conquest, even those who are most enthusiastic about the importance of increased sales disclaim an obsessive interest in growth. Charles G. Mortimer, who once called growth "a law of nature," elsewhere tempered his views by saying that a responsible chief executive is concerned about preserving the "good condition" of the corporation. Crawford H. Greenewalt was more specific about his reservations. "Growth per se," he said, "is meaningless. Rather it's a question of soundness and worth."

It is interesting to note that it is in regard to corporate survival that the different personal goals of management and stockholders are most likely to clash. There are times when it is to the interest of the latter to liquidate the company, but this is something to which management seldom acquiesces.

A striking example of such a conflict of goals was the struggle for control of the Endicott Johnson Corporation in 1960. The story began when Albert A. List, a wealthy financier, was persuaded by his friend J. M. Kaplan to make a bid for shares in Endicott Johnson, the old-time shoe-manufacturing company. Kaplan, who earlier in his career had built the Welch Grape Juice Company and more recently had spent much of his time in philanthropy, was a large Endicott Johnson stockholder and a member of the board of directors. He had tried to bring about a change in management policy that he thought would help to arrest the company's declining profits and sales. President Francis A. Johnson had resisted. Kaplan then interested Albert A. List, president of Glen Alden Corporation, a man of broad financial interests and, like Kaplan, heavily involved in philanthropy, to make a public offer to buy Endicott Johnson shares on the open market. The offer was made without advising management, and Johnson considered it a treacherous raid on the company. He called on the inhabitants of the three towns in New York's Susquehanna Valley where the company plants were located to take up arms against the invaders. He warned that a new management would close the plants for the purpose of cutting losses. Endicott Johnson had a long history of outstanding community activities, and so Johnson was able to persuade large numbers of grateful townspeople to use their savings to buy stock on the open market. This drove the market price above the Glen Alden offer and put substantial amounts of stock into the hands of friendly citizens.

In his first public statement about the stock offer, Johnson accused his enemy of waging a "blitz campaign." Afterward he vowed to fight to the end to retain control of the company and warned that the triple cities would become ghost towns if he lost. In the next few days violent opinions were expressed by the townspeople about the intentions of the invaders. Stock was bought up by plant employees, by church groups, by veterans' organizations, by the Chamber of Commerce. One group explained its actions as a means of preventing the "move . . . by outsiders to obtain control of this great American company that belongs to and is a part of Broome County." The Binghamton Furniture Company ran an advertisement, "Help EJ this week. Get free Endicott Johnson stock—this week only—with any $200 furniture purchase." And Johnson, in speeches to dozens of gatherings, said, "I couldn't live with myself if I left you people to him. I couldn't live with that and I won't."

The campaign was eminently successful. List was not able to buy enough stock to gain control, and he finally sold what he had to the employees' pension fund. Johnson was triumphant. When the shouting was over, *Barron's* reported that to all appearances the good citizens of Binghamton, Endicott and Johnson City had won a famous victory. "Far from applauding, however," the lead editorial stated, "*Barron's* is moved to wonder, like little Peterkin, what good will come of it."

The editor reflected the classic interests of the profit-oriented stockholder. Management had won its battle for the survival of the company, but the stockholders had lost an opportunity to arrest the decline in their assets. Unhappily, a year later the stockholders' equity was in worse shape than ever. The company lost over $12 million in 1961, and in 1962 the price of the stock dropped to less than one third of what it had been in 1960. The company had been saved from liquidation, which was what management wanted; but it was the stockholders who paid the price.

9

The validity of the third imperative of management theory, loyalty to the corporation, has been seriously challenged by the behavior of the executives responsible for the development of multidivisional or conglomerate corporations in the 1950s and 1960s. These companies are in effect corporate cannibals which swallow other companies to feed a new kind of appetite. In the process, old company loyalties are subverted and accommodation to corporate opportunism takes their place. The object of survival is no longer the corporation; it is the oligarchy itself.

This is not to say that the conglomerate executive is considered an intruder in the management elite. He may be resented by chief executives of companies that are subjected to raids, but his ability to show spectacular growth has made him something of a hero in management circles. The point I'm making here is that no one can admire the performance of these remarkable high flyers without acknowledging that "Dear Henry" letters are becoming obsolete.

Royal Little was one of the first to develop this method of merger and acquisition. He began his career in 1923 by starting an enterprise called Special Yarns Corporation. In 1944 he renamed his company Textron and tried to build a large combine that would be completely integrated from raw fibers to finished apparel. By 1949 he had found that this wasn't working too well, and he decided to pull the company apart. In 1952 he embarked on a new kind of acquisition program: he took over American Woolen, which had huge tax-loss credits and large liquid assets. This gave him the basis for a host of acquisitions (the largest and most ambitious was Bell Aircraft), which in ten years resulted in a corporate giant put together out of more than fifty large and small corporate entities.

At about the same time, James Spencer Love of Burlington Mills began putting together the biggest textile company in the world and in the 1950s acquired companies at an amazing rate; when he died in 1962, he had realized his ambition and was still going strong. He had pushed the thirty-six divisions of his company past the $1-billion mark. His expansion was so rapid that one of his associates once said, "It was like watching the Indian rope trick. One minute Spencer was standing there with nothing in his pocket but that one hocked cotton mill in North Carolina, his first acquisition. The next, he was climbing upward so fast he was practically out of sight." Another famous company acquirer was John Jay Hopkins, who built General Dynamics from a sales volume of $37 million in 1947 to $1.7 billion in 1957. His ambition was for his company to beat General Motors and become the largest company in the world, which conceivably it might have done if he hadn't been cut down by cancer in his prime and succeeded by a new management that made some catastrophic errors in judgment.

The technique of growth through acquisition is in some respects a modern variation of the Standard Oil trust-formation procedure of the nineteenth century. The present-day approach has led to what have been called "free-form" companies, not bound to any particular product or industry. This has become so extensive in the modern corporate world that in 1967 seventy-two of the five hundred largest corporations in the country had divisions in four different industry categories, and forty-six were in eight or more categories. One company, Litton Industries, had divisions in eighteen categories and included such diverse products as electronics, business equipment, aerospace, shipbuilding and medical instruments. Other major conglomerates were Gulf + Western, International Telephone & Telegraph, Walter Kidde, Ling-Temco-Vought, Teledyne, Textron. Some of these companies were moving so fast in their acquisition programs that one, Gulf + Western, picked up nine companies in one year, while another, Litton Industries, picked up eight. The Federal Trade Commission reported that in 1967 there were 1,496 mergers of manufacturers and mining companies, a rise from 995 mergers in 1966.

Theoretically, mergers can lead to greater profitability and growth for both companies involved in the action. Executives like to talk about a synergistic effect in which a fusion of resources produces a result which is more than the arithmetical sum of the parts. Through merger programs it is theoretically possible to acquire the best-qualified executives available and give them the greatest opportunity to use their talents. Also, production and marketing know-how in allied fields can be pooled to provide improved operations for merged companies. Sometimes the financial resources of a large company can help to stimulate the expansion of an acquired organization that has heretofore been starved for capital. Often unprofitable operations of an acquired company are closed down or sold off after a merger and the more promising segments are strengthened.

The fact that often these promises remain unfulfilled has not dampened the enthusiasm for this method of corporate expansion. One of the problems that have plagued multi-industry acquisitions is that companies which are acquired often continue to be managed exactly as they were before. As a result, the projected increase in profits may turn out to be illusory. Until recently the temporary illusion of greater earnings could be created if the purchase was made with convertible preferred stock. The common stock of the acquired company was then retired, and for a short while the earnings of the combined companies were applied to the number of shares of the acquiring company which remained constant. But once the convertibles were traded in, the stock was diluted and the earnings were spread over what in effect were the total number of shares of the two companies. (This practice was challenged by an American Institute of Public Accountants ruling in 1967 stating that per-share earnings must be based on convertible securities as well as common stock.) It is still possible for earnings to be increased for a short time if one of the companies has a sizable tax loss while the other is a big taxpayer; the old loss can be deducted from new profits for several years, which means that the stockholder will have the benefit of nontaxed earnings. But this is not a long-term benefit, either, since the tax loss is eventually used up and the surviving company may be burdened with the unprofitable operations that produced the tax loss in the first place. As a result of these and other factors, a study made by *Fortune* in 1967 found that over a period of time there was no significant difference between the earning performances of conglomerate and other companies.

Actually the synergistic effect of most merger programs is produced by the excitement that is created by a company which has a dynamic expansion program. There is an expectation that, somewhere along the road of an acquisition-minded company, profits will begin to multiply. This expectation is responsible for the extraordinary amount of trading that takes place in stocks of many companies with active acquisition programs, and for the often spectacular rises in their prices (sometimes in excess of fifty times earnings). In 1966–67 conglomerate companies were among the favorite growth stocks on the market and far outgained Dow averages in their rebound from earlier bear-market lows, with three of them—Teledyne, Ling-Temco-Vought and Gulf + Western—showing record gains.

To a large extent the success of conglomerate operations depends on the subordination of previous corporate identities to an enterprise which is constantly in the process of adding to itself. Unfortunately, loyalties which old employees took seriously cannot so easily be transferred, and the result is a general weakening of the basic sense of commitment to the corporate welfare. What was once a cohesive entity capable of creating an impressive history of accomplishments and inspiring deep commitments on the part of dedicated employees is rapidly becoming a volatile structure in which a particular group of ambitious oligarchs can at a given time build an effective power base.

The lack of cohesiveness among acquired companies led *Business Week* to call Borg-Warner, which almost doubled its size in ten years, a "fortress of permissive management." The company president, Robert S. Ingersoll, was quoted as saying in a speech to key executives, "We would like to have you temper your divisional interests wherever they conflict with over-all corporate interests. Better coordination than we have been able to achieve is demanded." The company's difficulty in achieving this coordination led *Business Week* to speculate that it had grown too fast.

But there have been many companies in the acquisition business that have grown far more rapidly than Borg-Warner. A study by Ruder & Finn of a company that had grown about twice as fast as Borg-Warner (in *five* years it had more than tripled its sales and had doubled its income of $250 million) showed that the difficulty inherent in the acquisition procedure is a matter of disappearing identity, not of growth rate. One of the major problems that faced the company, which had seventy-six plants engaged in a broad range of activities, was to make the individual divisions more parent-company-minded. "People in some places," said one top executive, "still remember a local division as the company it belonged to in the old days, before it became a division."

In a similar study of another highly diversified company with a dramatic growth record (its annual sales rose from $300 million to $800 million in five years), the comments were very much the same. One executive of a division that had been acquired said, "There's no point in trying to build up our old name now—that's all gone." Many wondered what the parent company was "up to." Others complained about the feeling of being a member of a small family in a big town.

The character of the oligarch in this new type of diversified corporation is quite different from that of the oligarch in the more traditional corporation. Acquisition-minded executives tend to be remarkably unemotional about their companies, and uninterested in setting up the large corporate staffs or impressive corporate offices that in the past were an important means of building a sense of history. These new oligarchs are extremely fast-moving, ambitious and efficient. As one division executive of the Ashland Oil & Refining Company said, "I can call up at eleven o'clock at night and usually get a decision on the spot. If not, I can get an awfully close reading on the situation." Another said, "I just don't think anybody can outmove us. We've already done it while others are still talking about it." There is great flexibility and little formality or red tape. And there is no sentimentality about the corporate tradition. Corporate identity for the parent company is important only if it contributes to improved performance. Whatever is unproductive is ignored. The whole idea of the corporation as an immortal enterprise seems to have faded from the minds of these corporate oligarchs. They are not working to create a great heritage. They are working to make the best-possible track record now, while they are in power; the future will take care of itself. They plan ahead—as Hopkins of General Dynamics did even on his deathbed—but it is in terms more of continuing the strategy than of erecting a permanent structure. They fully expect some other manager to come along after they are gone and rearrange the corporation to suit the expediencies of his day.

The increase of this type of executive in the corporate oligarchy is evident in the number of tender offers made recently. In the first six months of 1967 there were one hundred and twenty-three such tender offers, compared with only forty-six in the last half of 1966. The danger of invasion by these hungry oligarchs has become so great that some more tradition-minded executives who still feel a loyalty to the corporations in which they may have spent all their working lives have made secret pacts to come to each other's rescue in case of attack. Under the terms of agreement, one company will start buying its ally's stock if a third firm tries a takeover. This can drive the market price of the company's stock up high enough to foil a tender offer. Other executives have made what are known as "defensive mergers," seeking refuge with partners who are more to their own liking rather than permit themselves to be taken over by a raider. Still others have attempted to protect themselves by making some careful acquisitions of their own which do not threaten their identity but which, through an exchange of stock, put a substantial percentage of common stock in friendly hands. And, finally, many companies have made a concentrated effort to win public recognition for the excellence of their management's past record and future planning, in the hope that stockholder confidence will keep the price of the stock up and, therefore, less vulnerable to raids.

The oligarch of a traditional corporation who tries to defend himself has a sense of sovereignty about the enterprise over which he presides. The new, diversified manager is loyal to the *system*. He can change jobs at any time. His self-esteem is based on performance and power more than on position. He believes that the corporation is not an end to be served, but a means to be used in the effort to make the system work better and to increase his influence on the economic life of the nation.

The executives who control the destiny of the acquisition-minded companies have been called the "energetic tigers of corporate management." They have shown themselves ready to give a higher priority to earnings than to growth, although they maintain their interest in profits as "salt in the stew," for the benefit of stockholders. They have no respect for the survival of any corporation and are responsible for the demise of many. They are men in a hurry, and they know where they are going: to the top of the corporate world.

10

Thus the official doctrine of modern management fails to explain the nature of the corporate oligarch's real interests. He claims that he has replaced the old entrepreneur's concern about wealth and dynasty with profit, growth and company loyalty. This is not so. He is more likely to minimize than maximize profit, because the source of his power is his organization rather than his wealth, and he competes with stockholders for funds with which to expand the scope of company operations. He does not believe that growth per se is the goal of management; he is primarily interested in his own survival. He is loyal not to the corporation but to the oligarchy itself, which increasingly countenances the destruction of older corporations to further its ambitions. And he is more interested in naked power than in progress; when the two conflict, his inclination is to choose the former.

This is not to say that the oligarch has not made an impact on events in the contemporary world. It does mean that for the most part he is operating without clearly defined goals. What he assumes to be his corporate ideology is instead a mixture of clichés and outmoded theories. The robber-baron element in his personality is indeed on the wane; he is somewhat less interested in building a fortune and having his children succeed him as head of the corporation than his predecessors were. But he has not become the business professional he claims to be. The inconsistency between his professional ideology and his real behavior shows him to be a center of power without a convincing purpose.

7

*His Conflict
with the
Public Interest*

THE CHIEF DANGER TO MANKIND FROM THE LOVE OF POWER, Bertrand Russell observed, is that unchecked it leads to the oppression of peoples. Since corporate growth is not synonymous with social progress, it is clear that corporate power, like all other forms of power, must be checked if the public interest is to be protected. But, like all other men who love power, the corporate oligarch has always fought against any attempt to limit his freedom. He has vehemently opposed as "undemocratic" or "socialistic" any restrictive legislation aimed at curbing his power, and he has accused his critics of being sensationalist rabble-rousers who are more interested in seeing their names in newspapers than in serving the public. Top executives feel they have a "moral right," as Maurice Baum put it in an unpublished analysis of the ethics of the Kefauver Committee hearings on the drug industry, "to independent economic judgment as to the conduct of their privately-owned [*sic*] corporations, insofar as such conduct is not in violation of any known laws or accepted legal precedents."

The very idea of finding a new means of making a social assessment of business is puzzling to the corporate oligarch. He does not accept the idea that employees, stockholders, consumers and the general public need to be protected from the corporation. Indeed, he does not believe that he has the right, or that any self-appointed guardian of the public interest has the right, to decide what is good for people. People must decide this for themselves, and if they are free to make their own decisions, he believes, they will make the right choice.

This is a convenient theory, for it gives the oligarch license to sell anything the customer will buy. It also makes legitimate the attempt to create new consumer appetites by what Galbraith calls "the management of demand." For the theory does not insist that the customer make his "buy" decision without being influenced— or even led—by the seller. The customer's freedom is safeguarded so long as force is not used. Persuasion is fair game.

Opposition to this theory or earlier versions of it has been outspoken since Revolutionary days. Politicians, journalists, scholars, labor leaders and spokesmen for community groups have been worried that the power of the corporation could become so great as to jeopardize the freedom of the individual citizen. In a democratic society, they argue, the lives of people should not be controlled by the policies of commercial enterprises. Even competition does not guarantee democracy; the customer's purchase is no substitute for the citizen's vote. Because a company can sell its product it does not follow that the company is operating in the public interest. The public has a right to define its interests on the basis of noncommercial values and to call for government regulation when it thinks these values are threatened.

As an instrument for checking corporate power, the self-appointed critic of industry has often been remarkably effective. He is a man who feels his job has only begun when he exposes to public view those corporate practices which he thinks are harmful. He is usually an active reformer whose goal is to eliminate such practices. He often has a flair for publicity and seeks to bring an end to exploitation by using the power of the press to fight the power of big business.

The corporate oligarch's failure to appreciate or even respect contributions made by his critics has often made him an enemy— rather than the advocate he claims to be—of progress.

2

The earliest critics of industry thought that exploitation of the public was implicit in every act of incorporation. "Corporations with exclusive privileges," wrote "An Observer" in the January 7, 1792, edition of the Philadelphia *General Advertiser,* "have ever been deprecated as evils by the friends of equal liberty. Attempting to increase them in England was one of the causes of that civil war which brought Charles I to the scaffold; and in more modern times, it claims a share in producing an event still more important . . . the French Revolution. . . . If corporations . . . have created so much jealousy and fear in other countries, how much ought this to excite the same passions in this country." There was opposition among the legislatures to many of the corporations that were proposed, and not a few were voted down.

Public fear of corporations continued to be expressed in the early nineteenth century, climaxing in Andrew Jackson's administration when the leader of the New Democracy became the champion of the poor against the rich. One of Jackson's targets was the most powerful financial institution in his time, the second Bank of the United States. Critics called the bank a "monster" and a "hydra of corruption." In 1832 the men who controlled the bank attempted to get a bill passed by Congress to renew its charter. To help their campaign, they put financial pressure on key newspaper publishers to write editorials about the "fearful consequences of revolution, anarchy and despotism" which assuredly would ensue if Jackson were reelected that year. This behind-the-scenes pressure was brought to light by a subsequent Congressional investigation. One newspaper that had succumbed to the pressure was New York's *Courier and Enquirer*, which suddenly reversed its pro-Jackson position when the bank threatened to call a loan of $50,000.

Business interests won the first round when Congress passed the bill to recharter the bank. But they lost the fight when Jackson vetoed the bill. To justify his veto Jackson charged that the stockholders of the bank would have gained a windfall of $7 million through increased value of their stock if the bill became a law. By preventing this, Jackson added to his already considerable reputation as the first man of the people elected to the Presidency. In a closing paragraph of his message to the Senate (which subsequently upheld his veto) he asserted that "the rich and powerful too often bend the acts of government to their selfish purpose." His purpose was to check the growth of "moneyed power" which threatened to dictate the laws of the land. A few months later he was reelected, winning by an even larger margin than in 1828.

It wasn't until fifty years later that the practice of attacking business leaders in public became so popular a specialty for journalists that the press emerged as an effective counterforce to excessive corporate power. One of the earliest of a long series of sensational writers who, down to our own day, have prodded and irritated both the industrial tycoon and the corporate oligarch with abusive, often inaccurate but always provocative accusations was Henry Demarest Lloyd. Son of a New York minister, he first won recognition with a speech in 1880 to the Chicago Literary Club called "A Cure for Vanderbiltism." Lloyd called for railway regulation to end the abuses of the lords of industry. Shortly afterward he published an article in the *Atlantic Monthly* called "The Story of a Great Monopoly," which was extremely well received despite its many glaring errors and falsehoods about the Standard Oil Company. He accused the company of making forty-four per cent profit on every barrel of kerosene, but he included nothing in his calculations for the heavy cost of distribution and marketing, for capital investment, for plant depreciation, for the cost of barrels or for risks and incidentals; when all this was added in, the actual profit was less than three per cent. However, Lloyd did bring to national and international attention (the article was reprinted by the London *Railway News,* and thousands of copies were distributed to English investors) many rank practices of the time. He showed that monopolies were destroying their competition by obtaining secret rates from the railroads which enabled them to undersell the smaller companies, and that many of the big companies were using money taken from the public to influence newspapers, legislators and even courts.

So widespread was the reaction to Lloyd's attack that even Herbert Spencer, the leading philosopher of the day, said in a talk given in New York in 1882, "I hear that a great trader among you [Rockefeller] deliberately endeavored to crush out everyone whose business competed with his own."

More than a decade later Lloyd was still making a career out of his sensational attacks against Standard Oil. His book *Wealth Against Commonwealth* was published in 1894; like his initial article, it was bad history, full of errors and misleading biographical data, but it was widely read. Then ten years later a more careful critic appeared on the scene. In 1904 Ida M. Tarbell's *History of the Standard Oil Company* was published. Her argument was essentially that Rockefeller and his associates had built up a combination which was admirable in its organized efficiency and power, but that nearly every step of the construction of this vast industrial machine had been attended by fraud, coercion or special privilege, and that this had debased the whole standard of American business morality. Unlike Lloyd, Tarbell had a fine reputation as a brilliant and reliable writer, and her book was hailed then, and is still considered today, a classic in corporate criticism. In many ways it was the cornerstone for the muckraking era, a period which began strangely at the turn of the century and ended just as strangely a decade later.

3

Rockefeller's reaction to all of this criticism was silence. For almost thirty years he refused to reply publicly to the attacks against the Standard Oil Company. "If there was ever anything in this country," wrote J. C. Welch in 1883, "that was bolted and barred, hedged round, covered over, shielded before and behind, in itself and all its approaches, with secrecy, that thing is the Standard Oil Company." Many of Rockefeller's associates pleaded with him to speak up and clear the record, but he refused to "squabble with slanderers."

Other business figures of his day—Morgan, Hill, Frick, Harriman, Huntington—followed Rockefeller's lead and declined to speak up in their defense when attacked by critics. The result was a growing feeling that the men who headed the great corporations were guilty of the evils of which they were accused. "It dawned upon Americans," Charles Edward Russell wrote, ". . . that the republic could no more endure an oligarchy of capitalists than an oligarchy of slave-holders."

In October 1882 William Henry Vanderbilt uttered the legendary phrase which marked the high point in the industrial mogul's contempt for his critics. Vanderbilt had set out in a private train to survey his northwest empire, and at Michigan City, Indiana, he invited reporters to have a conference with him about his various interests. He discussed government rate regulations, to which he was vehemently opposed, and labor unions, which he thought were equally malodorous. He talked against antimonopoly politicians and claimed that they were the cheapest and most easily bought. He referred to one of his lines, the Chicago Limited, and explained that the only reason he kept it going was to compete with the Pennsylvania Railroad in passenger traffic. "But don't you run it for the public benefit?" asked a reporter. "The public be damned!" answered Mr. Vanderbilt. In later years he denied that he had uttered the legendary phrase, and everyone else in the New York Central denied that he had meant it, but it came to symbolize the height of irresponsibility in the attitude of the industrialist, proof that if he were to have his way the powerful head of large corporations would never hesitate to exploit the public to gain his own advantage.

Although Vanderbilt's remark has been vehemently disclaimed by later generations of businessmen (in 1939 *Fortune* published an article entitled "The Public Is Not Damned"), traces of his sentiment can still be found in the contemporary oligarch's scorn of the critic who claims to be a champion of public causes. If Vanderbilt said that he didn't care about the public, the modern executive believes that he knows what is best for the public, which is not very different. Charles E. Wilson's famous remark that what is good for General Motors is good for the country was an echo of Vanderbilt's sentiment. The two men would have agreed that business interests should be given the highest priority in the determination of American national policy.

4

Political action emerged as the real goal of business criticism in the late 1880s when concern about the sugar and oil trusts led to the Sherman Antitrust Act of 1890. Through clever maneuvering, Rockefeller and his associates managed to keep the Standard Oil Company intact, but persistent criticism over the next twenty-two years finally resulted in the enforced dissolution of the empire.

The political consequences of the attacks against big business were recognized by Theodore Roosevelt in the early 1900s. A liberal President, he enjoyed the reputation of a trust buster and welcomed the publicity that critics gave to practices he wanted to curb. At the same time, he cautioned writers against seeing evil everywhere in the corporate world. On April 14, 1906, he made an historic speech in which he coined the word "muckraker" as a derivation from the "Man with the Muckrake" in *Pilgrim's Progress.* "There is filth on the floor," he said, "and it must be scraped up with the muckrake; and there are times and places where this service is the most needed of all the services that can be performed. But the man who never does anything else, who never thinks or speaks or writes save of his feats with the muckrake, speedily becomes, not a help to society, not an incitement to good, but one of the most potent forces of evil." Judiciously he expressed the hope that the railway rate legislation he introduced that year would be "a first step in the direction of a policy of superintendence and control over corporate wealth engaged in interstate commerce," a policy which, however, would "not . . . be exercised in a spirit of malevolence toward the men who have created the wealth, but with the firm purpose both to do justice to them and to see that they in turn do justice to the public at large."

The serious prospect of legislation, curbing for the first time the freedom of the great entrepreneurs to conduct their business affairs as they saw fit, caused them to break their silence. Although Rockefeller still maintained that he was satisfied to let history judge the value of what he was doing, he decided to begin stating his case publicly in 1905. And, according to contemporaries, he did a good job at it. As Norman Hapgood noted in *Harper's Weekly,* Rockefeller was never guilty of an impatient comment and never in any public appearance betrayed the slightest irritation.

In succeeding years the government action against the Standard Oil trust intensified. By midsummer 1907 the national government had seven suits pending against the company and its various subsidiaries, while other suits were being pushed by state officers in Texas, Minnesota, Missouri, Tennessee, Ohio and Mississippi. To defend the company, Rockefeller gave an increasing number of newspaper interviews and permitted his speeches to be republished and distributed. In 1909 his book *Random Reminiscences of Men and Events* attempted to present a positive picture of the contributions made by businessmen to society. "Men of wealth," he wrote, ". . . have a just pride in their work and want to perfect the plans in which they have faith, or what is still of more consequence, they may feel the call to expand and build up for the benefit of their employees or associates . . ." It was a careful and honest attempt to present the positive side of the businessman's role in society by the man who was looked upon by the whole world as the richest and most powerful industrialist in history.

But the defense did not work. The long legislative battle against Rockefeller was finally won on May 15, 1911, when Chief Justice White read his twenty-thousand-word opinion ordering Standard Oil to divest itself of all subsidiaries.

5

Theodore Roosevelt saw the decrees of the courts against the monopolies of Standard Oil, the Northern Securities Company and the tobacco trust as an affirmation of the ability of the federal government to curb corporate power. The recent history of federal, state and municipal actions affecting corporate interests confirms the accuracy of his vision.

If the threat of such action had not emerged in the late nineteenth and early twentieth centuries, the businessman might have been less concerned about public criticism and taken a more philosophical attitude. After all, as Allan Nevins once wrote, "From the day of Titus Oates [the seventeenth-century English Joseph McCarthy], people have rejoiced in personification of evil; a prominent target always attracts missiles . . . Some of the best of Americans, from Jefferson to Franklin D. Roosevelt, have suffered from a spate of foul abuse, from whispering campaigns, from libels too gross to print; and rich men are always found guilty before they are tried." The businessman might have learned to ignore "the scum of libel which always floats on the stream of public discussion."

However, the problems which faced the captains of industry were more serious than libel. Criticism had become a part of the growing forces of reform, from the Populist movement in the 1890s to Theodore Roosevelt's Progressivism in the 1900s, to Woodrow Wilson's New Freedom during the war years and to Franklin D. Roosevelt's New Deal in the depression years. With the increasing strength of labor unions, the development of a critical press during the muckraking era, and an expanding antibusiness movement in succeeding decades, the corporate oligarch came to feel that battling both public criticism and threatened government action was part of his continuing management function.

This attitude produced a distinct pattern in the personality of the oligarch as regards public criticism. He no longer considered himself free to sit quietly and lick the wounds of personal insult as Cornelius Vanderbilt did after the panic of 1893, when he was accused of being a heartless, ruthless ogre. Nor was he free to explode impulsively as William Henry Vanderbilt did when he damned the public. He couldn't afford to be silent as Rockefeller was during most of his business life. Public criticism was something that had to be actively combated. The corporate oligarch needed positive endorsement from the community—not because he was looking for a vote of confidence, but because politicians were, and attacks against business were good politics. To protect himself the oligarch had to organize his response to criticism as if he were conducting a political campaign.

When the New Deal arrived with its vigorous measures to end the Great Depression, executive heads of large companies began to think of themselves as a homogeneous group that had to stand together to fight off the attacks of hostile journalists and politicians. Among the leaders of the attack against them was brain-truster Rexford G. Tugwell, who was appointed Assistant Secretary of Agriculture by Roosevelt and who wrote: "I am sick of a Nation's stenches/I am sick of propertied Czars . . ./I shall roll up my sleeves—make America over!" Tugwell argued that business had become "so huge and so interdependent that every action it takes is fraught with deep implications," and that the profit motive drives it into "non-useful or anti-social activities." An avalanche of books and articles supported his contention that business was the major cause of social and economic disorder. Some of the titles were *Partners in Plunder,* "The Cost of Business Dictatorship," "Messiahs of Feudalism," "Can Business Be Civilized?," "Can Business Manage Itself?," "Big Business, What Now?" (The last-named, published in *The Saturday Evening Post,* was authored by Joseph P. Kennedy.) Franklin D. Roosevelt's second inaugural address, in 1937, lashed out against the men of "entrenched greed" who sought "the restoration of their selfish power."

In the post–World War II years, the role of government in the regulation of business was firmly established. The critic was now the official scout for the politician, and virtually all serious anti-business articles in the press were followed by some kind of Congressional investigation. The corporate world came under attack in almost every quarter, and the oligarch took it for granted that for each attack there must be a counterattack to defend his power.

6

Some idea of the increasing pressure which has been exerted on corporations over the years can be gained from a cursory look at some legislative highlights.

In 1887 the Interstate Commerce Act was passed by Congress for the purpose of establishing rates that were "reasonable" and "just." The regulatory powers of the ICC were strengthened by the Hepburn Act of 1906 and the Mann-Elkins Act of 1910. Subsequently there were the Transportation Acts of 1920, 1940 and 1958. Similar controls were set up for other carriers in the Shipping Act of 1916, the Motor Carrier Act of 1935 and the Civil Aeronautics Act of 1938. Regulation of the field of broadcasting was established by the Radio Act of 1927 and the Communications Act of 1934, regulation of the stock exchange by the Securities Exchange Act of 1934, control over atomic energy by the Atomic Energy Acts of 1946 and 1954. The right of free competition was protected by the Sherman Act of 1890, the Clayton and Federal Trade Commission Acts of 1914, the Robinson-Patman Act of 1936. The Meat Inspection Act was passed in 1907 (one year after Upton Sinclair's book *The Jungle* was published). The first Pure Food and Drug Act was passed in 1906; a much stronger Food, Drug and Cosmetic Act was passed in 1938, with a pesticide amendment in 1954, a chemical-additive amendment in 1958, and a drug amendment (as a result of the Kefauver Committee hearings) in 1962. Other consumer products came under federal regulation with the Seafood Act of 1934, the Wool Products Labeling Act of 1937, the Fur Products Labeling Act of 1951, the Flammable Products Act of 1953, the Textile Products Identification Act of 1958, the Automobile Information Disclosure Act of 1958, the Hazardous Substance Labeling Act of 1960. Deceptive advertising practices were prohibited by the Wheeler-Lea Act of 1938. The "Truth in Packaging" bill was passed in 1966, and the "Truth in Lending" bill in 1968.

The purpose of most of this legislation was to protect the consumer, the investor and the public generally against fraud. In each case the heads of the corporations involved have insisted that they could be trusted to conduct themselves responsibly, and that it was unnecessary, indeed detrimental, to public interests to impose bureaucratic restrictions on the actions of responsible managers. There is no doubt that often the critics who attacked business achieved sensational publicity because of the extravagance rather than the validity of their accusations, and the public interest was sometimes ill-served. But in many cases the malpractices which were publicly aired by critics were scandalous, and the arguments advanced by the industry leaders in their own defense manifested a shocking lack of sensitivity to public health and safety. Over the years this continuing repetition of self-righteousness confirmed the already widespread conviction that the corporate oligarch was unscrupulous in his exercise of power, and that the country could be protected from his corrupt practices only by an extensive system of policing.

7

The corporate oligarch's blind pride in his own virtue not only incensed his detractors, it provoked public antagonism toward the entire business community. This tendency was well illustrated in the history of the nation's largest electric and gas utility, the Consolidated Edison Company of New York.

The electrical companies in New York City from which Con Ed was formed engaged in one of their earliest battles in 1889 when they refused to comply with a law ordering the removal of overhead wires. To enforce the law, Mayor Hugh J. Grant had to arm three crews of public-works men with snippers and axes and send them out to chop down the poles carrying the wires.

Almost eighty years later, with its 66,700-mile web of subterranean cables, Con Ed was making forty thousand excavations every year, and many people were talking as if they would be glad to take up arms once again. There were about three thousand interruptions in the company's electricity-distribution system each year. Three times in six years there were major blackouts in the city; the worst, in 1965, paralyzed the city, closing two of the metropolitan airports, depriving hospitals of power, trapping six hundred thousand passengers in subway trains, eliminating television and some radio stations from the air and creating monumental traffic jams in the streets. In this same period, Con Ed's customers had to pay for five rate increases totaling nearly $58 million, added to the highest residential-rate structure of any major utility in the nation.

As if this were not enough, air pollution experts pointed out that the belching smokestacks of Con Ed's plants were a major cause of the smog that was choking the city. The plan to build the world's biggest nuclear-power reactor in the Ravenswood section of Queens was vehemently attacked by such an eminent critic as David E. Lilienthal, former chairman of the AEC. And the project to build a plant at Storm King Mountain was criticized as an undertaking that would ruin the beauty of the Hudson River Valley, one of our country's great scenic attractions.

These were hard facts of corporate life which an enlightened management could face up to constructively only if it had the courage to admit its faults. But Con Ed was unwilling to do this. Its management had traditionally acted as if the company could do no wrong and that its only problem was public misunderstanding. Commenting on these attitudes, Washington utilities consultant David Kosh said: "I've been in the utilities business for thirty-four years and I can't think of a company that goes out of its way to alienate customers the way Con Edison does. They're so stiff-backed. I have yet to hear a Con Edison executive say, 'Maybe you have a point.' By definition, they always think they are right." *Fortune* attempted to find out why "Con Ed is the company you love to hate" and came to the conclusion that "most Con Edison executives have spent their lives within the protective womb of the company" and that, "old and embattled, proud and thick-skinned, the men who lead Con Edison look upon the company as their own personal creation." As of 1966, all three top executives had worked for the company more than thirty-three years. One would expect that a company beset with monumental crises would institute radical changes in its policies. But *Fortune* predicted there would be few such innovations at Con Ed. "Much of its plant is old," the editors said in summing up, "its rates are high, its profits are low, its growth is meager, its customers are furious. But at Con Edison the aging management assumes the mantle of martyrdom, and trusts that everything will turn out all right."

Not long after this article appeared, a new president was finally appointed—Charles F. Luce, former Undersecretary of the Interior. For the first time in its history company management seemed ready to admit that there was not only a problem of getting the public to understand Con Ed but of getting Con Ed to understand the public. After almost three quarters of a century of creat‑ ing animosity, the company publicly admitted that it had to find a new way to meet its obligations and properly serve the commu‑ nity interests. Con Ed had apparently found a chief executive who felt that the public had something legitimate to complain about.

8

Potentially more dangerous than the self-righteous manage- ment of an individual company have been organized groups of industry leaders operating as trade associations to stop govern- ment legislation. Lawyers have been careful to avoid violations of antitrust laws in such cooperative activities, but the public has had little protection from the combined pressures which a major industry can bring to bear in campaigns to protect its interests. The powerful lobbies of the defense industry, the gun industry and the oil industry, to name some well-known examples, have been remarkably successful in seeing to it that management's po- sition is given very serious consideration on all matters affecting the exercise of its power.

Representation in the formulation of government policy is, of course, no sin, and most trade association public-relations activity, even when it is addressed to legislative action, consists of above- board efforts to gain public visibility for an industry's point of view. But there have been some pretty nasty examples of indus- tries which have used an association to organize extensive behind- the-scenes schemes to silence their critics.

One of the most famous of these industry-wide campaigns was that waged by the patent-medicine industry shortly after the turn of the century, when labeling legislation was being introduced in practically every state of the union. To prevent passage of the proposed legislation, members of the industry association resorted to the same method used by the second Bank of the United States, updated to take advantage of twentieth-century business practices. The method was proudly described by F. J. Cheney, manufacturer of a catarrh cure, at an association meeting. "Inside of the last two years, [I] have made contracts with between fifteen and sixteen thousand newspapers," he told a group of his fellow producers. "This is what I have in every contract I make: 'It is hereby agreed that should your State, or the United States Government, pass any law that would interfere with or restrict the sale of proprietary medicines, this contract shall become void.' . . . In the State of Illinois a few years ago, they wanted to assess me three hundred dollars. I thought I had a better plan than this, so I wrote to about forty papers and merely said, 'Please look at your contract with me and take note that if this law passes you and I must stop doing business, and my contracts cease.' The next week every one of them had an article, and [the bill] had to go."

The J. C. Ayer Company, makers of Ayer's Sarsaparilla, went even further. Not only could there be no restrictive laws, but there could not even be criticism reported in the press. Ayer's contracts included a clause which stated, "It is agreed that the J. C. Ayer Company may cancel this contract, pro rata, . . . in case any matter otherwise detrimental to the J. C. Ayer Company's interests is permitted to appear in the reading columns or elsewhere in the paper."

According to the records of the Patent Medicine Association, most newspapers knuckled under to this pressure, but the national media did not. *Collier's* waged a continuing campaign even though it dropped $80,000 in advertising billing after publishing Samuel Hopkins Adams' series of articles, "The Great American Fraud," exposing the public deception involved in the sale of such products as Peruna, Lydia E. Pinkham's Vegetable Compound, Paine's Celery Compound and other nostrums. The General Federation of Women's Clubs organized a national campaign calling for legislation to protect consumers against misbranding and the adulteration of foods. And in 1906 the Pure Food and Drug Act was passed by Congress.

Thus the attack on the vested interests of the patent-medicine industry proved to be successful despite the tremendous pressures exerted by management to stifle the press; and the famous products of the early 1900s which were supposed to cure anything and everything passed out of existence.

9

A comic relief to the venality of the Patent Medicine Association's pressure tactics and similar campaigns can be found in the painful bleating of industry leaders who are attacked in public but who are not sophisticated enough or sufficiently well-organized to mount a coordinated counterattack. These executives often sound illiterate as well as ill-mannered in their spontaneous comments to the press, revealing a personality trait which is otherwise covered up in formal statements prepared by advisers.

One such example of management's natural intemperance occurred following the publication in 1963 of Jessica Mitford's book *The American Way of Death*. Partly because the funeral industry which she attacked did not include any major corporations and hence did not have the benefit of experienced public-relations counsel, the businessmen interviewed by the press felt free to speak their minds. The incident is worth recalling, not because these spokesmen were typical corporate oligarchs, but because as heads of relatively small companies they revealed a character trait which is equally common among heads of large companies, though the latter usually manage to disguise it.

An effective exposé of the wasteful extravagance of modern funerals and the deceptive practices of many funeral companies, Miss Mitford's book became a best seller almost as soon as it was published. Anticipating this sensational success and its consequences in the formation of public attitudes, industry leaders started worrying about their public relations while the book was still in galleys. At the time, several of them spoke to our firm about the problem, attributing their difficulties (as such executives usually do) to a few irresponsible companies whose scurrilous practices were about to give the whole industry a bad name. It was clear that the executives who talked to us were more concerned about the unpleasantness of bad publicity than about the possibility of legislation or a negative effect on sales, although these also contributed to their anxieties.

A preliminary investigation on our part suggested that it wouldn't do to try to place the blame on those guilty of the most extreme forms of deception; Jessica Mitford's argument that the basic commercial system by which funeral arrangements were made in this country exploited the grief of the survivors was convincing even to someone (like us) who listened carefully to the industry's point of view. If anything positive was to be done as a response to the attack, we felt, the legitimacy of much of her argument had to be acknowledged, and this should be used as the basis for making some needed changes in the general business practices of the industry. This approach, however, was never acted on, because no one was able to exert sufficient leadership to get the industry to agree to a united effort.

As a result, when the book appeared, several top executives of the industry made some incredible remarks to the press. Obviously these executives said what they really felt and not what a public-relations adviser had told them to say. Admittedly, this was more honest, but anyone who knew some of the more mature executives of the industry couldn't help but squirm at the foolishness of their less sensitive brethren who were quoted by reporters as speaking for the industry.

"The dames that write these books don't want to hear anything good," said the president of one company. "If you kill sentiment, you're a dead pigeon. The world runs on sentiment." The managing director of the National Selected Morticians angrily accused the author of trying to replace the American funeral service "with that practiced in Communistic countries such as the Soviet Union." The educational director of the same association was sure that the author was not a churchgoer and called her "a master of the false innuendo." Only one lonely voice, that of a funeral director named C. Harry Palm, of Fresno, California, was heard making a responsible statement. In a letter to a trade publication he asked why the industry wouldn't "admit that most of our poor 'public relations' are the result of our practices or actions." Instead of always being on the defensive against public opinion, he suggested, "let's listen to their complaints and adjust our thinking accordingly."

Since there was no official industry response, the sorry remarks quoted in the general press constituted the only record of top management's attitude. There is no doubt that if the issue had been a major one, and the industry had been more in the public eye, the folly of such a crude and hostile response to intelligent criticism would have created considerable difficulty for the men whose policies were being attacked.

10

Any adviser to a management group whose policies or products have been publicly attacked as being in conflict with the public interest (and which management's has not?) knows how disturbing such negative publicity can be to top executives. No doubt other men subjected to such criticism are also easily upset; the difference is that the corporate oligarch is so accustomed to the exercise of power in his environment that he is stunned when men of little consequence (by his standards) dare to question his actions. He has a particular difficulty in understanding the rights of the press in this regard. He knows that he can buy enormous amounts of space in his advertising campaigns, and that he can say virtually anything he likes in that space. He is therefore infuriated when something about his business which he doesn't like appears in the news columns of a newspaper or magazine, and when he discovers that, although such statements take up far less space than his own advertisements in the same media, he is powerless to change the wording of the article.

I confess that the traditional public-relations approach to this problem has probably not helped to further the interests of public welfare. If there is a real conflict between the power appetites of the oligarchy and the welfare of individual citizens, the more bluntly the conflict is presented the more likely the public interests will be served. Public-relations efforts to reduce the severity of criticism often disguise rather than reveal the essential conflicts involved. The purpose of such efforts is not to create an atmosphere in which the reforms demanded by critics will be made; it is to find a way to make the smallest possible concessions necessary to end the controversy. Only rarely is there a genuine willingness to face up to the real conflicts involved and to resolve them fairly.

One method that is used to appease vociferous critics of an industry is to set up a program of self-regulation. Corporate oligarchs hope that through such programs the extreme causes of irritation can be eliminated without the essential base of their economic power being affected, as might be the result if regulatory legislation were passed. This approach has been taken in the motion picture and tobacco industries with moderate success from the point of view of management. But the public has little reason to be satisfied by this compromise, since the removal of only the most extreme instances of irresponsibility, which is what self-regulation accomplishes, is usually a means of burying the real conflicts between corporate power and individual rights.

Again, I can cite an experience of a small industry to illustrate how this process works. The publishers of comic books in the United States can hardly be considered leaders of the corporate oligarchy, but their efforts to set up a program of self-regulation show in microcosm what happens when others closer to the center of power take this approach.

In the 1950s the industry had been experiencing a dangerous sales slippage due to competition from television, but its problems became greatly magnified when a well-known psychologist, Dr. Fredric Wertham, charged that the violence, cruelty and perversion pictured in many comic books were contributing to juvenile delinquency. Our firm acted as public-relations counsel to the Comic Magazine Association at the time, and I found it easy to join industry leaders in their conviction that Wertham's position was psychologically, sociologically and legally unsound. Once a childhood comic-book addict myself, I had never panicked about my own children's enthusiasm for the habit, although I thought there was probably a better way for them to spend their time. I had always been a strong believer in the ability of children to absorb the impact of even such horror stories as "Hansel and Gretel" and "Little Red Ridinghood." I was therefore an enthusiastic member of the "scorn Wertham" club. It wasn't until considerably later that I discovered that Dr. Wertham had a fine reputation among his peers, and that his judgments deserved to be taken seriously. This did not mean that he was correct in his criticism of comic books, but it did mean that those of us on the industry side of that debate who failed to show respect for his judgment, did not help explore the serious issues he raised.

The Wertham attack led to the threat, in many states, of legislation prohibiting the sale of comic books. Also, as a result of local agitation in support of Wertham's views, sales in some localities fell off more than ever. It was a major crisis for the industry, and no effort was spared in its defense.

The problem was resolved with the help of the industry's able legal counsel, an outstanding figure in the field of civil liberties, who stressed the evils of censorship which were implicit in the proposed legislation. Eventually, a program of self-regulation was designed around a new code of ethics, which prohibited extreme forms of horror and terror, and which would be administered by an industry czar. The man selected for the post was a judge who had experience in coping with problems of juvenile delinquency and who also, incidentally, seemed like a practical man who would recognize the problems of selling comic books in a declining market.

Once the program was set up, the judge administered the code with scrupulous care, and many civic leaders who had been outspoken in their criticism felt that they had won the battle. But the publishers felt it was they who had been victorious, because the code prohibited only the most extreme of the forms of violence to which Dr. Wertham had objected. It was clear that the change would create no serious obstacles to the continued publication of the same basic material which had always characterized their product. It was also clear that the industry had solved its problem without coming to grips with the basic social issues implicit in its business. And there was no immediate prospect that the heads of the companies would assume responsibility for the emotional consequences of their publications—whatever those consequences might be.

11

The unwillingness of the corporate oligarch to voluntarily moderate his policies with an adequate concern for public welfare is well illustrated by the recent history of the automobile industry.

For years it was management policy among the automobile companies to avoid reference to safety as a problem lest it create customer anxiety. Driving, it was thought, should be promoted as "comfortable" and "exciting," not "hazardous." When, for instance, the 1953 Buick Roadmaster had defects in its power-brake system that were serious enough for the company to issue two separate kits for replacement of the defective parts, agencies were instructed to make repairs without notice to the owners. According to testimony before the Supreme Court of Michigan in *Comstock v. General Motors Corporation* (1959), agencies were "not allowed" to advise owners to bring their cars in for the correction. "It was a hush thing," said an agency service representative. "They [the service department at Buick] didn't want the public to know the brakes were bad and they were very alarmed." The general service manager of Buick said that the dealers were free to do what they wanted, but conceded that the company had done nothing to seek out the owners of the cars to make sure the brakes were corrected.

During the 1950s the Public Health Service began making small grants to finance the study of techniques of crash-injury protection. In 1955 Ford and Chrysler agreed to help finance such a study at Cornell. General Motors, however, felt this was a mistake and refused to cooperate. In 1956, when Robert S. McNamara, then a vice-president in charge of the Ford Division, based his sales campaign on special safety features in his new models, General Motors officials were upset. They believed he not only would fail to sell his own cars but would frighten buyers away from other models as well. So much pressure was brought on McNamara that there were rumors he was going to be fired. He weathered the storm, but soon afterward the sales campaign was shelved.

In an article entitled "The War against the Automobile" Daniel P. Moynihan wrote:

> Students of American business ought really to try to learn what decision-making processes went on at this point in the 1950s when it became clear that automobiles were not safe as they might be. The largest and most profitable industry in the world faced the relatively simple problem of responding to criticism couched in terms of the public interest; and it could not do so. The industry gave almost no sign that it was aware of criticism; it was not so much a matter of responding badly as of not responding at all. The industry became more and more a caricature of an over-muscled, under-brained organism heading for disaster.

General Motors, which was the most recalcitrant of all in heeding the warnings of the safety prophets, had once prided itself on its ability to look at problems without prejudice. Alfred P. Sloan, Jr., had written that one of the company's most important assets was open-minded communication and objective consideration of facts. When James M. Roche was nominated as company president of General Motors he was described by an associate as a man with an open mind. He was said to have a willingness to listen, and to be a man who, as *Fortune* put it, "does not bristle at the first hint of censure; and he does not tend to personalize all criticism."

It was this "open-minded" management which behaved most badly in the bout with Ralph Nader, leader of the successful attack against the industry which began with the publication of his book *Unsafe at Any Speed.* As revealed in testimony before a Congressional committee, General Motors financed private investigations into Nader's private life in the hope of finding some personal scandal which might discredit him as a critic. When the attempt was exposed, Roche, to his credit, publicly apologized for this behavior, agreeing with Senator Abraham Ribicoff, Democrat of Connecticut and chairman of the Senate Subcommittee on Executive Reorganization, that such harassment was "most unworthy of American business." Board chairman Frederic G. Donner later conceded that the supposed open-mindedness at General Motors had existed only in relation to commercial facts. His top executives had lost touch with many of the larger national issues with which they should be concerned. "We have got a tradition in General Motors," Donner said, "of maybe too much sticking with our business problems." It appeared that GM managers had been unable to comprehend some of the more critical concerns of American life, and had been guilty of the "tunnel vision" and "narrowness and remoteness" referred to over the years by critics. Hopefully, they would now develop a broader perspective about their role in society.

The main thrust of management testimony at the Congressional hearings was that, with its new sense of responsibility about public safety, a program of self-regulation would be the best way to bring about the necessary changes. But the actions of General Motors and other companies were not such as to inspire public confidence in their promise to change their ways voluntarily, and the law-makers were not in the mood for face-saving solutions. The result was the National Traffic and Motor Vehicle Safety Act of 1966.

It is interesting to note that even after this public uproar the companies did not cover themselves with glory in the way they approached the safety problem. Although a number of safety features were introduced, the ballyhoo was more impressive than the protection. Critics of the industry claimed that most of the safety innovations that were made were superficial and ineffective. The professed concern about protecting the passenger sounded like a new sales pitch rather than a new sense of public responsibility on the part of management. The General Motors annual report following the Congressional hearing at which Roche made his dramatic apology did not even mention either Ralph Nader or the controversy. And two years later GM was again promoting reckless speed instead of safety in its latest models. The 1969 souped-up Chevelle SS 396 was advertised as "the class bully," and the Z–28 model Camaro as a car with "a mean streak" that is "built in." Open-mindedness and concern about the public interest had apparently yet to be accepted as the policy of General Motors or other large corporations—except when the government, with the help of outspoken critics, made it impossible to be otherwise.

12

At the height of the automobile-safety controversy Henry Ford II said of Ralph Nader, "He can read statistics, and he can look up a lot of facts that are in the public domain, but I don't think he knows anything about engineering safety into automobiles. I think if these critics who don't really know anything about safety will get out of our way, we can go ahead with our job."

There is no doubt that management is more knowledgeable about its own business than are its critics, but this superior knowledge is a cause of one of management's most serious blind spots. The critic is questioning not management's techniques but the premises on which it has based its policies. Management thinks that because it has employed the most highly skilled specialists to work on these problems its premises must be sound. But what is in conflict is a human issue rather than a technical one, and in this respect the critic is as well-qualified to express an opinion as the specialist.

Failure to recognize these qualifications was evident in the chemical industry's reaction to Rachel Carson's book *Silent Spring*, which warned that the indiscriminate use of insecticides was laying down such a barrage of poisons that one day the earth might become unfit for life.

"The history of the recent centuries," Miss Carson wrote, "has its black passages—the slaughter of the buffalo on the western plains, the massacre of the shore-birds by the market gunners, the near extermination of the egrets for their plumage. Now, to these and others like them, we are adding a new chapter and a new kind of havoc—the direct killing of birds, mammals, fishes, and indeed practically every form of wildlife by chemical insecticides indiscriminately sprayed on the land." She believed that "control of nature" was a "phrase conceived in arrogance," and that the practitioners of chemical control have brought to their task "no humility before the vast forces with which they tamper."

Published in 1962, *Silent Spring* was considered to be one of the books most widely read by government officials in recent years. Legislative bodies ranging from New England town meetings to the Congress applauded her contribution. Supreme Court Justice William O. Douglas declared, "We need a Bill of Rights against the twentieth-century poisoners of the human race." The New York *Times*, in an editorial, suggested that Miss Carson deserved the Nobel Prize for her great public service in arousing the public. Dr. Jerome B. Wiesner, chairman of President Kennedy's Science Advisory Committee, said in an official report on the subject that the uncontrolled use of poisonous chemicals, including pesticides, was "potentially a much greater hazard" than radioactive fallout.

Executives of the chemical companies, however, did not agree. They felt that scientists in the Public Health Service and in their own companies had more than taken into consideration any possible dangers from poisonous chemicals used for insect control. As far as they were concerned, it was self-evident that pesticides were essential to maintain and improve the nation's food supply and public health. That they must be thoroughly pretested for safety before use and that they must be carefully and wisely applied was also taken for granted. Accordingly, extensive programs had been developed to educate users and to minimize the risks. A report by the Manufacturing Chemists Association stated:

> Industry, government and non-profit institutions have labored to create these chemical tools, and to research, develop, test, and establish safety standards for them. Nevertheless, like other tools of our civilization, they are susceptible to misuse and abuse which can result in destruction to crops, harm to humans, and pollution of our environment. But instances of such misuse and abuse must not be allowed to obscure the fact that these tools are vital to the health and even the survival of humanity.

The oligarchs of the chemical industry felt that they had been dealing with the problem properly before Miss Carson's book was published. Like Mr. Ford, they didn't think an amateur who happened to write well was equipped to tell them how to engineer safety into their product. The 1963 annual report of the Monsanto Chemical Company stated: "A best-selling book which made some disturbing charges against weed and insect killers performed one useful service. It reminded the public that pesticides must be tested thoroughly, marketed responsibly and applied discriminately. Monsanto has always said so." The company's director of public relations was proud of this record. "No business can survive," he wrote in a letter to me on this subject, "—nor does any have a right to survive—unless first and foremost it is dedicated to the public interest. I happen to be fortunate enough to work for a company that both preaches and practices this philosophy."

But this same company, with its impressive record of research and concern about public welfare, attempted to counteract the effects of Miss Carson' book in a public campaign that did not acknowledge in any way that a writer who had been proposed for a Nobel Prize had raised a point worth considering. Monsanto issued a publication entitled *The Desolate Year* which denied that the public was being sold a "bill of goods" in the promotion of chemicals for insect control. What, the publication asked, would the world be like if it were deprived of insect control? "Life-slowing winter lay on the land that New Year's Day," the report began its imaginative forecast into the future, "the day that Nature was left to seek her own balance." It told how pests by the trillions multiplied, destroying crops and cattle, poultry and fish, causing famine, ruining homes and clothing, spreading disease and bringing death and agony to America. This was what would happen if Miss Carson were to have her way. Obviously she had been mistaken, or at best had overstated her case. Insecticides were a boon, not a threat, to mankind, and *Silent Spring* had introduced no new facts that the industry hadn't been aware of. Management had seen to it that minimal harm would come to the public from the use of its products, and no more could be asked of it.

The president of Monsanto, Charles H. Sommer, made a speech in December 1964 in which he suggested that both public and government attacks against the chemical industry showed a lack of knowledge about the great contributions made by chemical products. He said: "*We* know the tremendous good that has been accomplished by the proper use of such products as pharmaceuticals, polyethylene bags, detergents, food additives, chemical fertilizers and pesticides. Why, then, doesn't the public welcome these technical advances with the same degree of sophistication as it has shown toward television, electronic 'brains'—or today's high-powered automobile? These are questions which we must answer not only to our satisfaction but to the public's as well. Until we do, the best that we can hope for is that the public will tolerate us— apprehensively." He said it was up to the chemical companies to prove to the public that they were worthy of retaining their freedom of action, by showing how far they were willing to go on their own to insure the reliability and safety of their products, the ethical conduct of their business and the minimum of public hazard or nuisance in their operations.

In 1966 I wrote an article for *The Saturday Review* in which I criticized "the derisive tone" of Monsanto's *The Desolate Year.* "Derisive" was an unfortunate word and did not describe what I really meant; I wanted to say that this publication was an example of how executives of large corporations often fail to recognize the essential point in their critics' complaints. At the time I had not read Mr. Sommer's speech, but if I had I would have made the point that even such useful products as television, computers and automobiles may, in some respects, be detrimental to public interests, and that management should have the courage to face up to such shortcomings. Miss Carson had insisted that she never questioned the value of chemicals. "We must have insect control," she had asserted in a statement on *The Desolate Year.* "I do not favor turning nature over to insects. I favor sparing, selective and intelligent use of chemicals. It is the indiscriminate blanket spraying that I oppose." She had asked for humility and an awareness of the tragedy that had befallen us. "We live in an era," she had said in her book, "dominated by industry, in which the right to make a dollar at whatever cost is seldom challenged." She was challenging that right.

It seemed to me that industry leaders had not made it clear that they understood her plea. Moreover, it was disrespectful to the public figures who supported her thesis not to show a willingness to engage in some new soul searching. No one has the right to be so sure his assumptions are correct that he cannot benefit from serious and constructive criticism.

After my article appeared, the company's director of public

relations, who was noted for his thoughtful and responsible approach to public issues, wrote to me to ask whether I knew that the company "had solid scientific and governmental support" for its publication *The Desolate Year*. He expressed disappointment that I "—a presumed objective analyst of and occasional spokesman for the American business system—would be trapped into thinking our 'speaking up' for the role of pesticides against insects and disease would make us, ipso facto, a 'derisive' business defender!" He was right. My job as a public-relations practitioner is often to help management speak up in its own defense. And the language of my statement had been unjustified. But as a counselor to management I know better than most that top executives of large corporations are the ones who have difficulty in being objective, and that they often become so incensed by public criticism—especially when profits are labeled as an enemy of progress—that they will not see what their critics are trying to say. I thought that this was what was happening in the chemical industry. If management had been willing to listen respectfully it should have congratulated Miss Carson for what was obviously a fine piece of work in the public interest, albeit her book may have erred, as all books do, by giving too much emphasis to the points supporting her thesis.

I didn't intend then, and certainly don't now, to condemn the public-relations skill displayed in the publication of *The Desolate Year*. Given the problem of counteracting the effect of Miss Carson's book, it was, as one trade journalist put it, "a brilliant performance." I believe it is unfortunate, however, that public-relations techniques are employed more often (by my own firm as well as others, I'm sure) to rebut critics than to learn from them. This inhibits the forces which can lead to a meaningful social assessment of corporate behavior, and which should be able to direct the oligarch's power toward actions which will be of greatest public benefit.

13

The reluctance of the corporate oligarch to acknowledge the legitimacy of public criticism of his policies often tends to stifle independent thinking on the part of his subordinates and advisers. If there is an official rationale to justify management's position, as there almost always is, it is assumed that everybody in key positions of responsibility or influence in the company will endorse it. This expectation on the part of management may never be clearly articulated, but should anyone who is a member of or has a direct working relationship with top management ever be quoted in public as supporting a critical point of view on a touchy subject, he will not easily be forgiven.

This is not to say that the corporate oligarch uses coercion to enforce his opinion on those around him. No top executive I know has indulged in strong-arm methods to gain allies for his position, and it is even rare these days that economic pressure is used to keep subordinates in line. Although there have been a number of cases in the recent past in which men have lost jobs or agencies have lost clients because somebody spoke out of turn, I can report that in twenty years of experience in the public-relations business, our company has never been subjected to such an overt reprisal for opinions we have held or positions we have openly supported. I should add, however, that I can think of only two or three instances in which a client might have had cause to complain, and this, perhaps, is more to the point. For while it is true that progressive managers welcome the services of outside counsel precisely because he can speak his mind more freely than company employees in discussions of critical issues, it is also true that consultants feel obliged to be very careful about public positions they take as private citizens, lest they antagonize their clients. The constraints on employees against involving themselves publicly in controversial issues are, of course, even greater. This means that for those who have a working relationship with corporate oligarchs the right of dissent is limited by a form of pragmatic self-censorship rather than arm twisting.

To be sure, there are some who are so strongly opposed to official management positions that they would rather not work for a company than compromise their beliefs. In my own case, as a public-relations specialist who has been involved in many controversies, I have tried to be open-minded about as many questions as possible. But I have often wondered where open-mindedness ends and self-deception begins. A sampling of public issues in which our firm has represented management's point of view indicates, I think, the nature of the problem; television on the matter of violence; hobbies and the problem of glue sniffing; sugar and obesity; candy and dental caries; cosmetics and the values of natural beauty; pharmaceuticals and methods of promoting new drugs; cigarettes and health; packaging and deception; direct mail and the invasion of privacy; insecticides and the danger of excessive use; furs and the need for honest labeling. Anybody who has the normal allotment of prejudices about such matters may run into trouble when called upon to represent management's interest in so many diverse issues; and I'm sure that on occasion people working for our firm have felt dangerously close to being dishonest with themselves (although our policy is not to ask an executive to work on an account he feels uncomfortable about, and not to accept as a client of the firm any account which one of the principals finds objectionable).

It is, of course, legitimate for management counsel to help develop convincing public arguments in support of corporate policies. After all, it is reasonable to suppose that the corporate oligarch is right at least part of the time in his appraisal of the public interest. It is also fair to say that his point of view often gets short shrift because it is to the advantage of both journalists and politicians to attack a vested commercial interest whenever they can make a moderately respectable case in the press. Management has to work at least as hard as its detractors to gain attention for its point of view, for no matter how sound its position may be, the accuser is bound to make the bigger headlines.

Moreover, since the issues are always far more complex than a casual reader of the daily press imagines, anybody who becomes professionally involved in an argument is bound to find that his previously held convictions were based on superficial and often inaccurate information. Nowhere is this more evident than in the controversy which has confronted management of the tobacco industry in recent years. To keep abreast of new developments, top executives have been obliged to do a tremendous amount of reading of research reports. The record of the scientific aspect of cigarette smoking is probably the most voluminous of any such literature in the history of commerce, and there are very few if any members of top management who are not familiar with it. I know, for instance, that key executives of Philip Morris, a long-time client of ours, are often more knowledgeable about evidence used by their critics than the critics are themselves. Indeed, one of the great public-relations problems of the industry is to find some way, in the face of the many sensational stories which appear regularly in the press, to make it clear that the men who make the decisions in the tobacco companies are not inhuman ogres wilfully deceiving the public: they are men who feel their responsibilities keenly and are conscientiously searching for sound answers to extremely difficult questions.

The trouble in many industries, however, is that top executives are so entrenched in their position of power that they presume everyone in their circle will automatically side with them against their critics. These executives cannot imagine that associates who share the same economic interests may differ in regard to social, cultural or intellectual values, and that this may lead to a major divergence of opinion as to what the corporation should do in relation to a sensitive issue. They are not aware that such differences can be healthy and constructive, or that wiser decisions for all concerned may result if frank and open debate is permitted.

"He whose bread I eat his song I sing," was the impatient comment one of my associates used to make when members of our staff complained that their conscience was troubled about a position taken by top management of a client company. I shuddered whenever he said it. It always seemed to me that one of our great obligations, and perhaps the hardest job we had to do in the face of pressures and temptations to compromise our beliefs, was to maintain our integrity. Near my home in New Rochelle, N.Y., is a commemorative statue of Thomas Paine; on the pedestal is engraved the following quotation from his writings: "It is necessary to the happiness of man that he be mentally faithful to himself. Infidelity does not consist in believing or disbelieving but consists in professing to believe what he does not believe." I do not know whether my associate's raw candor about the compulsion to accept management's beliefs is more realistic than Thomas Paine's injunction to be mentally faithful to oneself, but there can be little doubt that proximity to the corporate oligarch can and often does subject one to severe personal pressures, and sometimes this leads to acts of mental infidelity—both in what one feels obliged to say and constrained not to say—that are profoundly disturbing to the human spirit.

14

Does this mean that the corporate oligarch and those who work for him are psychologically incapable of recognizing or acknowledging the faults in their own argument or listening attentively to what their critics have to say? Not necessarily. Their future prospects may be better than their past record.

Clarence Randall, former board chairman of Inland Steel, thinks the trend is the other way. He wrote recently, "The men at the top of our great corporations, those who direct the vast enterprises that mean so much both to our economy and to our social welfare, so live their lives that they no longer take the wind directly in their faces. . . . As a man's authority increases, so do the barriers that cut him off from direct contact with the world about him. . . . The consequence is that when the great storm comes, as it does sooner or later to every large corporation, and he is driven out into the turbulence of public opinion, he may not be ready to go on deck." With business success, Randall argued, comes a sharp reduction of personal exposure to divergent opinions. In the years that the oligarch travels in a chauffeured car and in a private airplane, eats in a private club and plays golf or fishes, hunts or goes yachting, with prearranged companions, he seldom sees anyone except those who show him deference, and almost never those who talk back. The corporate oligarch, therefore, comes to expect all right-thinking men to agree with him. He forgets that men can differ on what is truth. "Preoccupied with the complex affairs of their own corporations, they [top executives] cut themselves off from the source of facts and ideas by which mass judgments are formed in our country. Their thinking on the great questions is borrowed and the opinions they hold are seldom tested by controversy."

Randall recommended that when the top business executive meets a reporter, or a Senator, and is moved to try out some of his ideas about world affairs, he should "leave his public-relations man at home, ignore his trade association's Washington man, and do the job strictly on his own."

There is no doubt that Randall's perception of the isolation which exists at the top of the corporation is accurate. But I think his sense of history is wrong when he suggests that chief executives have become worse in recent years. A vast change has taken place since the days of the muckraker, when the leaders of industry thought they could either ignore their critics or crush them with economic pressure. The corporate oligarch today at least knows that a vocal critic must be intelligently answered. The trouble is that his progress is more a result of increasingly aggressive legislation which threatens him from every side than a clarification of his role as a leader concerned with public welfare.

On the other hand, I think Randall overestimates the chief executive's personal ability to react constructively to his conflict with public interests should he divest himself of his public-relations advisers. He is, to be sure, more respectful of public opinion than were the tycoons of the nineteenth century. He is also more responsible in the way he fights his critics than were the business leaders at the time of the patent-medicine-industry scandal. But left on his own he would still be as intemperate in his response as were the heads of the funeral industry when it was attacked in the early 1960s. Unfortunately, the public-relations approach which aims at giving a polished look to statements by corporate oligarchs has often impeded rather than aided the honest resolution of conflict with public interests. However, I believe the desire to appear more sophisticated in public is at least a sign that management is becoming aware that an unrestrained appetite for power is not consistent with the ideals of a civilized society.

There is no doubt that the corporate oligarch is still capable of using and abusing power in ways that can be dangerous to mankind. But the men who preside over the destinies of our major corporations today are faced by critics with unprecedented skill and power of their own. As a result some corporate oligarchs are becoming aware of the need to respond constructively rather than defensively to criticism. Most hopeful is the emergence of men like Randall, who seem to recognize that conflicts between corporate power and public welfare do exist and that top management must actively and seriously participate in efforts to arrive at a meaningful resolution if the cause of mankind is to be properly served.

8

His Desire
for a
Better Image

AN INCREASINGLY IMPORTANT FACTOR IN THE CORPORATE OLIGARCH'S
reluctant awakening to the realities of public criticism is his hope
that some means can be found to project a better image.

This desire seems to have been initially aroused at the height of
the muckraking period, when industrial leaders began to worry
about the consequences of negative public attitudes. The new
concern was expressed in 1909 by E. K. Hall, vice-president of
American Telephone & Telegraph, which was to become a pioneer
in public-relations efforts to create a good image. He suggested
that because the public does not know the men responsible for
corporate policies, "they misunderstand us, they mistrust us, and
there is a continued tendency to believe that our intentions toward them are not fair." He went so far as to call this "general
attitude of the public mind . . . the only serious danger confront-
ing the company."

A new trend in popular fiction generated by the mood of reform at the time helped to reinforce the damaging stereotypes of businessmen that were becoming part of basic cultural attitudes. The villainous businessman in these novels was not simply a personification of the old aristocratic aversion to "being in trade"; the characterization was the result of a literary rebellion against the earlier businessman-hero novels of Horatio Alger, Jr., and William Dean Howells. It was also a response to the works of Karl Marx, which had recently been translated into English. The earliest of the new antibusiness novels were written by Frank Norris (*The Octopus*, 1902), Upton Sinclair (*The Jungle*, 1906), and Theodore Dreiser (*The Financier*, 1912); and they portrayed businessmen as depraved, ruthless, savage characters who thought nothing of sacrificing human welfare for private gain. Sinclair Lewis' *Babbitt* appeared in 1922, describing the new American businessman as a petty, uncreative conformist who was corrupting American values by his lack of commitment to any ideal. *Beggar on Horseback*, a play by Marc Connelly and George S. Kaufman, produced in 1924, satirized the insensitive businessman to whom nothing was sacred that could be packaged and sold at a profit. F. Scott Fitzgerald's *The Great Gatsby*, published in 1925, portrayed a self-made tycoon who realized that success in the business world was meaningless, and that life for the man who "made it" was empty and sterile. In 1934 Thomas Wolfe's *You Can't Go Home Again* described the frantic madness of the depression-years top executive, creating still another character type that was not calculated to endear the businessman to the reading public.

This trend in twentieth-century fiction (which continued after World War II with such novels as *The Man in the Gray Flannel Suit* and *Executive Suite*) represented a formidable literary attack on the personality and character of the corporate oligarch. Although many of the novels condemned specific practices found in particular industries, the cumulative effect created a picture in the public mind of a man with few, if any, redeeming features. He was the great threat to American civilization rather than the pillar he considered himself to be. Since many of these books enjoyed widespread popularity in their time and some of them were later judged to be classics of American literature (which of course the dated Horatio Alger novels were not), the negative stereotype of the big businessman was deeply ingrained in the public mind. It was an image that would be hard to change.

2

Embittered and somewhat unnerved by this unflattering picture, the corporate oligarch was able to see how extensively it affected (or reflected) popular impressions when Elmo Roper conducted his first public-opinion studies in the late 1930s. Fifteen years of poll taking were summed up in an article Roper wrote for *The Harvard Business Review* in 1949, entitled "The Public Looks at Business," in which he reported that the picture was not as bleak as some feared. He observed that the public was impressed by the achievements of big business, although it was apprehensive over the possible abuses of corporate power. On the basis of his findings he suggested that "the attitude of the people toward business will be determined . . . by how well people can remember the good things which business has done for them." Two years later a research group at the University of Michigan published the first full-scale public-opinion study of big business, laying the foundation for what were later to be called "image profiles." In 1953 David Lilienthal's book *Big Business: A New Era* attempted to develop a blueprint for a program that he thought would evoke positive and affirmative public attitudes toward industry. In 1954 a book appeared by J. D. Glover, entitled *The Attack on Big Business,* suggesting that the administrators of business should "clarify their own thinking about the fundamental nature and purposes of large business organizations." If they could develop more meaningful goals for their corporations, he believed, public hostility could be overcome.

The significant contribution made by these authors was a belief that something could be done to dispel the stereotypes of businessmen that had become so popular in the first few decades of the twentieth century. A note of caution was struck by Glover, who warned that "the intellectual critics of big business—including Supreme Court Justices, Congressmen, professors, and ministers of religion—cannot be moved from their positions by slogans coined by 'hucksters.' " But what intrigued the corporate oligarch was the possibility that he might be able to change his profile and put on a new face which would more accurately represent his character.

Early in 1955 several articles appeared on the new technique of motivation research and how it might help change public attitudes. Then late in the same year an article appeared in *The Harvard Business Review* entitled "The Mass Image of Big Business," by Burleigh B. Gardner and Lee Rainwater. This was probably the first time the word "image" was used in connection with business, and the authors suggested that a "more realistic knowledge of public thinking on big business can lead to the abandonment of the many pervasive stereotypes that plague this field of discussion." They believed that the "middle majority" mass-market group, considered to be sixty-five per cent of the population, was impressed by the many contributions of big business, but that it was also fearful that the power of the corporation might get out of hand and work against public interests. Public-relations techniques might be able to relieve these apprehensions, but the authors warned, "Rule by pollsters . . . applied to economic affairs could create a complete tyranny of the consumer."

This analysis gave a hint of the new idea that would rapidly become popular among corporate oligarchs, that the criticism of business was more often due to a bad image that could be corrected than to the policies being questioned. The fear that the power of the corporation was becoming too great was the result of a stereotype; all one must do to eliminate the fear was to eliminate (or change) the stereotype.

In 1956 the Oil Industry Information Committee conducted a searching self-examination of broad policies and approaches to the problem of bigness in industry. The final report quoted top executives of large companies who felt that the image of big business was out of date. Du Pont's president, Crawford Greenewalt, said that "the old type-casting of the businessman as materialistic, selfish, . . . and insatiable in his pursuit of money . . . has made its mark and has created in the mind of the average person the myth that the public welfare is in some way in danger, that society needs protection from these businessmen in caricature." At fault, said the report, were the events of earlier American capitalism that produced the muckrakers, the Sherman Act, Theodore Roosevelt's "Big Stick" against the "malefactors of great wealth," and the New Deal's antagonism to the "economic royalists." The antibusiness stereotypes which resulted from this history, together with the modern-day departure from the classical capitalist ideal of competition, had aggravated public apprehensions about the possible misuse of power by big business, and about its supposedly "monopolistic" or "oligopolistic" character.

According to Robert E. Wilson, chairman of the board of the Standard Oil Company (Indiana), "modern American capitalism is truly a new thing in the history of the world." Theodore V. Hauser, chairman of the board of Sears, Roebuck, found it ludicrous that our system is being challenged on the basis of a "philosophy one hundred years old and directed against a capitalism very different from what we Americans have." A General Electric advertisement about "People's Capitalism" declared: "Our brand of capitalism is distinctive . . ." The writers of the oil-industry report acknowledged that the nature of the new capitalism had not yet been fully clarified, but one significant proposition was believed to be what Barbara Ward called "the revolution of the profit motive" from the quest for private gain to the fulfillment of a social function for the mass market.

An explanation of public apprehension about big business was given in Herrymon van Maurer's book *Great Enterprise*. "Individually," he wrote, "the people feel they cannot adequately enforce the rules which they think business should follow. But through their government they feel they *can* have a voice in making sure that certain standards are lived up to by business. Government is looked upon, therefore, as a source of checks and balances on business excesses." The only way this belief could be counteracted, he suggested, would be to make it clear that corporations today do not conform to the ideas of the classical economists and that "the social responsibilities and economic activities of large corporations are so inextricably mingled as to amount to the same thing."

The oil-industry report endorsed Maurer's call for "the development of a rationale of great enterprise by which the large corporation can understand itself and explain itself." But in the meanwhile, it suggested, the public should be shown evidence of industry's moral "good citizenship" *as well as* its economic utility. Toward that end, certain themes should be emphasized in corporate communications programs—namely, the contribution of business to material plenty, its role in guaranteeing economic security, its evolution toward a system that reflects the democratic ideals and applies them to the larger society, its recognition of the spiritual objectives and worth of the individual human life, and its role in an enterprising and diverse society and in the development of individual opportunities and individual creativeness. At the same time, the report cautioned its readers that "any effort to change deeply ingrained images of an institution must anticipate the long pull rather than the short, spectacular dash."

This was the foundation on which the whole image-building strategy of the following decades was constructed. There was enough good sense and thoughtful self-evaluation in it for the idea to be credible. The oligarchy wanted to tell the truth about itself—as it conceived the truth to be. It could convince the public that corporate growth was synonomous with progress by publicizing all the contributions modern business makes to society. This would change the image of big business and make the public less receptive to attacks against business interests.

3

Imagism was a school of poetry which originated in London around 1912 and lasted for several years. Its adherents included Ezra Pound, Hilda Doolittle, Amy Lowell, James Joyce and Richard Aldington. Visionaries of a new era, their precise phrases were like pieces of sculpture, fixing images in frozen gestures.

In 1922 Walter Lippmann's *Public Opinion* established the bridge between artfully constructed poetic images and the passively received stereotyped images of people, nations and events which form the basis of public opinion. The same process was involved; but while poetic images were distillations of truth, stereotyped images, Lippmann pointed out, were ingredients of illusion.

An important source of material for Lippmann's analysis was the World War I propaganda efforts to present a positive picture of events that were taking place on the battlefront. These activities were primitive, however, when compared to the propaganda programs of World War II, particularly those conducted under the direction of Joseph Goebbels, Hitler's minister of enlightenment and propaganda. Goebbels' dramatic successes made it clear that if one man exercised strict control over every possible outlet for public information it would be possible to convince millions that his view of what was happening in the world was correct. The effectiveness of Goebbels' campaigns, matched to a large degree by those conducted under Stalin in the U.S.S.R., stimulated George Orwell to write the novel *1984* (published in 1949) in which the practice of "double think" was described with frightening realism. This projected the art of image making as one of the most dangerous innovations of the twentieth century.

A more sober and responsible concept was developed in 1956 with the publication of Kenneth E. Boulding's *The Image*. Boulding described a "public image" as "a record in more or less permanent form which can be handed down from generation to generation." He concluded that there was a need for a new science which he called Eiconics, based on an "image of the image capable of developing researchable hypotheses, testable propositions, and of producing an orderly growth of theoretical insight." In this way, institutionalized images could become instruments of progress rather than deception.

The communications techniques by which the corporate oligarch eventually believed images could be created in the public mind was a hybrid of wartime propaganda, the theory of Eiconics, and the practice of political campaigning and consumer-product marketing in the 1940s and 1950s.

In the post–World War II years both of the latter specialties became highly sophisticated, taking a page or two from Goebbels, without, it was hoped, his irreverence for facts; and a paragraph or two from Boulding, without, unfortunately, an appreciation of his probing search for truth. The proliferation of trained public-relations practitioners, public-opinion pollsters, motivation-research experts, package designers and specialists in a host of other relatively new types of mass communications created the expectation of a breakthrough in the process of persuasion. The discovery by the commercial world of subliminal perception and, subsequently, multisensory experiences and multimedia techniques suggested that a new era had arrived. Image making came to be used as the general term which embraced all these techniques insofar as they could help create positive thinking and friendliness toward a person, a product, a corporation, an industry, a nation or any other classification in contemporary society.

To dramatize the importance of a good image in personal selling, McGraw-Hill published a classic full-page advertisement in 1958. Filling the top half of the page was a photograph of a hard-bitten executive sitting hunched at his desk, staring suspiciously at the reader and saying, "I don't know who you are. I don't know your company. I don't know your company's product. I don't know what your company stands for. I don't know your company's customers. I don't know your company's record. I don't know your company's reputation. Now—what was it you wanted to tell me?" The message was clear. A good image precedes the salesman, softens up sales resistance, creates friendly attitudes, puts the customer in a mood to buy.

Because individual companies were interested to see how well they were doing in over-all communications, the first industry-wide "corporate-image profiles" were published by the Opinion Research Corporation in its 1959 Public Opinion Index for Industry. Twenty-two leading U.S. companies were rated comparatively on such characteristics as product reliability (from a low of five per cent to a high of sixty per cent); company solidarity (from a low of twelve per cent to a high of fifty-eight per cent); attention to human values (from a low of seven per cent to a high of twenty-two per cent); record for steady work (from a low of six per cent to a high of forty per cent). Altogether there were fifty characteristics rated in what was described as a "cafeteria of attitudes." This could be used as a guide for the corporate oligarch who was concerned about the total picture of his company.

That same year the work of graphic designers to create new visual images for corporations resulted in a spurt of new registered trademarks, a rise of twenty per cent over the previous year, including new ones for General Dynamics, U.S. Steel, U.S. Plywood, and Cities Service. In June 1959 the American Management Association organized its first seminar on "Developing the Corporate Image." In 1962 Irwin Ross's *Image Merchants* was published; in it public-relations practitioners were called "men who endlessly create, delineate, adumbrate, and project the most flattering available 'images' of their clients."

In retailing it became popular to talk about the importance of store images. Phil S. Harris, president of S. Klein, New York, predicted that when price advantages were equalized among competitive outlets a "battle of images" would take place in which customers would be attracted on the basis of reputation for service. The Super Market Institute in cooperation with *McCall's* initiated an annual award for the advertising campaign which most effectively built a store image. Producers of brand-name products experimented with advertising and promotion campaigns to increase sales through image identification. A typical program was conducted by Armour and Company, which found that after twelve consecutive four-color advertisements in *Better Homes and Gardens* over-all brand awareness rose from 55.1 per cent to 65.5 per cent, with varying degrees of success showing up for different categories of products (bacon, hot dogs, canned hams and luncheon meat). On brand attributes Armour showed a net change of plus 12.3 per cent. Ninety-eight similar case histories were published in 1962 by the National Industrial Conference Board, which concluded that "making people aware of a company, its trademarks and brands, its products and services, and the uses of its products, are important advertising objectives."

4

Unfortunately, the popularity of corporate images encouraged the belief that the new selling techniques which had been developed could compensate for serious product or corporate faults. The possibility that a good image could be created for *anything* provided the right techniques were used encouraged some top executives to worry less about solving problems or meeting criticism than about putting up a good front.

This was illustrated by the experience of General Electric following the price-fixing scandal of 1960 and 1961. GE had had an excellent record of socially responsible policies under a series of outstanding top executives from Charles Coffin to Edwin Rice, Gerard Swope, Owen D. Young, Charles E. Wilson, Philip D. Reed and Ralph J. Cordiner. The company had sponsored scientific work of such men as Steinmetz, William Coolidge and Irving Langmuir. It had originated the plan under which the company matched the employee's contribution to his alma mater. It had been the first to make medical catastrophe insurance policies available to employees. Little, if any, of this activity had been conducted for the express purpose of impressing the public. Policies had been developed because they were believed to be sound, not because the company wanted to be liked.

But in 1957 GE management caught the image fever and became interested in attitude measurement. During the following two years two massive studies were conducted in cooperation with Alcoa, Du Pont, Texaco, U.S. Steel and Westinghouse to determine what people thought of these and other large corporations in the country. General Electric management was undoubtedly pleased to find itself the best-known and best-liked company in the country (a projected 64.1 million were supposed to know GE "well" or "fair," as compared to U.S. Steel's 37.5 million). It was not made clear why precisely this was an important accomplishment, but the impression given was that if friendliness was a quality that could be measured as accurately as sales and earnings, GE wanted to be first. It also wanted to continue improving itself in the future. Rather than pat itself on the back complacently, management expressed concern that GE was not increasing its familiarity rating as rapidly as others (four per cent over the two-year period as compared to eight per cent for Westinghouse and Du Pont). The conclusion was that "getting more intimately known to the public" was a legitimate management goal, and that the job of "commanding public attention" would require "sustained, planned programming over a long term."

A subsequent survey, conducted in 1961, indicated a drop by GE from its position of preeminence to a second-place rating. This was quite a blow to those who considered the company's prestige in the industrial community an important index of success. According to the December 1961 issue of the company's internal house organ, *Monogram,* the decline was due to an antitrust action that put General Electric in the headlines, plus a brief but well-publicized strike, plus the big-business controversy that arose in connection with a national election, and finally to a short economic recession. The fact that more ground was not lost as a result of these negative factors was considered to be a tribute to "the work that the General Electric people have done to earn public recognition for good quality and high integrity." Was the loss a permanent one? Dr. Horace J. De Podwin, head of the company's public-affairs research work, thought it was too early to tell. "Effective communications efforts by the company," the house organ concluded, "are at work in the rebuilding effort. But the communication will be wasted without the kind of good work and fair dealing by people throughout General Electric that made us Number One in the public esteem in the past—and should make us Number One tomorrow."

These observations were remarkably gentle in view of what had in fact taken place during the course of the year. The antitrust action referred to so tactfully by *Monogram* was the price-fixing scandal that in February 1961 resulted in jail sentences for seven of the highest executives in the electrical industry. Editorial writers throughout the country had expressed shock at the immorality exposed in Congressional hearings; the Washington *Post* had stated, "We believe that new top management is needed in General Electric, which is the fourth largest industrial corporation in the United States." Henry Ford II, a member of the board of directors of GE, had called on U.S. business to put its house in order. "World Communism," he had said, "could not ask for a better gift than this [scandal]." At the April stockholders' meeting in Syracuse, New York, several stockholders demanded the resignation of Ralph Cordiner, the company president. And in June, having survived the attack, Cordiner testified before the Kefauver Committee that the conspiracies had been a "humbling experience," that he had been "deeply grieved" and "shocked" by what had happened, that "we've learned a lot" and that such acts must be prevented in the future by teaching individuals moral character.

What priority would management give this new program of moral education? Perhaps that would depend on how badly the company's image was affected. Happily (or unhappily), subsequent image studies showed there was little to worry about. The public had a short memory, and public awareness of the scandal dropped from sixty per cent to forty-seven per cent in four months. *Monogram* reported the good news and interpreted the results of a new survey to mean that even those who were most concerned "feel by a very substantial margin that General Electric customers still got their money's worth in the products involved, and they tend to reject any contention that the company has gotten either too big or too diversified to manage."

The implication was that a good corporate image had a higher priority than improved moral character, and that a continuing program of selling the former could help relieve top management's concern about the latter.

5

The superficial attitudes toward corporate problems created by eager corporate imagists is thought by some to be more than compensated for by the heightened sensitivity to the public interests which they brought to management. The desire to win public approval, however, is not the same as being responsive to public needs. Like politicians who take any stand that promises to win votes, corporate oligarchs who worry about their images are not likely to be courageous leaders. They may make more speeches, sponsor more cultural activities, design better institutional advertising programs, support more worthy causes; but to protect their corporate image they will tend to avoid taking positions on major public issues lest the company be identified with points of view which some stockholders or customers might find disagreeable.

An incident in 1962 illustrated how constricting a policy of protecting the corporate image can be. Mr. J. M. Shea, Jr., senior vice-president and a director of American Petrofina, had once been an obscure, prosperous Dallas businessman somewhat active in civic activities. For a long time he had been disturbed by the growth of political fanaticism in Dallas, but he had not been outspoken about his concern. Then came the assassination of President Kennedy and what to Mr. Shea was a shocking aftermath. He heard a small group of extremists angrily scolding the priest at his local Catholic church for holding a requiem mass for the dead President. Others accused Pope John XXIII of having been influenced by Communists. Mr. Shea decided to speak up, and wrote an article for *Look* denouncing Dallas' leaders for coddling the extremists. In Dallas, he asserted, there were "so many Americans vowing vengeance upon their President that a known Communist would seem to veteran security men like a lesser menace." In later talks on the subject, he called on responsible citizens to speak out and urged, as a start, that the Texas School Book Depository be transformed into a center for municipal studies dedicated to the memory of the late President.

As a result of these statements, American Petrofina received some letters deploring the position taken by the company executive, and enclosed with many of the letters were torn-up credit cards for Fina gas stations. Petrofina officials then asked Mr. Shea to agree to an arrangement whereby his public utterances would be screened by the company. Mr. Shea considered this an infringement of his right of free speech and promptly resigned. *Saturday Review* published an editorial on the case, suggesting that corporations did not have the moral or constitutional right to demand "clearance" of employees' personal views. It was an issue that had come up previously when Bethlehem Steel dismissed a community-relations aide who, as a private citizen, had joined a local group working to improve race relations in Bethlehem, Pennsylvania; and when top executives of U.S. Steel did not appear to exert leadership in the troubled racial situation in Birmingham, Alabama. If the corporate image were to become a major consideration in the formation of management policies, employees would soon find themselves imprisoned in a mental straitjacket.

Unfortunately, many corporate-image planners do not recognize this danger. They see employees as instruments of the corporate image and do not realize that using them to represent company policy in the community can be an infringement of their personal rights. In an article in *Public Utilities Fortnightly*, A. R. Newell, division manager of the West Penn Power Company, Washington, Pennsylvania, suggested that management take advantage of the fact that employees are "active in every facet of community life: church, social clubs, union, charitable organizations, service clubs, politics, P.T.A., Chambers of Commerce, schools, cultural organizations—you name it! . . . To the public and customers they are the company and what they do and say greatly influences the ultimate Corporate Image." The same observation was made in a report from the Opinion Research Corporation stating that any company which paid close attention to the employees' role in the public contacts could build a statistically verifiable favorable image in the minds of the national public. The way to achieve this benefit, according to the report, was to exercise "image control," starting with "conscious formulation by the chief executive and his associates of the corporate character to be projected." An industrial designer, Crawford Dunn, suggested that such image control be called "corporate ikonogenics." He recommended that all "unenfranchised sources of noise" be eliminated, and suggested that this could be accomplished by curbing the tendencies toward creative expression found too frequently among employers and by arming the program "with the means of effectively quarantining the corporate kibitzers, however well-meaning they may be."

6

The greatest danger in the practice of corporate imagery is that the top executive may become blind to the realities of corporate life which are apparent to everybody else. As Mary McCarthy once wrote, "Those who seek to project an 'image' are unaware of how they look. The truth they are revealing has become invisible to them."

One example of such self-deception was the announcement by the design firm of Lippincott and Margulies that in 1959 the Consolidated Edison Company had changed its image from "a firm which had a personality problem if ever one existed" to "a friendly, informal, progressive company." It was all supposed to have been accomplished through a new "jolly" trademark, new "bright" company colors, a new "cheerful" sign with the apology "Dig We Must," an "owlish, lovable" Uncle Wethbee on TV, and "a new (really new) kind of ad—the documentary candid which eschews slickness, impressiveness, glamour and beauty for the sake of plain old realism."

This supposed triumph of corporate-image making impressed no one but its creators. Those who were critical of Con Edison continued to object to its policies. Notwithstanding the excellent professional work of Lippincott and Margulies, Con Ed's personality problem was far from cured. (A curious postscript to this story appeared in a *Wall Street Journal* article on August 26, 1968, which stated that Lippincott and Margulies were hired again in 1967 to improve Con Ed's identity. "They [company executives] thought that the entire problem was one of image," Walter Margulies was quoted as saying; "but our study showed that the problem went much deeper than that." Apparently the image-making efforts of the previous decade were conveniently forgotten.)

The tendency to consider an impressive-looking campaign an adequate substitute for needed changes in the policies or character of management is familiar to many public-relations specialists. Programs aimed at curing corporate ills by trying to project a better corporate image are always abortive. To give a typical example, in the early 1960s our firm worked for a company that was experiencing a serious decline in sales. We made an analysis which showed that customers, competitors and, most of all, employees felt a lack of direction on the part of management. Although at one time, when the father of the current president had been the chief executive officer, the company had been recognized as one of the leaders in its field, it was now looked upon as a second- or third-rate operation. The current president expected us to do something about the "facelessness" of the company, and we earnestly set about to do so. As a result of our efforts articles began to appear about the company's achievements; speeches, brochures and seminars helped to focus attention on management development programs; a new look was given to company literature, and so on. But, alas, there was little evidence that anything of substantial value was being accomplished. The president of the company honestly thought he was doing something to help the company improve itself, but everyone else knew that he had merely found an excuse not to look at the real problem—his own shortcomings. What had caused the bad reputation was bad management, and the best public-relations program in the world could not compensate for this failure. The poor image was deserved, as most poor images are. We would have made a far more important contribution to the president and his company if we had helped him recognize what the real problem was, and, following the principles of Kenneth Boulding's theory of Eiconics, stimulated the process of bringing about inner change.

7

Although the image mania of the late 1950s began to be ridiculed as a fad, in the early 1960s interest in image making showed no signs of abating. The insensitivity to public attitudes which had characterized previous generations of business leaders now was dramatically reversed by what often seemed to be an oversensitivity bordering on institutionalized paranoia.

This was not only true about corporations. To see how extensive this sensitivity had become I asked Burrelle's Press Clipping Bureau to keep an eye out for newspaper stories in the spring of 1962 that contained the word "image." I was soon inundated with clippings describing people who were worried about the images of such diverse subjects as Hawaii, Mexico, Siberia, Chicago, Pittsburgh, Cleveland, Kansas City, Boston, Orthodox Judaism, the

Catholic Church, prizefighting, the medical profession, the legal profession, controllership, agricultural colleges, the small-animal clinician, the wives of clergymen, Nobel Prize winners, astronauts, college students, American women, the bachelor and Elvis Presley.

In less than a decade the word "image" had emerged from its respected state of quiet beauty and dignity to become an expression of widespread self-consciousness. What had once been "a word of art," as Archibald MacLeish put it, "employed with rigorous precision by disciplined poets who knew exactly what they meant by it . . . has now become a trade term . . . used in a muzzy, fuzzy, girlish sort of way to mean what people think of you."

Former Secretary of State Dean G. Acheson suggested that the spreading interest in images was due to a "narcissus psychosis" caused by an inferiority complex which made people fearful of and hence sensitive to criticism. He thought this was a harmful development in international affairs; the nervous compulsion to overreact to criticism would lead nations to adopt only those policies which would create a good image rather than those which would achieve valued objectives. "A country half slave—or all slave—to foreign criticism cannot stand, except as a mental institution." The courage to deal with real problems could be regained only if "we exorcise image worship." The cartoonist Jules Feiffer anticipated the creation of a State Department Bureau of Images. The historian Daniel Boorstin wrote a book called *The Image: Or What Happened to the American Dream*, in which he bemoaned the flood of "pseudo-events" which are artificially created to make trivia seem important, and image-making promotion efforts which try "to salve mediocrity by mediocre appeals for 'excellence.'" The columnist Hal Boyle wrote that a corporation worrying about its image was "pretty much like looking at yourself in a crazy mirror in an amusement park and hoping that passers-by won't think the reflection is the real you." The television critic John Crosby wondered if the confusion between images and reality had gotten so bad that "the American people don't even see images of images of images any more." Tom Patterson, the education editor of the Riverside *Press Enterprise* wrote that "today's exorbitant concern with image-building is like heating the bath water by vigorously rubbing the thermometer." The St. Joseph, Michigan, *Herald-Press* published an editorial stating that the "overwhelming preoccupation" with images "creates the false goal of spending undue time and energy on establishing an outward impression at the expense of the more vital problem of internal improvement." A cartoon in *The New Yorker* showed a worried man waking up in the middle of the night, pointing out to his bewildered wife a nightmare vision of himself in the darkness and crying, "There it is again! That damned goofed-up corporate image of ours." The New York *Times Magazine* published an article calling for an end to "Creeping Imagism" and making the suggestion that "the next time someone starts talking to you about Stevenson's egghead image or Rockefeller's progressive image, don't sit there. Grab the image. And then stomp it to bits."

There were many suggestions for changing the word "image" to something else to avoid stereotyped thinking and face up to realities. Sam Feinberg wrote in *Women's Wear Daily*: "Image is wishful thinking. Identity is what a company *is* . . . Image is a statue in search of a pedestal. Identity is the whole works. . . . It's time for a change—from image to identity." Walter Barlow of Opinion Research Corporation said, "A tremendous amount of utter nonsense has been written on the subject of 'corporate image' and only yesterday I was asked for about the nth time if researchers or somebody could find a better phrase. We have experimented with a number, and I find myself reaching for such synonyms as 'total reputation,' 'the collected experience gained by people from whatever source,' and the like." The advertising agency Chirurg & Cairns, Inc., believed that the word "*character* is a good substitute because it is a real and measurable quality, while *image* is only a reflection of something real." The public-relations firm Robert S. Taplinger Associates, Inc., announced the formation of a Society to Scotch the Word "Image." Members were invited to suggest alternative words, and a case of Scotch whiskey was promised to the person who proposed the best replacement.

In 1962 I wrote an article for *Harper's* entitled "Stop Worrying About Your Image," which ended with the conclusion "An executive working for a large corporation, or a politician, or an entertainer, has as much right to search for an image that will help him find meaning in his life as does an artist, philosopher or scientist. But his pursuit of reality will be illusory if he continues to fool around with the modern debasement of one of the most beautiful words in the English language. Instead he should stop worrying altogether and concentrate on trying to find himself."

But the corporate oligarch has not stopped worrying about his image. I think now that the impulses which underlie corporate imagism are sometimes more significant than many of us thought they were a few years ago. These impulses may be rationalized to fit into archaic corporate concepts, but they can also manifest a desire to find new values in corporate life. Amidst all the shallow sloganeering about corporate images in the 1960s one can find evidence that some oligarchs are trying to redefine their function in society, not in order to create a better-selling image but in order to live up to an image of what they think they ought to be.

This occurred to me after years of struggling to avoid the word "image" in business conversations. I had been blue-penciling out "images" in every program or proposal that came across my desk, and every time a client mentioned the word I took the time to explain why I didn't like it. Eventually I began to wonder whether my efforts to avoid the cliché in speech and on paper were not misdirected. The modern executive who is thinking ahead feels that in "image" he has found a word that can help him come to grips with a reassessment of his basic motivations; perhaps my job as a public-relations specialist should be to help such oligarchs use this new tool effectively rather than scold them for their abuse of the English language.

His Desire for a Better Image

"All of us know," James Baldwin once wrote, "whether or not we are able to admit it, that mirrors can only lie . . ." The question is, will the corporate oligarch's interest in his corporate image cause him to believe in the lies that mirrors project or help him find some new truths about himself? Primping before a mirror accomplishes little if what we want is to better ourselves. What we really are is never the reflection of a self-flattering pose. If appearance has some relation to reality, then we reveal ourselves to preceptive observers by how we look to them in unguarded moments. To improve ourselves we must learn to see ourselves as others see us.

The corporate oligarch, powerful leader that he is, is not eager to acknowledge unpleasant truths about himself. He would like to think that he has problems with the public because his real assets are not recognized rather than because there are any basic deficiencies in his makeup. His interest in image making suggests that he may be trying to solve his problems by advertising his virtues rather than by correcting his faults. But it can also mean that he is searching for a way to perform a leadership role in society that is broader than the moneymaking role he has played in the past.

It is undoubtedly true that most often when the corporate oligarch talks about his corporate image he sounds as if he is thinking of the former. He complains that his achievements have never been adequately described to the public. "We have made no record of our accomplishments for the public, the government and even our own industry," said Myer B. Marcus, executive vice-president of Food Fair Stores, recommending to the National Association of Food Chains that a thirty-page insert in *Reader's Digest* describe the contributions of the food industry to the American way of life. "The commercial banking industry does not enjoy the favorable image to which it is entitled on the basis of its contribution to the community and the nation," said Samuel M. Fleming, head of the American Bankers Association and president of the Third National Bank of Nashville, Tennessee. The problem was that "not enough is known about the system and the part it plays in our economy." These sentiments have been echoed in every segment of the American business community. The oligarchy appears to feel that the time has come to let the public know the contribution that each company, each industry and American business as a whole is making to the country.

This more superficial desire for an improved image is in some respects no more than a rebellion against anonymity. Chief executives are frustrated because their success has been ignored by the public. They consider the corporate-image idea a rationale for trying to establish a public reputation for their companies and themselves. They want publicity. They want honor. They want fame. They want to be considered persons of distinction. They want to project themselves and their companies into the permanent record of their time.

Some have gone so far as to imagine that an impressive corporate image can bring them immortality. Thus, a fine mausoleum in suburban Westchester County erected in memory of a New York businessman bears his name, not in the usual austere mortuary letters, but in a delightfully elaborate script familiar to millions of customers as the trademark of his chocolate-candy company. The corporate image was apparently such an important symbol of this oligarch's accomplishments that he wanted to take it with him to the grave!

To others, acquiring a corporate image is like buying a new suit of clothes or a new house. One company president told me, "I've become a rich man from my business. My company is doing fine and running pretty much by itself. I've tried to think of what I should work for now, and I guess it ought to be an image." The wife of another company president once complained that when her husband walked down the street in Palm Beach no one recognized him, while others who were worth much less were greeted by every other person. She wanted him to have an image so that he would be recognized by everybody who saw him. This was a democratic family: the husband also wanted his wife to have an image. When she bought a new fur coat, there was no reason, he thought, why it shouldn't be front-page fashion news, and when she went to the first night of the opera he wanted her to be singled out as the most glamorous lady in the audience.

Still another company president, a lady this time, was so infatuated with her good looks that she had literally hundreds of portrait photographs taken under corporate auspices. In one of the most bizarre episodes that ever came to my attention as a public-relations consultant, this company president encouraged a false rumor that she was afflicted with a mortal illness in order to justify an intense campaign of personal publicity—to produce a public image which she could enjoy before her supposedly imminent demise.

The inflated sense of one's own importance which is created by the appetite for acclaim has long been identified with successful businessmen. Just over a century ago, Dostoyevsky wrote in *Crime and Punishment* about a character "who had made his way up from insignificance, was morbidly given to self-admiration, had the highest opinion of his intelligence and capacities, and sometimes even gloated in solitude over his image in the glass." Dostoyevsky's character felt that his hard-earned wealth was what most satisfied his ego. "What he valued above all," Dostoyevsky wrote, "was the money he had amassed by his labor and by all sorts of devices; that money made him the equal of all who had been his superiors." The corporate oligarch who thinks of images in terms of status has simply elevated himself from private gloating over the size of his fortune to public boasting about his importance in the corporate world.

But there is another kind of interest in corporate images which reveals, I think, a more serious and creditable aspiration. This is found among top executives who feel embarrassed by the vainglories which are often associated with image making. They may enjoy the boost to one's ego which comes from occasional personal publicity, but they are not obsessed with a desire to see their "pictures in the papers" or to have their corporate success hailed as one of the great achievements of modern times. They are far more anxious to overcome the shortcomings of their companies as pointed out by men they respect than to get self-glorifying statements into print. Their interest in improving their corporate image reflects a willingness to respond to criticism rather than a wish to fight it or deflect it or even counteract it.

These top executives listen with great attentiveness when their public-relations counselors give them a report of what leading investment analysts, newspaper editors, key employees, large customers and others think about their company, not as an index of its popularity but as a frank appraisal of its strong and weak points. A technique which is being used increasingly to help top management gauge its public-relations problems, these confidential reports (in which only the position, not the name of the person interviewed, is disclosed, which encourages more straightforward replies than would ordinarily be given) provide the corporate oligarch with a rare and valuable insight into his own worth as a manager and the position of his company in the community. When he studies the comments in such an analysis he is not making the traditional mistake of looking in the mirror to see how handsome he is; he is trying to improve himself by facing up to what others honestly think of him.

One of the most important developments of this mature approach to corporate images is a growing awareness on the part of some top executives that they must pay more attention to the human elements of their enterprises and display a capability of managing more than sales charts and balance sheets. Instead of trying to prove that what their corporations have done in the past is better than people give them credit for, they recognize that something more must be done in the future. The problem is that the phrase "corporate image" still conjures up some of the more superficial tendencies in the top executive's personality; it is often painfully clear that he has yet to find the language in which a real sense of responsibility to the community can be meaningfully expressed.

9

His Impulse
to Render
a Public Service

THE DESIRE OF MEN WHO HOLD POSITIONS OF GREAT ECONOMIC power to make a noneconomic contribution to the community is not, of course, unique to these pioneering corporate oligarchs. The Maecenas and Medici traditions of the past demonstrated that a relationship could be established between power and patronage and that economic, political, social and cultural aspirations were not incompatible with one another. The organizers of sixteenth- and seventeenth-century corporations which were dedicated to the opening up of new worlds had an ability to mix a degree of community idealism with personal ambition. Even in the nineteenth century, when the robber barons of the New World were given legal sanction to plunder public property to build their own fortunes, there were some visionary industrial leaders who gave a high priority to the needs of society. There were only a few of these powerful figures of the past, however, who would have considered that a possible conflict between commercial gain and community good should ever be voluntarily resolved in favor of the latter.

The revolutionary change which is in prospect with the advent of the socially oriented corporate oligarch of the 1960s is that, against the backdrop of an increasingly mature interest in corporate images, the leaders of the commercial world may be approaching the day when they will officially declare moneymaking subordinate to community welfare in setting the goals of their corporate power.

On the face of it this is farfetched. But a review of the precedents which have brought the corporate oligarch to this stage shows that the prospect is not as unreasonable as it seems. By analyzing the motivations behind his past and present activities in the public service, and facing squarely the significance of his many failures as well as the promise implicit in his few successes, one can find some basis for optimism. He still has a long way to go before developing a fundamentally different outlook on his role in society, but not to recognize the possibilities of a revolutionary change is to miss, I believe, the most important feature of the corporate oligarch's present condition.

2

One of the most famous of the early industrial leaders who were concerned about the welfare of their fellow man was Robert Owen. His experiment in industrial utopia, New Harmony, Indiana, lasted only three years (from 1825 to 1828) and cost him most of his fortune, but it was a significant landmark. Because it failed, later industrial leaders with his inclinations adopted a benevolent approach to running their companies instead of trying to plan model industrial communities. Abram S. Hewitt, one of the first of these benevolent entrepreneurs, had been a teacher of mathematics at Columbia University. He made his fortune in the mid-nineteenth century in the manufacture of iron girders and beams in partnership with Edward Cooper, son of Peter Cooper. When

Hewitt's company became an important supplier to the United States government during the Civil War, he refused to take any profit. He considered the work of his company a patriotic duty. This was, incidentally, an interesting contrast to the Civil War enterprise of his contemporary Jay Cooke, who made sizable commissions by selling government bonds to the public to help finance the Union cause. Cooke preferred to marry patriotism with profit rather than sacrifice one for the other. Hewitt, on the other hand, was so willing to go to the other extreme that in the depression years 1873–78 (a depression partly brought on by the failure of Cooke's banking firm) he ran his plant at an annual loss of $100,000 so that he could give his employees fair wages. He was elected mayor of New York in 1886 (the opposition candidates were Henry George and Theodore Roosevelt), and he summed up his philosophy when he said, "A nation is not great because it is rich, any more than a man is a hero because he is a millionaire. The question is not how much riches we have accumulated but what we are doing with them."

"Pious" John Wanamaker was another early businessman who attempted to express his public-spirited ideas in the way he ran his company. A pioneer in retail merchandising who later became Postmaster General in President Benjamin Harrison's administration (1889–93), Wanamaker developed schools, libraries, savings funds, pensions and insurance programs to put his theories into practice. He believed that "a tremendous responsibility rests upon employers towards their intelligent, painstaking employees, who spend their lives year in and year out under the same roof." In 1902 J. C. Penney developed his variation of the same theme when he opened his first "Golden Rule Store" and proclaimed his belief that the businessman's sacred duty is to be of service to his fellow man. Penney felt that customers were neighbors "whom it is our neighborly privilege to assist toward buying what they need and want at the lowest fair prices." Only by performing this function with scrupulous honesty, he preached, could the businessman achieve salvation.

As the corporate oligarch emerged in the early twentieth century, the somewhat patronizing and often sanctimonious benevolence of these few individualists gave way to a somewhat more organized form of social consciousness. The dictum of personal morality was replaced by a vague sense of corporate responsibility. One of the first chief executives to express this new point of view was John H. Patterson, president of the National Cash Register Company, who was looked upon as a social reformer as well as an outstanding executive. He believed that only through enthusiastic devotion could employees do a good job, and he built modern factories with elaborate facilities to prove his point. His management provided showers for employees on company premises, dining rooms which served meals at cost, entertainment, schools, clubs, libraries and parks. Patterson trained a number of executives who later became leading exponents of enlightened management policies. Among these were Thomas J. Watson, founder of IBM, Charles F. Kettering of General Motors, Alvan Macauley, long-time head of Packard, and Richard R. H. Grant, president of Delco Light and of Frigidaire. Watson, particularly, pioneered many new concepts of human relations in corporate life; one of them, a company policy against factory layoffs, had its first test in the Great Depression, when IBM kept men at their jobs by producing parts that were put away in storehouses as inventory.

3

A different but related strain of magnanimity in the corporate oligarch is the philanthropic impulse which he shares with other men of wealth. The injunction to impose on oneself a tithe of one's personal possessions to fulfill one's religious obligations and care for the needy is of ancient origin. The history of the American industrial leader contains repeated manifestations of this method of fulfilling the dictates of conscience.

An early example of philanthropy among American businessmen was the disposition of the estate of Stephen Girard, the wealthy shipping magnate, who died in 1831. Although he had never been charitable during his lifetime, his bequests reflected what at the time was an unprecedented interest in philanthropy. He created a $6-million trust for the creation and endowment of a college for "poor white male orphans" which was subsequently named after him. (The college was situated in an area of North Philadelphia which later became a predominantly Negro neighborhood, and in 1954 a suit was initiated to end the segregation stipulated in Girard's will. The action was brought to a successful conclusion in 1968 when the Supreme Court denied the appeal of trustees of the estate to reverse a lower-court ruling in favor of desegregation.) Girard also left large sums to hospitals, orphan societies and other charitable associations; $500,000 went to the city of Philadelphia for certain civic improvements, $300,000 went for the canals of Pennsylvania. In the words of a contemporary, Edward Everett, "Few persons . . . enjoyed less personal popularity in the community in which he lived. . . . A citizen and a patriot he lived in his modest dwelling and plain garb; appropriating to his last personal wants the smallest pittance from his princely income; living to the last in the dark and narrow street in which he made his fortune; and when he died bequeathed it for the education of orphan children. For the public I do not believe he could have done better."

The argument that businessmen who became rich by selling the public their wares should return the favor through private philanthropy (there was no income tax at the time) seemed so reasonable following Girard's death that there were public outcries against those who showed no philanthropic instinct at all. This was the case when John Jacob Astor died in 1848 a much richer man than Girard and left most of his estate to his son William. A famous newspaper editor, James Gordon Bennett, protested the absence of public bequests in the will and stated that at least one half of Astor's immense fortune rightfully belonged to the people of New York.

It is hard to estimate the number of nineteenth-century entrepreneurs who made a serious attempt to balance accounts with the communities that made them rich, but there certainly were many who did. Israel Pemberton devoted himself to Quaker causes and especially to the Indians, with whom he was sympathetic. He was sometimes called "King Wampum" and is said to have given most of his money and time to support the Friendly Association for Regaining and Preserving Peace with Indians by Pacific Measures. Samuel Vaughan Merrick did much the same in projects to help educate Negroes in the South after the Civil War, and he is believed to have made many generous gifts which he carefully concealed from the general public's knowledge. In 1873 Commodore Vanderbilt gave nearly a half-million dollars to a little Methodist Episcopal school in the South, which appropriately was renamed Vanderbilt University.

John D. Rockefeller showed a philanthropic bent from the day he started to earn a living. By the time he was twenty-one he had contributed to the Erie Street Baptist Church in Cleveland, to a Cincinnati Negro to buy his slave wife, to a Catholic orphanage, to a Negro mute-and-blind society, to an industrial school, and to a Swedish mission in Illinois. In his later years, when he became the richest man in the world, he gave more than half his fortune away to create giant foundations for education, medical research and other public causes. Andrew Carnegie, whose pattern of giving was very similar, formulated a "gospel of wealth" which he hoped would convert the industrial world to the ideal of philanthropy as the only legitimate utilization of privately accumulated capital. He believed the millionaire should not be a hoarder of useless millions but should administer his entire estate for the good of his fellows and in the end give all his money away. He should die a poor man, and in that way he would be "twenty times a millionaire still in the affection, gratitude and admiration of his fellow-men."

The practice of philanthropy during this period had little to do with corporate goals. It was assumed by most of these philanthropists that the purpose of business was to make money by whatever means one could. Their nobler sentiments were addressed only to the use of wealth once it was accumulated. It was part of their religious heritage to believe that charity was the only method by which the corruption of excessive riches could be avoided. Thus, the Baptist minister Frederick T. Gates urged his friend John D. Rockefeller to give away his money faster than he made it lest his fortune crush him and his children and his children's children.

Recipients of philanthropy often took it for granted that wealthy businessmen gave money away as a form of penance. It was supposed, for instance, that Alfred Nobel, the Swedish chemist and engineer who amassed a great fortune in the nineteenth century from the manufacture of dynamite and other explosives, left the bulk of his fortune in trust to establish the famous Nobel prizes for just this reason. Resentment against any such attempt to make up for the harm done in the pursuit of material gain led to the famous "tainted money" controversy around the turn of the century, when the Reverend Washington Gladden, a Congregational minister, denounced the benefactions of the rich "pirates of industry" as a transparent means of buying public favor and heavenly salvation. The world would be better served, he said, if the industrialist were more human, made less money and stopped trying to make up for his sins through supposedly generous charities.

It was certainly not uncommon then and it is not uncommon today for great philanthropists to be ruthless businessmen. Corporate critics have repeatedly accused philanthropists of squeezing the poor laborers to acquire fortunes with which they can glorify their own names. Gustavus Myers described the dismal lot of the early-nineteenth-century workers whose hearts were broken and whose health was destroyed by the tragic circumstances in which they struggled to earn a living—a significant contrast and sequel, he wrote, "to the accumulations of multimillionaires of which Girard was then the archetype."

In my own experience as a consultant to men who simultaneously direct the affairs of great corporations and manage their own private foundations, I have often been struck by similar contrasts. As executives they are perfectly comfortable about discharging employees en masse, canceling pension programs, refusing to spend money on modernizing plants, and taking many other actions which clearly give a higher priority to corporate power than to human welfare. Yet as philanthropists they are capable of being deeply touched by the gratitude of a single individual whose life has been significantly changed as a result of their benefactions.

I cannot say, however, that I have ever detected either a sense of guilt about their management policies or a feeling of expiation about their philanthropy. Although the possibility of a relationship between the two is an attractive theory, I rather doubt its validity. If anything, a philanthropically oriented businessman attempts to use his business as a means of earning enough money to support his favorite causes. This is not a matter of purifying one's soul; it is a strategy for financing one's pet projects. This is true even when the effects of a business enterprise seem to run counter to the purposes of a personal interest, as when a manufacturer of military products uses his personal income to support peace-research projects. I have known one such individual for many years, and he has lived his double life with what appears to be remarkable equanimity. He justifies his business endeavor as a legitimate enterprise which serves a real need so long as nations feel obliged to maintain a defense posture, and he finds it personally rewarding to spend as much time and money as he can in the search for means to relieve tension in the world so that one day defense postures will be unnecessary. I believe he would consider his life a great success if his philanthropic contributions to the search for peace should one day succeed in eliminating the market for his military products.

4

The possibility of a convergence of private philanthropic inclinations and public corporate ambitions arose in the twentieth century, when the corporate oligarch began to be concerned about the danger of negative public attitudes toward business.

A meager start in corporate philanthropy was made as a response to the patriotic fervor of World War I. In the 1920s and 1930s corporate giving was primarily directed toward community-chest and depression causes. Then, under the proddings of community-chest leaders, the federal Revenue Act of 1935 was passed, making it possible for corporations to deduct from taxable earnings charitable contributions amounting to five per cent of net profits. The philanthropy which had heretofore been a sporadic feature of the corporate world, practiced only by those industrial leaders with charitable inclinations, now became an official concern of management. The corporate oligarch could earmark part of his company's profits for charitable purposes without imposing a heavy burden on stockholders and without reducing his own personal capital. He also had available to him an important new technique by which to persuade the public that corporate management was concerned about the welfare of the community.

By 1961, American corporations were giving more than a half-billion dollars annually to philanthropic appeals. By 1964, nearly half of all corporations with a thousand or more employees had operating foundations or trusts to handle their philanthropies. In 1964 the Ford Motor Company Fund alone made grants totaling $6,446,829. In 1965 the Esso Education Foundation—established ten years earlier by the Standard Oil Company (New Jersey) and six affiliated companies—made grants totaling $2,197,538. That same year the General Electric Foundation gave $4,100,000 to educational programs. In 1966 General Motors' financial aid to education amounted to $11,400,000. That year the Chrysler Corporation Fund (which had been incorporated in 1953) contributed $3,000,000 to the Detroit United Foundation's 1966 capital-fund drive. Another record gift, $3,627,108, was made that same year by the Corporation Fund and Chrysler Corporation employees to the Torch Drive. Also in 1966, U.S. Steel's contributions for educational and charitable purposes were $7,000,000. In 1967, Mobil Oil's worldwide contributions to health and welfare organizations, professional societies and education were estimated at more than $5,500,000.

With the entry of philanthropy into the corporate environment, the idea that charity can bring some tangible reward became popular. Because such substantial amounts of money were involved and the goals were so important to the corporation, most companies made control of contributions a top-management function. The reward was not likely to be immediate or even measurable, but, since the corporate oligarch believed that a positive public attitude toward his company was a valuable asset, directing charitable gifts in the company's name, particularly if they could be well publicized, was considered an important part of over-all corporate strategy.

The promise that charity will pay off in some way has, of course, been made frequently by professionals in the world of fund raising. This has been true not only in regard to corporations; most individuals too appreciate some form of public credit for their benefactions. Thus, one of the great friends of the city of New York will long be remembered for his Delacorte Amphitheater in Central Park, the Delacorte Mobile Theater and the Margarita Delacorte Memorial fountain in Columbus Circle. The forest of plaques covering the walls of American institutions make it clear how common this appeal is to contributors of all sorts. The bigger and more important the building to which the plaque is attached, the more secure the giver feels about the piece of immortality he has acquired. One leading hotel-business executive known for his shrewd assessment of real-estate values recently called his $2-million contribution for a university building which would be named after his father "a hell of a buy."

Recognition from one's peers is another reward of philanthropy. This is why the idea that "people give to people" is an axiom for all professional fund raisers. A man who is inclined to make large donations likes to be asked by another who is himself generous. This puts the giver in the same company as the asker who is already widely respected in the community. Thus, one wealthy oligarch once told me that he gave $1 million to Lincoln Center because he was personally asked to do so by John D. Rockefeller III. Of course there were other reasons, but the opportunity of being able to give Rockefeller a million dollars was no small satisfaction. This consideration also has a negative aspect; how does one say no to a cause which one doesn't believe in but which is represented by an eminent citizen whom a top executive can't easily refuse? The answer is to give as little as possible. "I find," reported one businessman to the *Wall Street Journal*, "that a $1,000 donation will get practically anybody off your back."

Concern about appearances has not by any means become the overriding concern in all philanthropy. There are still many prominent citizens who prefer to make their gifts without any fanfare. When André Meyer of Lazard Frères gave $2.5 million for the construction of a new physics building at New York University he permitted his name to be publicly identified only because university officials thought it would be helpful to them. "I'm terribly allergic to any kind of article about me," he was quoted by the New York *Times* as saying. Alfred P. Sloan, Jr., had some of the same instincts, although many of his benefactions did carry his name (he accumulated a personal fortune of $250 million in his lifetime, but gave away over $300 million). Once, long after his retirement as chairman of General Motors, he showed his distaste for public recognition by declining to be interviewed on his birthday, with a note which stated, "I would like to 'fade away' and be forgotten. I think having lived to the present age justifies my so doing. I am sorry. I do not want to be discourteous. I cannot afford to be. But I most earnestly ask to be excused." In the obituary of Mrs. Moses L. Annenberg, widow of a leading figure in the publishing business, it was reported that some of her philanthropic contributions had been made anonymously and others had been made on the condition that there be no publicity. A large number of the 2,811 libraries built with funds from Andrew Carnegie did not carry his name. John Burroughs, the celebrated naturalist, once reported to a friend: "Mr. Ford, of automobile fame, is a great admirer of my books—says there are few persons in the world who have given him the pleasure I have. He wants to do something for me—he wants to present me with an automobile all complete and send a man to teach Julian how to run it. His sole motive is his admiration for me and my work—there shall be no publicity in connection with it." A recent gift by Charles S. Mott, director and largest single stockholder of General Motors, of $128 million to a foundation administered by the Board of Education of Flint, Michigan, was made without any publicity. The huge stock transfer came to light in a routine report required by law to be filed with the New York Stock Exchange and the Securities Exchange Commission.

But such modesty is not particularly consistent with the corporate character. Although there are some examples of gifts being made anonymously from corporate foundations, it is generally understood that management wants the company name (or the name of the top executive officers) identified with its benefactions.

5

The third element in the corporate oligarch's expanding interest in community affairs was his skill in using public service as a sales promotion device. Machiavelli admired "the qualities of the fox and the lion" among Renaissance princes; the sales-oriented business leader of the twentieth century developed a variation of this combination through his mastery of the "soft" and the "hard" sell.

Part of his cleverness was to know how to provide tangential benefits to potential customers as a "soft sell" technique to interest them in his product.

It was not by accident that John H. Patterson, the National Cash Register Company president who was looked upon by many of his contemporaries in the early twentieth century as a social reformer, was also considered the father of modern salesmanship. It was also in character for "Pious" John Wanamaker to finance a variety of cultural events as a means of promoting sales. Any great salesman, whether or not he is interested in public affairs, knows that a good deed can be good business. As P. T. Barnum put it, "The liberal man will command patronage."

Public-service sales promotion was a far more direct way of cashing in on a contribution to the community than either corporate philanthropy or executive participation in community affairs. In the 1950s and 1960s it came to be looked upon as the ideal form of image-building activity, for it paid for itself in sales while supposedly helping to create positive public attitudes toward the corporation.

Typical of these public-service sales campaigns was the "Seat Belts for Safety" promotion developed in 1962 by the Standard Oil Company (California). For several months Chevron stations offered drivers seat belts at less than half their ordinary price, with no charge for installation. The advertisement announcing the promotion stated: "Today, you can get this auto seat belt for $5.95 each at most Chevron Stations, installed free. Why? Simply because Chevron believes that seat belts belong in your car and in every car. Is this a good deal? Yes, it is. Many have paid $12.95 for this same belt, plus installation." The belts were of high quality, surpassing the rigid requirements of the National Safety Council and other organizations, including the United States government. The company said the program was non–profit-making. But its purpose was merchandising, and the measure of its success was that it helped to build traffic at service stations. Within two weeks of the initial deliveries of thirty-five thousand belts to stations, dealers had started reordering to handle a waiting list of customers. It was considered an outstanding performance, and at the same time management felt it had created what one trade paper called "a better public-service image of the company."

To give another example, a "Penfriend" program was launched by the Parker Pen Company at the 1964–65 New York World's Fair. The company erected its own pavilion at the fair, and visitors were invited to be matched with an overseas friend with the help of a computer which recorded language capability, sex, age bracket, hobbies. Sixty writing desks with a selection of Parker pens attached served the needs of those wishing to begin their Penfriend correspondence at once. Over two million people entered the pavilion, and six hundred thousand visitors started Penfriend correspondence. The project, which resulted in worldwide publicity, formed the basis of a well-planned sales promotion for dealers and distributors. Name-gathering manuals prepared for each distributor's locality were issued, and Parker representatives in different countries were guided on advertising and publicity techniques, and on how to establish contact with schools and business and professional groups to obtain Penfriend applications which could be fed into the computer.

Even when a public-service program did not have a direct product connection, it could be accepted by top management as a reasonable sales promotion strategy. Thus, a bicycle safety program begun in 1956 by Johnson & Johnson was concerned with the idea that it would enhance the company's reputation as a reliable source of surgical dressings. Strictly speaking, fewer accidents could mean fewer surgical dressings sold, but if Johnson & Johnson could show that it was genuinely interested in the health and safety of its customers it would earn the respect, and presumably the loyalty, of parents, doctors and nurses who were interested in reducing accidents. The details of the program were worked out in cooperation with the National Safety Council, the Bicycle Institute of America and the National Education Association. Materials were produced for teachers, including rules of the road, safety tests both written and mechanical, application forms for licenses, inspection forms, operators' certificates, and a draft ordinance for local vehicle codes. The layout for a test-riding course was included, with all the details for setting up and running the program. A twenty-seven-minute film was produced. Posters were distributed for classroom use, and several cities used them on their buses, trolleys and taxicabs. Over three thousand communities used the materials. An estimated 24,521,780 people were exposed to the program. Johnson & Johnson considered this an outstanding public relations achievement.

Public-service advertising campaigns also became popular during this period. Even though these too were not directly tied to sales, management felt they were sound investments. Moreover, the responsibility for seeing to it that the investments produced dividends was assumed by sales departments, which usually conceived the campaign in the first place, and which made sure to "merchandise" the advertisements to customers and potential customers. Among the companies cited by *Saturday Review* for outstanding public-service advertising campaigns in 1967 were Olin Mathieson Chemical Corporation, St. Regis Paper Company, Metropolitan Life Insurance Company, Seagram Distillers Company, Sears, Roebuck & Company, American Telephone & Telegraph Company. The subjects of these campaigns included a description of an historic water-purification program in Vietnam (Olin), how to safeguard children from drowning (Metropolitan Life), and why young people should not drink (Seagram).

6

A tacit assumption of public-service sales-promotion campaigns is that they have the advantage of satisfying the personal desire of the corporate oligarch to be a public benefactor while also, hopefully, providing valuable support to sales efforts. This is not discussed openly by executives, because corporate oligarchs don't like the idea that company funds are being spent merely to please them. But it is the common experience of sales executives and public-relations specialists that these campaigns are more likely to arouse interest on the part of top management than almost any other kind of promotion program.

Nowhere is this more apparent than in the sponsorship of cultural events. And the marked increase in this type of corporate activity is another index of the corporate oligarch's increasing tendency to use corporate resources to further noneconomic goals under the guise of a theoretical aid to sales or to customer relations.

In 1963 *Time* reported that U.S. corporations spent more than $25 million in support of art, literature and music, and that this expenditure was decidedly on the increase. During the 1960s the public saw evidence of this trend in the mass media, particularly in broadcasting, where, for instance, the Humble Oil and Refining Company sponsored "An Age of Kings" on educational television stations, U.S. Steel sponsored commercial TV programs showing the story of Christ as depicted in paintings from the late Middle Ages and the Renaissance, and Texaco continued its sponsorship of the Metropolitan Opera weekly radio broadcasts. In addition, many corporations acquired important art collections for a variety of purposes. One of the first corporate art patrons was Abbott Laboratories, which purchased paintings to reproduce in its house organ. During the 1939 New York World's Fair IBM exhibited a collection of paintings taken from each of the seventy-nine countries in which the company did business. It later opened an art gallery in its headquarters building in New York. The Container Corporation of America commissioned works of art for its advertising campaigns. In 1960 the Chase Manhattan Bank purchased more than $500,000 worth of paintings and sculpture for its headquarters building. That year the Whitney Museum commemorated the trend with an exhibition called "Business Buys American Art." Subsequently, the S. C. Johnson Company amassed a $750,-000 collection of art works, probably the largest art purchases ever made by a single corporation. Other companies like the

Mead Corporation, Philip Morris and Clairol organized art exhibitions which traveled around the country or around the world.

The sales theory behind many of these programs is that "culture consumers" represent an important market for American business; by exposing a corporate name to an audience which has such extensive purchasing power, the company can gain a significant commercial benefit. *Fortune* estimated that in 1960 Americans spent or donated at least $3 billion for culture, seventy per cent more than a comparable estimate for 1950. The Stanford Research Institute predicted that by 1970 the figure would reach $7 billion. Attendance at major museums rose from approximately 150,-000,000 in 1957 to approximately 300,000,000 in 1967.

Testimony in support of the theory that sponsorship of the arts is good business was available from many sources. Typical was the following statement from Arnold Gingrich, publisher of *Esquire*, who helped form an Arts Advisory Council to encourage more corporations to sponsor cultural programs. "I work for a magazine," he said, "that has for better than a decade now been working the cultural side of the street, so to speak, and if you've seen how fat our current issue is then you know I'd be an arrant hypocrite if I didn't come right out and admit that we've found its cultural involvement most rewarding in every respect. So the only axe I have to grind is such an obvious one that there'd be no point in searching me for any concealed weapons."

Leo H. Schoenhofen, Jr., president of the Container Corporation of America, said, "There is nothing either new or sinister in the fact that we are using fine art for our own ends. This has almost always been true of art patrons. . . . When industry truly begins to believe in the arts, to believe in them enough to use them selfishly—to put them to *work* for business rather than serving merely as corporate decoration—then, truly, a new Renaissance will be upon us."

Despite these confident statements, the connection between good business and good art is visible only to those who respect the importance of both. A clever sales executive can learn to use almost any publicity-producing project to help establish a relationship with prospective customers, but there's nothing unusual about art which makes it more effective or appropriate for promotional tie-ups than other fields of public interest such as sports, entertainment, education. Nothing unusual, that is, unless somebody in top management has a special interest in art and would like to see the company make a contribution to the cultural life of the community. The Container Corporation of America's famous advertising program, "Great Ideas of Western Man," was initiated when Walter P. Paepke was president of the company. Paepke, who also founded the Aspen Institute of Humanistic Studies, was once asked whether his interest in good design really helped sell products. He is reported to have snapped back, "Hell, I don't know. But I don't know that getting the customer drunk does, either!" If the president of a company is interested in art, it is natural for him to show that interest in the way he runs his company. Presumably if he's interested in getting drunk he does that instead.

Another example of an art program which reflected a top executive's personal interests was Mead's "Art Across America" series of exhibitions. Arthur I. Harris, then president of the packaging division, which sponsored the program, was himself an art collector and believed that "the artist is the natural partner of the paper and packaging industry." A number of salesmen and customers complained about the company's program because it included what they called "beatnik art." One irate businessman wrote, "Our country, at present, is in enough turmoil and strife caused by rebellious participants . . ." Mead should not be "publishing paintings, condoning and encouraging this rebellious action." The program was in "very poor taste" and "untimely," and it "completely misrepresented the corporate image of Mead." But the more sophisticated top executives of the company realized that if this was what one of their associates wanted they could find ways to capitalize on it. J. W. McSwiney, executive vice-president of the Mead Corporation, said that the program facilitated making contacts with prospective customers and civic leaders, "contacts you can't make any other way." With a little effort this could be a valuable tool for any imaginative salesman.

7

Beginning in the late 1940s a fourth type of community activity made its appearance as an official policy among corporate oligarchs: their personal participation in public affairs. As was the case with their interest in philanthropy, this too had precedents dating back to the nineteenth century, when so many wealthy industrial leaders entered government service that the U.S. Senate was called "a millionaires' club." (In 1968 twenty per cent of U.S. Senators were still millionaires according to an Associated Press survey.) A public career has long been considered a privilege of the wealthy in America. In the post–World War II years when top management was becoming increasingly concerned about public criticism, and when philanthropy had become an accepted corporate function, many companies began to encourage their executives to spend time on community affairs as part of their regular duties.

One of the first to institute such a policy was General Motors, which, shortly after the war, issued a formal resolution stating: "Apart from any personal responsibility as a citizen of the community in which he resides, every corporation and divisional executive has an obligation to help maintain the position of General Motors as a good responsible citizen of the community." Less than twenty years later a survey indicated that eighty per cent of General Motors executives were active in more than one hundred different types of civic, charitable, educational and other organizations.

A public discussion of this new idea took place in 1951 when the Corning Glass Company sponsored a two-day conference of businessmen, sociologists and other scholars, journalists and other officials on the theme "Living in Industrial Civilization." There was considerable talk by participants about the disappearance of the "soulless" corporation and the advent of a new era in which top management was at last showing some intelligence about its role in society.

That same year Frank W. Abrams, board chairman of Standard Oil (New Jersey), wrote an article for *The Harvard Business Review* in which he suggested that personal involvement in community affairs was an important management function. He lamented that too many top executives were still isolated in a business aristocracy created by "mingling and talking only with ourselves." He felt that active participation in dealing with the problems of a complex world was the only method to extend the horizons of the corporate officer.

The trend toward community involvement was given an important boost in 1953 when the New Jersey Supreme Court, in *A. P. Smith Manufacturing Co. v. Barlow*, recognized the right of corporations to support public projects. In part the New Jersey decision stated, "modern conditions require that corporations discharge social as well as private responsibilities . . . to insure and strengthen the society which gives them existence."

In 1956 there was another conference on industrial community relations. This one was held at Cornell University, and it reaffirmed the need to involve corporate officers in public-service activities. At about the same time C. L. Shartle completed his study *Executive Performance and Leadership* and reported that the major single activity of the heads of large firms was public relations.

Another study, this one conducted by the National Industrial Conference Board and published in 1966, reported that of 1,033 corporations, 815 had some form of public-affairs program. In addition, this study revealed that forty per cent of the top executive officers of these companies reported they were spending from six to twenty-five hours a week on this activity.

Among those companies which encouraged such community activities on the part of top management was the Chrysler Corporation. Lynn Townsend, chairman and chief executive officer, served as chairman of the capital-fund drive of the United Foundation of Metropolitan Detroit and as national chairman of the Industrial Payroll Savings Committee of the U.S. Treasury Department. Speaking at a United Fund committee meeting, Townsend said, "Duty in the interest of a community stretches a man's imagination, makes him grow and helps to make him a better businessman and a finer human being." At General Electric, senior officers made it a practice to be active in many national programs; for example, chairman Gerald L. Phillippe was chairman of an advisory committee to the Office of Economic Opportunity, and president Fred J. Birch served on a commitee to study the overhaul of the Post Office Department, as well as on the President's Business Council. At Mobil Oil, board chairman Albert L. Nickerson was chairman of the Business Council and of the Balance of Payments Committee of the U.S. Department of Commerce, a trustee of Rockefeller University and the American Museum of Natural History, a trustee emeritus of International House, a fellow of Harvard College and a member of the corporation of Radio Free Europe. Roger M. Blough, board chairman of U.S. Steel, believed that top management must play an important part in community activities because people "look to big business to discharge fully its obligations as a corporate citizen of the community. Beyond the heavy burden of taxation that it bears, they expect it to contribute both time and money to civic improvements, charity drives, hospitals, schools and recreation facilities."

In 1967 *Look* did a roundup story on corporate involvement in community affairs and reported that some top executives admit—"though not to avaricious stockholders"—that they do good in eighty per cent of their company time. The benign impulses of these oligarchs transformed them from "blue chip chiefs, drawing $40 to $252 an hour," into "a bunch of social workers." *Look* was puzzled by what appeared to be a sudden outbreak of public conscience and speculated that it might have had something to do with the race crisis and the secret pressure exerted on major corporations by Presidents Kennedy and Johnson to hire Negro workers and executives, which, together with the subsequent Poverty Program, seemed to have turned loose "a reforming force on the upper floors of capitalism."

8

There is no question that in the social crisis that hit America in the 1960s management became more involved in community activities than at any time in the history of the corporation. This heightened involvement was accompanied by a shift in the oligarchy's point of view toward public affairs. A note of urgency was introduced into the public remarks of top executives about the new role of the corporation in society. It almost seemed, as David Riesman once put it, that the businessmen who had been trying to manipulate the public into thinking more positively about the corporation had unwittingly manipulated themselves into being socially responsible, and even to *feeling* socially responsible. There were also, of course, very practical considerations. Top executives were aware that with the growing militancy of community leaders, particularly in the black community, a new threat to corporate security had to be reckoned with. Unless corporations began to take some positive action they would be in trouble. Thus what had often been little more than a marginal interest on the part of top executives to gain some community-affairs credits for their corporate biographies now became a matter of serious concern.

Many of the programs undertaken by major corporations in the light of this new development were quite remarkable. For example, in 1968 Smith, Kline and French organized a self-help program in the Spring Garden area of Philadelphia to clear the streets; it also provided job training and undertook the rehabilitation of sixty brownstone-type houses (aided by a fifty per cent state income tax credit on the first $150,000 spent on the project). Inland Steel Corporation broadcast job openings on a television

"Opportunity Line" show and produced jobs for three thousand unemployed or underemployed in five weeks. Xerox initiated Project Step Up to pay prospective employees while they attended classes which would enable them to meet Xerox job entry requirements. Lockheed-Georgia (a division of Lockheed Aircraft), Atlanta's largest employer, hired over six hundred hard-core-unemployed Negroes in the first few weeks of 1968. Hallmark undertook to build Crown Center, a $115-million project to comprise some fifty buildings in downtown Kansas City, Missouri, in what would be one of the largest downtown urban-renewal projects in the country. Other urban-renewal and housing-renovation programs were undertaken by corporations in Pittsburgh, Cleveland, Hartford, Providence, Albany, Buffalo, New York, Chicago. One company, U.S. Gypsum, undertook programs in three of these cities and announced plans to open a computer-cable plant which would give jobs to three hundred hard-core unemployed in the Bedford-Stuyvesant area of New York City. Acrojet-General Corporation established a branch plant in the Watts section of Los Angeles. Other companies planned to build plants in areas of Minneapolis, Boston and Warm Springs, Oregon —the last-named to give jobs to Indians in the area. Ford Motor Company, General Motors and Chrysler hired nearly fifty thousand employees from the inner city of Detroit and were strong supporters of the New Detroit Committee, which provided such services as health, recreation, education, employment and legal- and financial-problem solving to residents of the ghetto. The life insurance industry made available $1 billion for use in twenty-four cities as seed money in programs to bring proper housing to ghetto residents. Eastman Kodak changed its employment standards by reducing its educational and police-record requirements and making way for increased employment of minority groups. The Chase Manhattan Bank and the National City Bank initiated programs to hire and train high-school dropouts. Litton Industries, Westinghouse, Burroughs, RCA, Xerox, IBM, Hotel Corporation of America, Eastern Gas and Fuel Associates and Bristol-

Myers also sponsored major projects to aid minority groups and hard core unemployed.

One of the most interesting aspects of these programs was that many executives were taking an interest in community needs without paying too much attention to how this might help their corporate image. For once it seemed to be the deed more than the credit which concerned them. One large corporation to whom Ruder & Finn recently recommended an extensive program of hiring and training Negroes approved everything but that section aimed at publicizing the new policy. "Let's make sure we do a good job," a top executive said, "before we try to blow our horn." It was a refreshing experience for public-relations specialists who so often feel under the gun to get publicity whenever management has even thought of doing something worthwhile for the community.

An outstanding program in this respect was that launched by the Advertising Council, an organization that was formed in the early 1940s for the purpose of helping the country mobilize its resources for the war—and, incidentally, to refute the accusation that the advertising industry was headed by men without a conscience. A former president of the Advertising Council, Theodore S. Repplier, had once called its motive "Simon-pure *pro bono publico*," because the advertising industry which supported it had no other motive than doing good. The campaign it developed in 1968 to tackle the problem of the slums was one of its proudest accomplishments. The media would contribute approximately $25 million in free space to promote the JOBS program of the National Alliance of Businessmen, the President's Council on Youth Opportunity, and Urban America, Inc. A typical headline in the new advertisements was: "Youth needs your help this summer. Not a lot of Yak." Another was: "Most kids live in the city. So do most rats." A third: "Give money. Give jobs. Give a damn."

Whether it was conscience or fear or, as is likely, a combination of the two which was responsible for these activities, the oligarchy appeared to be making a substantial effort to get the corporation moving on a new track. And it was clear that the direction was coming from nowhere else but top management. A report by Public Affairs Communications, Inc., stated that middle management was not nearly as enthusiastic about social action, and there were many instances in which active hostility on the part of supervisors and foremen caused programs to bog down. Leo Beebe, a vice-president of Ford who later became the executive vice-chairman of the National Alliance of Businessmen, recently confessed, "I used to sit in my office at Ford and receive memo after memo from Mr. Ford telling me I'd better hire some Negroes. I kept throwing the memos away. Mr. Ford was dedicated to that approach, but I wasn't." In addition, the heads of medium- and small-sized businesses were generally not as inclined as heads of major corporations to undertake social-action programs. Clearly, if a change was to be made in the social attitudes of American industry, the pressure would have to be sustained by senior corporate officers. There was evidence that the oligarchy was aware of this need and was willing to exercise the leadership necessary to push its programs through.

9

With corporate philanthropy, public-service sales promotions, community involvement and social action all having become part of management's official function, the question is, to what extent has this brought about a fundamental change in the outlook of the corporate oligarch in regard to his role in society? To answer this, one must try to make a realistic assessment of the impact of these new efforts on the community.

First let us look at the record of activities closest to home: management's contribution to the welfare of company employees. There can be little doubt that, aside from the few concerned business leaders mentioned earlier, the oligarchy has obstructed rather than contributed to the improvement of working conditions in the United States. Moreover many of the exponents of "welfare capitalism" were the worst enemies of organized labor. As the La Follette investigating committee of the late 1930s brought to light, many employers of the 1920s engaged in a widely practiced industrial militarism, including the establishment of arsenals, "standing armies," and a well-organized espionage system. Moreover, the historic breakthrough of the National Labor Relations (Wagner) Act of 1935, which created the foundation for collective bargaining, was made against tremendous pressures brought by corporate management. One of the practices forbidden by the act was employer domination of employee organizations; this forecast the doom of company unions, which were the favorite of so-called enlightened management. In the next several years the explosive growth of union power in the steel industry, the building industry, the automobile industry, the electrical, radio and machine-tool industries, the textile industry, the transportation industry, the meat-packing industry and the retailing industry created a new environment in which the oligarch could no longer function as a benevolent ruler of his corporate kingdom. While progressive labor-relations policies could still produce additional fringe benefits for employees, the major advances in wages, security and working conditions were a consequence of the growing power of the unions, not the magnanimity of a few corporate oligarchs. By 1950 there were approximately 16 million workers who were union members, and who found that the best method of solving their problem with management was to accumulate enough power of their own for them to be treated as equals. Corporate oligarchs who declared that employee welfare was one of the major goals of their management received little credit; they had, after all, no choice. Working conditions were being improved steadily, but this was not because management had changed its priorities. It was clear that only if such a change took place would the corporate oligarch have any chance of exercising real leadership for his employees and of defining goals which would help realize some of their aspirations, as well as his, to improve the conditions of society.

Secondly, with all the remarkable advances in the field of corporate philanthropy since the 1930s, the amount of money involved is still relatively small. In 1961 a total of $10 billion was contributed by Americans to charitable enterprises; corporations gave only five per cent of that amount ($500 million). That year corporate profits amounted to about $46 billion; the five per cent allowable as deductions would have amounted to over $2 billion. The actual contribution of $500 million was therefore less than twenty-five per cent of the amount that corporations were entitled to give. Thus, the corporate oligarch has made only a start toward establishing philanthropy as a major goal of his business life. It is an important beginning, but he has a long way to go.

In addition, the corporate oligarch's record of giving reveals serious deficiencies in his philanthropic decisions. This is due, in part, to his lack of qualifications to evaluate the needs of society. As Carnegie and Rockefeller both observed, success in making money does not provide one with the experience necessary to give it away wisely. The problem is compounded by the corporate oligarch's interest in public-relations considerations as distinguished from the worthiness of the causes he supports. A survey conducted by the Russell Sage Foundation in 1950 revealed that over one third of all corporate contributions go to the "safest" recipient of all, the local united fund or community chest. Indeed, most united-fund campaigns are organized around corporate leadership, and about two thirds of the money they receive comes from corporations and their employees (often through a payroll deduction plan).

Still another weakness of corporate philanthropy is the tendency of some oligarchs to steer contributions toward enterprises which further the economic interests of big business. An example of this is the support given by corporations to Harding College in Searcy, Arkansas, which acts as a propaganda machine for ultra-conservative causes and which has received ninety per cent of its funds from corporations; in 1949 Alfred P. Sloan, then president of General Motors, contributed $300,000 to help launch its right-wing motion picture service. The utilization of tax-free dollars for enterprises of this sort which are thought to serve the interests of corporate power can be a dangerous trend. And as Congressman Wright Patman's report in 1962 indicated, the likelihood of such a trend's developing is enhanced by the growing links between foundations and corporations, links which are forged both by businessmen who serve as trustees of major foundations and by foundations which own stock in major corporations. (His report stated that foundations owned ten per cent of the stock of two hundred and sixty-three corporations, including some of the largest in the country.)

The third method of performing a public service, and the one which comes most naturally to the corporate oligarch, suffers from a different shortcoming. Since the object of public-service sales promotion is to gain some commercial value for the corporation, polish and salesmanship are more important than authenticity. So long as the campaign can be publicized as a contribution to society, and customers accept it as such, the promotion is considered sound. If, on the other hand, it should prove to be controversial in any way, or even if customers or the company's own salesmen fail to be enthusiastic about the enterprise, it will be abandoned. The actual contribution made to the community means nothing if those whom management is trying to impress fail to respond.

The unfortunate consequences of this approach to public service have been particularly evident in cultural projects. To become interested in the arts exclusively as a means of attracting public interest means paying more attention to audiences than to content. This may prove to be effective as sales promotion; it may be gratifying to the artistic sensitivities of executives in the company who are interested in art; it may even make some passing contribution to public enjoyment of the arts. But if management lacks conviction about the importance of maintaining quality in its art programs, they will be little more than a dip in the sea of culture, refreshing for a moment but quickly forgotten.

The prevalence of this failing was noted by Emily Genauer,

the art critic, who wrote after attending a conference on business and the arts in 1967 that many of the executives who advocate cultural programs are "so small minded, so niggardly, so unimaginative, so bound by Babbitry, so ignorant of art's role in our contemporary lives, so tied in with packaging . . . My feeling, as I listened to the cant being spouted all that dreary day, was that if this is the kind of brains, the combination of practicality and vision it takes to run big business, many first-class artists I know could do the job part-time." The essence of her complaint was that apparently "art is on the town, to be chucked under the chin by every passing gallant," and that so long as this is the spirit with which corporations are sponsoring art projects, they aren't doing anybody a favor. The same observation was made by Howard Taubman, writing in the New York *Times* about the Business Committee for the Arts, a national advisory group of corporate executives under the chairmanship of C. Douglas Dillon. "Many business contributions," Taubman wrote, "whether of money, services or enthusiasm will be useful, and some will be wholly admirable. But unless there is an increase in sensitivity and sophistication, these will be undertakings of dubious value by sponsors who have no true understanding of art or who are intent only on self-serving projects."

Moreover, there is little promise of consistency in public-service sales-promotion projects. If a company develops a good promotion one year around the idea of public service, it may switch to a letter-writing contest the following year, and introduce trading stamps the year after that. Top management may be disappointed in such a change because it likes the image bonus of a public-service promotion. On the other hand, if sales targets are met it cannot complain. Besides, many practical-minded sales executives are skeptical about the whole idea of the "soft sell" in today's marketing world. They think that pretending to be a public benefactor is no more than an excuse to help top management gain some ego satisfaction, and they would not be unhappy if the public-service approach to promotion could become less popular in the future. A possible trend in this direction was indicated in a study of consumer attitudes toward banks conducted by Lippincott and Margulies. The report suggested that the idea of friendliness as a means of building a public image had been overworked. Friendliness, they believed, may even have a detrimental effect on a bank's business. By questioning one hundred men and one hundred women at random in the New York City area, the researchers found that people tend to be wary of the "overfriendly" bank, that small neighborhood banks and banks which offer easy loans often seem unreliable as compared to big banks which have many corporate accounts and extensive foreign interests. While Lippincott and Margulies did not recommend that all special banking services be abandoned, it did suggest that the most effective image for a bank should combine polite consideration with authority and the bearing of a stern father, "the iron hand in the velvet glove." If top management is confronted by enough reports of this kind it may be embarrassed into restraining its interest in public service and even encouraging sales executives to concentrate on other types of promotions to accomplish their purposes.

The fourth type of public service engaged in by the corporate oligarch, personal participation in community affairs, also has its serious limitations. Not surprisingly, many top executives have difficulty adapting themselves to an activity that does not come naturally to them. As a result, they frequently do a poor job for the institutions they are trying to help. Often, wrote Eloise Spaeth in a New York *Times* article on the subject, the businessman member of a museum board is "out to prove that the public's money isn't wasted. He may veto the purchase of a painting he considers too expensive, only to see the same canvas triple in price within a year. Or with his feet planted firmly on the books, he will veto a salary raise for a curator, only to find that in this narrow field a higher salary has to be paid when the disenchanted curator picks up and leaves." Because of the frequency of bad judgments, she observed, many museum directors have been "savagely burned by ignorant and arrogant trustees."

Henry Ford was a classic case of an industrial leader whose bad judgments about the general concerns of the community posed a serious problem. "When he turned to fields in which he lacked skill and experience," Allan Nevins wrote in his biography of Ford ". . . his intuitions often led him utterly astray; . . . his capacity for rash acts . . . disclosed a combination of ignorance, impulsiveness and bad judgment that would have wrecked a man of less appealing personality, less faith in his own instincts, and less dazzling constructive achievements, past and potential." Ford would have been scornful of an artist or writer who meddled with the machine shop at Highland Park. But, being an intuitive thinker, with a trust in his own star—or comet—he could not comprehend why men were scornful of his meddling with complex national, international and racial problems.

The tendency of the contemporary corporate oligarch to misjudge social needs and to concentrate on the wrong aspect of a basic problem was indicated in a recent survey by the National Industrial Conference Board. Mayors of one hundred major American cities were asked to describe the cooperation they were receiving from local corporations in urban-development programs. One of their major complaints was that business leaders tended to concentrate on those activities related to the economic prosperity of the city rather than those which represented the most pressing social needs.

The oligarch's lack of training and experience in assessing and responding to public needs has often been as much a cause of concern for him as it has been for the community. Surveys of management attitudes made by Warner and Abegglen, Wayne Hodges, *The Harvard Business Review* and *Fortune* all report that top executives tend to feel awkward when they first become involved in community work. Many confess that they have agreed to engage in these activities only because they believe it to be "for the good of the company." As *Fortune* put it, such executives feel that their involvement is "more entrapment than free choice." And even if they later learn to enjoy their work, as most of them eventually do, they are too often called on to make judgments for which they have no background rather than given an opportunity to use their talents as managers for the benefit of the community.

10

All this suggests that the mountain of recent speeches, articles and reports describing the new sense of corporate responsibility in top-management circles rests on very insecure ground indeed. Executives are saying many self-flattering things about their new corporate goals, and many claim to be making a serious effort to devote corporate resources and their own time to support non–profit-oriented causes. But there is far more talk than action. And even those who talk haven't yet found a way to articulate a new point of view which would justify a major change in priorities.

The problem is rooted in the corporate oligarch's misunderstanding of his legal responsibilities and in the unreality of his official ideology. So long as he believes that his primary duty is to provide a fair return on investment for his stockholders, and that he can best perform that duty by maximizing profits and growth through loyal devotion to the corporation, he will never be able to do more than make a token contribution to the social progress of his era. Only when he recognizes that his major accountability is to humanity and that the immense power he controls should be devoted to the goals of mankind will he be able to assume the leadership role in the community to which he aspires.

Nowhere are the consequences of his attempt to beg this crucial question more apparent than in regard to the problems of the hard-core unemployed, the urban slums in the big cities, civil rights and fair employment practices. Confronted by the need for fundamental changes in American society, many corporate oligarchs have responded by sponsoring the action programs mentioned above, and by giving their support to such new programs as the Urban Coalition, the National Alliance of Businessmen, the U.S. Chamber of Commerce's Forward America and the National Association of Manufacturer's STEP. But in most of these efforts the actual corporate contributions have so far dealt only with the fringes of the problem. They may have given management the satisfaction of believing that *something* is being done, but the basic economic orientation of big business—which was undoubtedly a factor in causing the problem in the first place—has not actually been changed.

The rationale which is presently offered by management to justify its social-action programs is not that its goal has been redefined and that the betterment of society is now its primary aim. Instead, the corporate oligarch talks about saving American society from destruction *lest the corporation itself be destroyed in the process!* This hardly represents a change in priorities. He still worries about what is best for the corporation rather than what is best for society. "If the cities continue to deteriorate, our investments will inevitably deteriorate with them," said Western Electric's Paul A. Gorman. "It is a very reasonable expectation that business will experience a serious degradation of the climate which allows it to operate profitably," said U.S. Steel's Roger M. Blough. There is nothing inconsistent, according to Chase Manhattan's George Champion, between the corporation's social responsibility to the community and its economic responsibility to stockholders. Successful businesses are always willing to invest in research and plant facilities that won't pay off for a decade or more. "This is no mere exercise in altruism," Champion insisted, "but just good business sense." And it is on this point that the new programs are foundering.

The tragic error in the corporate oligarch's approach to the major social problems of his age is that corporate power (which in his mind goes under the name of "profit") is still considered the end and social action the means to that end, instead of vice versa. Riots must be prevented because they can ultimately be bad for business; so management gives jobs to black Americans, sponsors summer educational and cultural programs in ghetto areas, and provides help for housing-rehabilitation projects. But at the same time it takes pains to reassure stockholders that it has profits uppermost in its mind. It even calls for larger government tax credits to relieve the corporation of the economic burdens of social-action programs. Nothing must be done to jeopardize the earnings per share or impede corporate growth. The old world must go on as it was; that, after all, is what most top executives think they are trying to preserve.

Thus, despite the leadership abilities he has displayed by initiating his action programs, the corporate oligarch has shown little inclination to make community betterment his goal. And so long as he feels obliged to state that nothing he does will lessen corporate profits, that the basic financial interests he is trying to protect will not be affected, he will be limited to half measures. "It is clear," said David Sarnoff recently, "that neither RCA nor any other company can be content with its record of past performance." This is a vast understatement. The size of corporate management's contribution comes nowhere near the need.

To give one striking example of how far short of the target the corporate contribution has been, the 1968 summer-job program for New York City organized by the National Alliance of Business hoped to produce 37,500 jobs, but in early July the *Times* reported that only 2,400 jobs, little more than six per cent of the target figure, had been found. Mayor John V. Lindsay's aides were quoted as saying that the Alliance program was "a total failure." This seemed to give substance to the warning by John W. Gardner, chairman of the Urban Coalition, that in dealing with such a major problem "the big danger is dabbling. You can get tied up in some fascinating little project endlessly. What we are talking about now is eliminating the ghettos. We want something so big that it will take every resource we have."

There is no doubt that what many large corporations have undertaken in the late 1960s is unprecedented. But seen in the context of the enormous social, economic, cultural and educational changes which must take place in the 1970s, most of this corporate activity is precisely the kind of dabbling to which Gardner referred.

The social-action programs, therefore, which appeared to herald a new outlook for the corporate oligarch, have instead merely produced another variation of earlier efforts to perform some kind of public service. In keeping with the tradition of corporate philanthropy and sales promotion, today's social-action programs are no more than a marginal concern of top management. As a public-relations consultant who has discussed all varieties of public-service programs with top management, I know how far down the line of priorities they truly are. There are some executives who are genuinely concerned and who are eager to make an important contribution to the community; but even the most ambitious social or cultural undertaking has to be squeezed in between the "more important" things which management feels it has to take care of. It is a rare executive who believes that corporate growth represents an abuse of power so long as it is not dedicated to the improvement of society. Most oligarchs seem to think that public service is a sort of premium that gives the corporate package a special appeal. "We have reached the point," said Virgil E. Boyd, president of the Chrysler Corporation, "where business as usual—advertising and selling of products, making a profit and paying our taxes—is no longer enough. A new dimension has been added, and that is advertising and selling the ideas and the fact of a socially responsible company." If the oligarchy is to become a major factor in a national effort to realize great ideals, an additive will not do the job. The crux of the problem is whether the oligarch wants to consider his responsibility to his fellow human beings as an extra dimension or the basic dimension of his working life.

Is it possible that the impulse to perform a public service can ever become the central force behind American corporate power? I think it can, primarily because the impulse is potentially a very strong one. Does this mean that management will one day consider some specific social action, such as giving jobs to the disadvantaged, as the primary purpose of business? Not at all. Business is too complex an operation for such single-mindedness. But there is no reason why the primary goal of management cannot eventually be defined as the utilization of corporate resources for the service of public interests in every way possible. This will require putting the old maxims of profit, growth and corporate benefit where they truly belong, in the junkyard of outmoded symbols, and, in their place, raising a new standard which will make it clear that the corporate oligarch's mission is to build a just society capable of fulfilling the potentialities of all its citizens. The likelihood of effecting this change depends on his willingness to make idealism a central rather than an incidental part of the management function. I believe he has—or can develop—the ability to create such a conceptual framework, but whether he will actually do so remains to be seen.

10

His Efforts
to Be
Articulate

To LEAD THE CORPORATION IN A NEW DIRECTION AND GIVE IT AN
opportunity to become a vital and constructive force for progress
in society, the corporate oligarch must do some fresh thinking on
his own. No one can come up with the answers for him. If he
depends on his advisers to articulate the principles on which new
forms of corporate behavior may be based, they will most likely
provide the clichés with which they think he feels most comfortable. He can buy the best talent available to make analyses, do
research, make forecasts and write acceptable speeches, articles
and books for his signature; but unless he takes the time to think
clearly about what it is he wants to accomplish and how he can fit
together in a cohesive plan his personal ambitions, the aspirations
of those who work for him and those who invest in his company,
the concerns and welfare of those who buy his products, and the
needs and ideals of the society in which his business is conducted,

he will remain a prisoner of the same old stuffy and sterile ideas with which he has so long been surrounded.

The art of composing one's thoughts on abstract questions does not come easily to the corporate oligarch. He is a busy man, a man of action, not a thinker. He can write a letter or memorandum at the drop of a hat if it has to do with something that takes only a few minutes to work out in his mind; but any statement which requires a few hours or a few days of concentration is considered an excessive burden. He thinks his time is too valuable for such protracted undertakings. A master of delegation, he knows the value of staff work in any project that threatens to be time-consuming. It is consistent with his entire approach to management to assign all serious writing to specialists. The measure of the specialist's effectiveness is how little direction he needs from management in order to come up with a good product. The writer who does his job well will develop his own creative ideas and not depend on the oligarch for suggestions.

The same is often true of what the corporate oligarch reads. He has all he can do to keep up with daily newspapers, business and trade publications, general magazines and his daily correspondence; he rarely finds the time for any serious reading about the social, economic and cultural trends which could affect his approach to corporate policy making. Even lengthy reports from members of his staff sometimes create a problem. One top executive I know has a rule that if a report is longer than a single page he automatically returns it to the sender unread.

So unused is the corporate oligarch to the rigors of disciplined study and conceptualization that if he ever departs from his usual routine and tries to work out a major article or speech on his own he is surprised and sometimes a little embarrassed by the amount of time it takes to do a reasonably good job. He tends to assume that what takes another man a week to accomplish he can polish off in half an hour. On the other hand, if he produces an original thought or two, he is likely to be secretly pleased by the discovery that a faculty which he has not used for such a long time has not withered.

A refreshing and revealing description of this experience was given by Walter Beinecke, Jr., vice-president of the Sperry and Hutchinson Company, in a talk at Yankton College in Yankton, South Dakota, in 1958. His topic was "Conflict and the Democratic Spirit," and he touched on the right of dissent, the rights of special-interest groups and the value of individualism in American society. In his opening remarks he said, "I appreciate your invitation to be here today. I am not, however, at all sure that I am the person who should be standing here talking to you. I am not a scholar. I am not learned in political theory, in economics, or in sociology. I am just what I appear to be—an American businessman who plays a part in running an old and successful business." Later on he said, "My colleagues prevailed upon me to make this talk. They said businessmen do not do enough talking. I had thought usually they do too much. As it turns out, I am glad I accepted the assignment. As many of you sitting here today know —those of you who are businessmen—we do not often sit back to assess what might be termed 'the larger picture.' We are too busy running our business. In fact, as businessmen, we are perhaps sometimes too much inclined to leave the theories and the larger thinking to others." But Beinecke welcomed the opportunity to broaden his outlook. "In preparing to address you here today," he said, "I found it important to do some searching and some reading. I felt it necessary to organize my thinking about the affairs of the country. . . . It was a fruitful experience for me. I enjoyed it. So, if it turns out that anything I say here today is helpful or interesting, I shall be doubly pleased."

2

In the early nineteenth century, when the Industrial Revolution first came to America, businessmen made no pretensions to being interested in abstract questions. This was observed by Alexis de Tocqueville, who wrote: "Ambitious men in democracies are less engrossed than any others with the interests and judgments of posterity; the present moment alone engages and absorbs them. . . . They care much more for success than for fame."

It was not until the middle of the nineteenth century that the industrial leader began to recognize that his position required him to state his policies in a somewhat permanent form. In 1840 the Lowell Cotton Mills published what may have been the first company newspaper, called the *Lowell Offering*. Presumably its purpose was to provide management with a means by which it could inform employees about company activities and raise morale by appealing to the workers' sense of belonging to a communal undertaking. Other pioneer publications created for similar purposes were *The Mechanic* (first published in 1847) of the H. B. Smith Machine Company of Smithville, New Jersey, *The Locomotive* (1867) of the Hartford Steam Boiler Inspection and Insurance Company, and *The Travelers Record* (1865) of the Travelers Insurance Company. The last-named publication at one point enjoyed a circulation of fifty thousand, rivaling the consumer publications of its time.

But even these efforts were not serious attempts to present a thoughtful view of the corporate mission. Rarely did the entrepreneur take the trouble to describe his goals in relation to the historic development of the country. The problem was how to get people to work hard to produce goods that could be sold at a profit. The company literature still reflected a concern for immediate results rather than long-term benefits.

As the nineteenth century progressed and the intellectual life of the country developed, a few captains of industry showed literary or scholarly inclinations. One of them, Jay Gould, was a writer before he became a businessman; in 1856, when he was twenty years old, he published *The History of Delaware County and the Border Wars of New York*. Fifteen years later Gould's questionable dealings with the Erie Railroad were the subject of a book by another businessman, Charles Francis Adams, who subsequently became chairman of the board of the Union Pacific Railroad (from which position he was ultimately ousted by Gould). Adams, who was the grandson and great-grandson of the two Adams Presidents and the brother of Henry Adams, wrote several other historical and biographical works. Another businessman-historian of the time was Henry Charles Lea, who made his fortune in the publishing business, then retired to work on *A History of the Inquisition in the Middle Ages,* which was published in 1888. Sparing no expense on his project, Lea sent agents exploring the libraries of Europe in search of data, and the result was a monumental work which was recognized by historians as a major contribution. Still another with a literary turn of mind was B. B. Comegys, a Philadelphia banker who in 1893 published *A Tour Through My Library and Other Papers.*

The first major effort by an industrialist to be articulate about the businessman's mission in society was made by Andrew Carnegie. Between 1880 and 1909 seven books setting forth his ideas were published. He wrote about democracy, about the problems of his day, about his experiences as an American living in Great Britain, and, of course, about his "gospel of wealth." Only one of his books had to do with the more commonplace subjects of "how to win a fortune" and "the road to business success"; this was a collection of essays. In his last years he wrote his autobiography (he lived to be eighty-four and it was published posthumously).

So broad was Carnegie's range of interests that one reviewer commented, "He was thought to be socialistic by the conservatives and conservative by the socialists." He seemed to identify with both the enlightened upper class, of which he was a member, and the masses, about which he professed great sympathy. His concentration in later life on his philanthropies, and even the sale of his company to the Morgan interests to help create the corporate structure of U.S. Steel, were direct products of the concepts he developed in the writing of his books.

The weakness of Carnegie's literary efforts was that he was a dilettante in his conceptual formulations and he mistook pontification for philosophy. As a youth he had spent time in libraries, had memorized much of Shakespeare and had studied Darwin and Spencer, and when he was successful he sought out the company of the learned and the literary. But his books betrayed an undisciplined mind when it came to developing his own ideas about society.

3

Although an increasing number of industrial leaders tried to follow Carnegie's book-writing example, the results were often little more than sentimental reflections on their own success stories. These were echoes of the rags-to-riches novels published by Horatio Alger, Jr., toward the end of the nineteenth century. Curiously, Alger's novels did not idealize wealth. He often deplored what he considered to be the idle life of the men who occupied the Fifth Avenue mansions, and expressed sympathy for the unfortunate poor who lived so close by. Alger's heroes achieved their success through hard work and virtuous conduct. Many industrialist authors tried to prove that they were real-life versions of Ragged Dick and hence deserving of the immortality which Alger postulated for his fictional character.

This was the spirit, for instance, of the seven books written over Henry Ford's name. Three of them, written with a collaborator, Samuel Crowther, were variations on the theme of how he built the Ford Motor Company. They were straightforward and rather unimaginative descriptions of how a determined young man fulfilled his dream of mass-producing the automobile for the American public. The fourth book, also written with Crowther, was an appreciative recollection of Thomas A. Edison. The fifth was an authorized interview by Fay Leone Faurote, *My Philosophy of Industry*, and it contains many comments about machinery as a new Messiah, about success and progress. All these books were written between the ages of sixty and sixty-eight (he lived to be eighty-four), when Ford was apparently in a reflective mood, eager to tell the world his version of the Horatio Alger story. A seventh book entitled *The International Jew*, published in Leipzig, was an example of Ford's failings as a world thinker and of the potentially dangerous consequences of a top executive's irresponsible social philosophies.

The same degree of autobiographical self-consciousness can be found in John D. Rockefeller's *Random Reminiscences of Men and Events*, published in 1909. It also characterized Harvey Firestone's *Men and Rubber: The Story of Business* (written with Ford's collaborator, Samuel Crowther). J. C. Penney wrote three books in the last thirty years of his life—all telling his own rags-to-riches-through-hard-work-and-virtuous-conduct story. Jean Paul Getty wrote his autobiography when he was seventy-four years old, following the same general pattern.

This strain of writing, however, tended to diminish as the more impersonal corporate oligarch came into power. The difference can be seen by comparing the chapters of an anthology published in 1967, *How to Get What You Want Out of Life*. Those written by men whose lives followed the pattern of earlier generations of business tycoons were given to the same old poverty-to-success view of their careers. Conrad Hilton told how he had started out in life as a storekeeper and, by "thinking big," had built a giant chain of hotels. Howard Johnson began his business career with $500 and a rented shack which eventually turned into a vast network of roadside restaurants. Joyce Hall's first job was in a small book and stationery store, after which he founded the company which became the largest publisher of greeting cards in the world. But such melodramatic tales were absent in the chapters by William T. Brady of the Corn Products Company, John G. Martin of Heublein, Inc., and James E. Robinson of Indian Head Mills. The new managers made little or no reference to their modest beginnings. Their emphasis was on how to do a good job as an ambitious executive. They told their readers that a good performer can climb to the top of the corporate ladder if he has the right spirit and works hard.

Thus, in place of autobiographical, self-congratulatory versions of the Horatio Alger story, the modern corporate oligarch developed a different kind of inspirational approach to his success story. How he started out in life was not as important as the spirit he showed in his job as a company executive. He believed that his success as a top executive rested largely on his ability to inspire the same kind of spirit among his subordinates. This sense of mission became characteristic of much of his writings.

4

The emergence of the chief executive officer as the professional head of a large organization was accompanied by the development of a management technology. The latter was commemorated by a series of books, articles and speeches describing successful corporate performances. One of the first and most prolific writers of "how-to" management was Edward A. Filene, a pioneer retailer. Between 1924 and 1939 he published seven books describing practical management techniques. One of his titles was *More Profits from Merchandising*; another, suggesting that business methods could help solve world problems, was called *The Way Out: A Businessman Looks at the World*. Thomas J. Watson wrote along similar lines in a book called *Men—Minutes—Money*, published in the 1930s, and in the 1950s he wrote another book, *As a Man Thinks*. In 1937 Charles P. McCormick, president of McCormick & Company, Inc., wrote a book, *Multiple Management*, describing his experiences in setting up "a democratic method of government for business," in which decision making was divided among a series of responsible boards rather than concentrated in the hands of a few executives.

A high point in management's ability to conceptualize about the processes of administration was achieved in 1938 with the publication of *The Functions of the Executive,* by Chester I. Barnard, president of the New Jersey Bell Telephone Company. This was distinguished from earlier—and later—writings by its sophistication, perceptiveness and scholarship. It was probably the most thoughtful book ever written by a chief executive officer of a major corporation. Unlike so many other books by business leaders which became quickly dated, Barnard's analysis was a serious philosophical work and made a lasting contribution to the study of large organizations. First presented in a series of lectures given at the Lowell Institute in Boston, his essay was the product of the extensive management and administrative experience of a man who was capable, as he put it, of submitting his mental processes to inspection. It was not, he said, the work of a scientist or a scholar, but rather of an interested student of affairs. The final manuscript was completed at the urging of the dean of the Harvard Graduate School of Business. When it was published, the *American Journal of Sociology* called it "a major contribution to the understanding of our society."

Barnard's thesis was that the major structure of developed societies was its complex of formal organizations. He described organizations as cooperative systems with moral purposes that are distillations of attitudes, values, ideals and hopes impressed upon the emotions of man through countless channels of physical, biological and social experiences. An increasing degree of cooperation implies an increasing moral complexity. The strategic factor in cooperation is leadership with a high capacity for both technological attainments and moral complexity. The strategic factor in the dynamic expression of leadership is moral creativeness, and the strategic factor in social integration is the development of and selection of leaders.

Barnard estimated that there were one hundred thousand executives in the United States who occupied high management positions, yet, he believed, there was no commonly accepted conceptual scheme which permitted them to productively exchange ideas. Much abortive management, he felt, was the product of "almost total disregard, in *thinking*, of the subjective aspects of authority." Informal organizations essential to the vitality of business enterprises were being ignored. The moral factors upon which the vitality of organization depends were treated mostly as "subjects for glowing generalities in inspirational addresses." He hoped his book would help in the development of a science of cooperation and organization. He ended with a declaration of faith:

> I believe in the power of the cooperation of men of free will to make men free to cooperate; that only as they choose to work together can they achieve the fullness of personal development; that only as each accepts a responsibility for choice can they enter into that communion of men from which arise the higher purposes of individual and cooperative behavior alike. I believe that the expansion of cooperation and the development of the individual are mutually dependent realities, and that a due proportion or balance between them is a necessary condition of human welfare. Because it is subjective with respect both to society as a whole and to the individual, what this proportion is I believe science cannot say. It is a question for philosophy and religion.

Unfortunately, few corporate oligarchs appear to have studied Barnard's work. It proved to be of greater interest to the academic world than to the world of affairs. The relevance of philosophy, religion and the higher purposes of man did not become a favorite theme of subsequent businessmen-authors.

The writing of top executives after World War II was largely devoted to practical expositions of specific management problems. The American Management Association began publishing its descriptions of corporate accomplishments. A foundation formed by the management consultant firm McKinsey & Company made a grant to the Graduate School of Business of Columbia University for a series of lectures (later published as books) by outstanding industrial leaders. Among those who contributed were Roger

M. Blough, Ralph J. Cordiner, Marion B. Folsom, Crawford H. Greenewalt, Theodore V. Houser, Frederick R. Kappel, Charles G. Mortimer, David Rockefeller and Thomas J. Watson, Jr. Another book-producing lecture series was established by Charles C. Moskowitz at the School of Commerce, Accounts and Finance of New York University. Still another was called Careers in Depth and was aimed at giving advice to young people with business aspirations. There was also the Management Science Series, in which top executives described the practices of their industries for a reference library on contemporary business.

In addition, there was a virtual eruption of addresses by leading corporate executives. Many of these addresses were reprinted in *Vital Speeches* magazine, which in one year (1965) published speeches by the presidents or board chairmen of Standard Oil (New Jersey), Chrysler, Continental Oil, U.S. Steel, Chase Manhattan Bank, CBS, General Foods, Burroughs, Bell & Howell, National Biscuit Company, Republic Steel, General Electric, Procter & Gamble and McGraw-Hill.

Another trend was the evolution of articles in magazines based on interviews of top executives. Notable among these was the "Lessons in Leadership" series in *Nation's Business*, which in 1965 featured the ideas of chief executives of Sears, Roebuck; Bank of America; Kroger Company; Du Pont; Howard Johnson's; and Goldman, Sachs and Company. A similar article series was published in *Business Management* magazine, and a third was the "President's Panel" of *Dun's Review and Modern Industry.*

In 1967 the publication of *My Years with General Motors*, by Alfred P. Sloan, Jr. (edited by John McDonald of *Fortune* together with Catherine Stevens), presented the most authoritative history of a large corporation ever written by its chief executive officer. In contrast to Barnard's abstract formulations, Sloan gave a day-to-day report of his experiences. "The end product," he wrote, "of what I have described in this book is efficiency, using that concept in its broadest sense." It was considered by many the greatest corporate story ever told by a member of the oligarchy.

It cannot be said, however, that this tremendous outpouring of publications produced a literature worth preserving. Although the oligarch succeeded in becoming a prolific author, he failed for the most part to make a significant contribution to the world of ideas. At best, the enormous mass of speeches, articles and books that have come out of the public-relations offices of major corporations in this century are of historical interest. They provide authentic but dull records of management's official position on a great variety of subjects. One has to search thoroughly to find a passage that shows a memorable insight into the human condition or an expression that contains even the most limited of universal truths.

It is hardly an impressive defense to claim that management had few pretensions to such grandiose achievements in its writings. If that were the case, why bother? The fact is that the corporate oligarch's effort to be articulate too often represented a corruption of the function of the printed or, more accurately, the published word. As a public-relations specialist, I take my full share of blame for this unfortunate episode in publishing history. Our purpose most often was to gain what we call in our sophisticated jargon "visibility" for top management. This means getting his name into print rather than encouraging him to take on the painful burden of doing some writing himself if he has any ideas that are worth stating publicly. Our job was to help him gain the prestige which supposedly comes from having an article appear in a respected publication, or a book distributed under the imprint of a well-known publisher, or a speech delivered to an important audience. Never mind that almost all of this literature was ghostwritten (not infrequently by public-relations men who knew less about their subjects than their readers did); that so many of the books were subsidized by "guaranteed" sales (bought by the company for distribution to key employees and customers); that so many of the articles were presold (by arranging to have an author acceptable to a magazine editor commissioned to do the piece for the executive's signature); and that so many of the speeches were canned (using the same phrases and concepts over and over again). The main value of the undertaking was in the "merchandising" of the finished product to captive audiences. It wasn't important whether the content had any substance; no one had to read or listen to the words. It didn't matter that the most serious written expositions by top executives were artificially protected from the market influences which these same oligarchs were so loudly praising and which enabled the consumer to reject inferior products in commercial lines of merchandise. All that counted was that the trade be exposed to management's name under impressive auspices, and that the company's reputation be thereby enhanced.

The problems created by these practices were described by Clarence B. Randall, former board chairman of Inland Steel and one of the most articulate corporate oligarchs in recent time. Between the ages of sixty-one and seventy-four he published eight books, which is something of a record for a business executive. (Only Roger Ward Babson, who wrote over thirty books, had a greater output; but Babson was in the publishing business and his books were, in a sense, part of his business.)

Randall's first book, *A Creed for Free Enterprise*, showed that he was a creditable writer capable of organizing his thoughts about society and presenting them with force, intelligence and persuasiveness. He wrote in a journalistic style and was given somewhat to generalities, but he was a maverick in his thinking and had the courage to attack official management dogma. In a later book, *The Folklore of Management*, Randall warned that the top executive could become an effective leader only if he spent the time to think through "the whole meaning of what he is seeking to accomplish." Pointing out that this is not a responsibility that can be delegated, he stated that if the executive cannot write his own speech he should make none.

> If he is tongue-tied in public it is because he is tongue-tied in private; he simply has nothing of significance to say. Let him be himself at all times. Let the public know him as he is. Let

him stand up and say to an audience precisely what he said to his seatmate on the 8:04 that morning or what he said to his associates at lunch, disagreeable as the results may be in terms of public relations. It is the views of the man himself the public seeks to probe, not those of his script technician. In the Greek tragedies, the actors wore masks; but that time has passed. Today, the public is not easily fooled. It says, as did Isaac, "The voice is Jacob's voice, but the hands are the hands of Esau." Only the speaker is deceived. When he quotes Shakespeare or Herodotus he proclaims himself a fraud, and all that he says thereafter is appropriately discounted by those who hear him.

I think Randall overstated his case, but his point was valid. There is, after all, a legitimate role for staff assistants in the preparation of major pieces of writing by public figures. *Life* has pointed out that the phrase "and that government of the people, by the people, for the people, shall not perish from this earth" was written by Theodore Parker; "the only thing we have to fear is fear itself," by Louis Howe; "ask not what your country can do for you; ask what you can do for your country," by Oliver Wendell Holmes. If statesmen can make judicious use of preparatory work by writers and researchers, top executives whose literary skills and knowledge are generally more limited can learn to do so also. The trouble is that the corporate oligarch so often fails to recognize the major role he himself must play in the development of a speech or an article. He would be relieved if his assistants could do all the work for him and leave him free to devote his time to more important things.

It is one of the scandals of modern management that many top executives do not even take the trouble to read, let alone write, articles or books published in their names. And too often when they do read what has been prepared for them, the changes they make betray a small-mindedness and superficiality found among men who have not learned to subject their thinking to critical analysis.

Public statements by corporate oligarchs are dull and uninspiring, therefore, not because the words are written by somebody else, but because the executive signing the statement too often has nothing important to say. The executive's fault is not only that he devotes too little time preparing—or working with his writers to prepare—his material, but that he has not taken enough time to think deeply about the purposes of his job and its relation to other purposes which are of vital concern to his fellow man.

5

It was in 1906 that the anthracite coal industry hired Ivy Lee, the journalist turned publicist, to represent its point of view to the public. Lee distributed to newspaper city editors a "Declaration of Principles" on behalf of his client, stating that his intention was "frankly and openly, on behalf of business concerns and public institutions, to supply to the press and public of the United States prompt and accurate information concerning subjects which it is of value and interest to the public to know about."

History was not kind to these efforts, and, as in so many subsequent campaigns, management's point of view did not prevail. But it was especially harsh to the writings of J. Ogden Armour, whose book *The Packers, the Private Car Lines and the People,* also published in 1906, attempted to refute the muckraking attacks against the meat industry. Almost simultaneously, Upton Sinclair's *The Jungle* made its scathing attack on the inhumanity of the meat packers. So great was the impact of this novel that more than sixty years later President Johnson invited Sinclair to attend the signing of the 1967 meat-inspection bill, designed to eliminate unsanitary conditions and adulterated meat still found in some sections of the industry.

Today the public statements of chief executive officers of large corporations under attack are more refined than those of previous generations. In 1965, when control of the price of steel was a national issue, *Fortune* published a well-written statement on the industry's point of view by U.S. Steel president Roger M. Blough. That same year Charles G. Mortimer, chairman of the board of General Foods, wrote an article for *Look* entitled "Let's Keep Politics Out of the Pantry," warning against allowing government to dictate rules for the shopper. The alert housewife, he asserted, was the best policeman for unethical packaging. Also in 1965, Robert Kintner, president of the National Broadcasting Company, wrote a three-part series of articles for *Harper's*, "Television and the World of Politics," in which he analyzed the role played by television in recent elections and explained why he thought it was making an important contribution.

These highly professional performances do not seem to be faring very much better than the cruder essays of earlier industrial leaders. Thoughtful readers are impressed but not persuaded by the articulateness with which industry's views are presented, and by the public-relations ingenuity by which management's official doctrines have been translated into language that meets the criteria of some of the country's most critical editors. I can report that many of these articles take months, sometimes years, to get into print, and that the jockeying back and forth with sentences and concepts that must please the editor, the writer and members of top management who have been charged with the responsibility of formulating positions on major issues (to say nothing of the executive in whose name the article is being written) requires great agility, tact and perseverance. It is one of the public-relations man's most difficult assignments, and when he succeeds it is often considered a major triumph. But I think he deceives himself if he mistakes a self-serving attempt to applaud the corporate oligarch's accomplishment for an honest or even useful exploration of the issues involved. If the carefully chosen phrases merely disguise the reluctance of leading corporate executives to stray from the official position of their companies or their industries in regard to the public consequences of their corporate policies, there is little to be proud of. Even the reader who is sympathetic to management's position is likely to see through the veneer. And it may well be that the more polished the article the less convincing it is to the reader who is undecided. If top executives reveal themselves to be entirely one-sided in their views, they will be recognized not as men of vision but as spokesmen for a corporate party line which is aimed at preserving corporate power rather than serving public welfare.

Only rarely does an individual corporate oligarch have the courage to rise above the group thinking so popular among defenders of his industry and to articulate a genuinely new and constructive point of view. One such was John I. Snyder, chief executive officer of U.S. Industries, Inc. He once told an international group of government officials, labor leaders, industrialists, journalists and scholars gathered in Geneva, "As the head of a corporation that designs and manufactures automation machinery, I feel a deep and abiding responsibility to inform anyone who will listen about the true facts of automation. If I may, I'd like to suggest that we might start a campaign here today to educate the uneducated, fight fantasy with fact, and make people wake up to the stark realities of the technology that surrounds them. . . . The birth-agonies of the Industrial Revolution were attributable to failures in social and economic innovation. It is here we must strengthen and embolden ourselves. Business and industrial management, labor leadership, the organized professions must recognize the primacy of long-range national and international interests over the short-range commercial ones which now too much determine our course." He was quoted by *Life* as saying that the new machines now being developed will bring about "a total reorientation of human society. Humans will become wards of the machines, supported by the machines. But the great unanswerable question is, what, then, will happen to the souls of people? We will have to build things from the inside out. People—living, breathing, feeling and thinking people—somehow will have to learn to do nothing in a constructive way."

U.S. Industries was a Ruder & Finn client when John Snyder

made those statements, and I know that his words reflected deep inner convictions. I also know that although he had been responsible for a remarkable industrial performance he was often criticized by the world of big business for worrying too much about social problems and not paying enough attention to company earnings. Snyder had taken a bankrupt railroad-car business and built it into a modern forward-looking industrial complex with annual sales of well over $100 million. Yet as a top executive he managed his company as if he were more interested in making an important contribution to the advancement of society than producing a maximum return on investment for stockholders. He believed that his stockholders could be persuaded that the company should work toward social as well as financial rewards, and his confidence was borne out by the continuation of his management through many difficult periods (although he himself was only a minority stockholder). But John Snyder died in office, and he was succeeded by his executive vice-president, I. John Billera, who had a more traditional view of responsibilities to stockholders. Billera subsequently told a *Business Week* reporter that under Snyder's reign the company "could have been justifiably accused of having its head above the clouds. Now we have brought our feet down to touch the ground." U.S. Industries' per-share earnings rose thirty per cent in the first year of Billera's management, made possible at least partially by the elimination of supposedly peripheral activities, including contributions to the Automation Foundation, which Snyder helped found and helped support through a self-imposed tithe on the sale of automation equipment.

By most accepted business standards, the successor management was more responsible and more effective than the one it replaced; but many thoughtful observers felt that, with John Snyder's death, the oligarchy had lost a rare top executive who had the courage to challenge the archaic rules which bound it to the past and to articulate a daring concept in corporate management which pointed the way to a new kind of leadership in the future.

6

The communications which are supposed to reflect most accurately what top management thinks about its business and the corporation's role in society are company house organs and annual reports to stockholders.

In the three-year period from 1948 to 1951, five hundred new company journals, many of them edited by professional journalists, came into being. By 1965 there were ten thousand being published. *The Ford Times* developed a readership of over one and a half million; the Standard Oil Co. (N.J.) *Lamp*, 850,000; IBM's *Think*, 130,000. The National Cash Register Company's *Factory News*, inaugurated as a twelve-page journal in 1890, expanded to as many as one hundred pages. The total corporate investment in these publications is estimated today as well over $500 million and the combined circulation at three hundred million per issue.

This sudden burst of communication activity clearly signaled the corporate oligarch's recognition that he needed a voice to express his point of view to employees, customers and other special audiences. But the format and the content of most of these publications did not reflect the slightest interest on the part of top management in how his message was conveyed. Although the cumulative amount of money spent on house organs was substantial, editorial responsibility was often placed in the hands of inexperienced personnel, revealing once again the corporate oligarch's tendency to judge a piece of writing by the package in which it is contained rather than the ideas it expresses. So long as the company name is on the cover and there are enough statements inside which are in some way identified with company management, the communications mission is considered accomplished. It is extremely rare that the kind of editorial judgment which makes commercial publications of equal circulation readable is applied to these supposed expressions of management philosophies.

The potential of this form of communication when management accepts it as one of its important functions can be seen from the outstanding achievements of the *Kaiser Aluminum News,* which has devoted special issues to explorations of changes in the contemporary world. The remarkable clarity, maturity and originality of these professionally written essays reflect a corporate outlook which is open to new concepts and embraces advanced thinking about the needs and opportunities of a rapidly developing society. "The Promised Land" was a study of changes in the ways that we look at and use our environment. "Communication" described how the ability to communicate is acquired, how the inner process of perception differs from what happens in the outside world, and how communication can be improved to reduce misunderstandings. "Telemobility" explored the transition from a largely mechanical environment to an electronic environment in which human experience is increasingly based on the manipulation of wave lengths in the electromagnetic spectrum. None of these were presented as having a relationship to the business of Kaiser Aluminum, but they provided evidence to anyone who was interested that top executives of the company were aware of and concerned about many significant trends of contemporary society.

Company annual reports to stockholders, with their traditional "Letter from the President," have grown so elaborate in recent years that the printing cost alone is thought to exceed $100 million. Among the top one hundred companies of the *Fortune* 500 list in 1966, fifty-four annual reports had more than thirty pages, two had more than fifty pages. Eighty were printed in color, ninety-six used photographs or line drawings to illustrate the text. Some of the reports took seven or eight months to complete, with the expenditure of an enormous amount of costly executive time in all phases of preparation.

Again, the bulk of these pages reflects the narrow, archaic set of management principles subscribed to by most members of the oligarchy. The very process of developing material for these publications all but precludes the possibility of articulating important ideas. "After revisions through countless drafts by accountants, auditors, treasurers, banker-directors, lawyers, union negotiators, engineers, scientists and purchasing agents," wrote William Dinsmore in a *Harper's* article, "the typical corporate message ends up freighted with vague generalizations, clichés, half-truths, total omissions, unsubstantiated claims and downright distortions."

The overriding consideration in the preparation and design of annual reports is making a good impression. The report is a sales tool by which management tries to convince shareholders that the stock they own is a good investment. This is certainly a legitimate purpose, but it does not justify the pretentious, often unctuous, manner in which the year's record is so often placed before the reader. The annual State of the Union message by the President of the United States is not expected to restrict itself to the rosy aspects of American life; why cannot a State of the Corporation message be equally frank? The answer, of course, is that it is in his annual report that the corporate oligarch feels under the greatest obligation to mouth the platitudes with which he describes his official ideology. By the same token, the nervousness which prompts him to seek a consensus on each word reveals the insecurity which lurks behind the saccharine phrases. As a man who cannot abide criticism, he fears that his annual report may reveal some failure to meet the formal criteria of corporate success, and that confidence in his management will accordingly be shaken.

Occasionally top executives have made an effort to rise above this timidity and incorporate in their annual report an authentic statement about some broad social or economic trend which transcends company interests. One company which has followed this approach is Litton Industries. In 1965 its annual report featured an excellent essay on the subject of "Leadership in the Marketplace"; in 1966 management invited historian Allan Nevins to write an introductory essay on the subject of "Managing Ideas"; in 1967 the report was written on the theme of "Building a Creative Environment." These reports obviously reflected top management's desire to publish documents that would be respected by serious thinkers. Although some feel that even these essays suffered somewhat from the self-consciousness of an editorial con- trol that was aimed to please rather than to articulate new points of view, they pointed in the direction of an annual report that could put new leadership ideas to the test of intelligent and criti- cal readership.

7

The best hope that management will eventually utilize the plat- forms that are available to it—books, articles, speeches, house or- gans, annual reports—to present new definitions of the corporate function, and to raise the oligarch to a level of true leadership in society, is the gravitation of men with highly developed intellec- tual capacities into top management positions. This does not sim- ply mean men with graduate or postgraduate degrees. The task of developing a new outlook for corporate management can be ac- complished only by persons who can think broadly about commu- nity needs, who have creative interests in more than one field of human endeavor, who have some understanding of the wisdom which determines the priorities of civilized human beings, and who recognize that the responsible exercise of power in a literate society requires an ability to articulate forward-looking ideas with clarity and conviction.

To encourage men with intellectual and creative resources to enter the field of management, A. L. Nickerson, president of So- cony-Mobil Oil Company, said he would like to see top executive positions filled by men trained in the liberal arts. "The field of humanities—literature, philosophy, and art," said Inland Steel's Clarence B. Randall, "is more firmly linked to management than science is to production." Roger M. Blough called upon intellec- tuals to join the ranks of management, where, he wrote in a *Har- vard Business Review* article, they would find a unique variety of experiences to challenge, broaden, intrigue, tax, diversify, reward and stimulate them.

The activities and statements of David Rockefeller, chairman of the Chase Manhattan Bank, provide an outstanding example of how broad intellectual interests can help a corporate oligarch exert national and international leadership. He once proposed the creation of a managerial task force of free enterprise to act as business consultants for developing countries. On another occasion he made specific recommendations for the encouragement of private enterprise in Latin America. On a third occasion he introduced his ideas for the establishment of a National Council on Business and the Arts. When he addressed the 1968 annual management conference at the University of Chicago, he told executives, "What we as businessmen must do is to demonstrate through action that the profit motive, properly employed, constitutes a powerful tool with which to achieve the goals that the best of our young people profess to want." He urged business leaders "to display in our professional lives precisely those qualities which our youthful critics say we lack—open-mindedness, intellectual honesty and commitment to responsible social progress."

One of the first intellectuals to join the ranks of top management was Dr. Thomas Sovereign Gates, senior partner in both J. P. Morgan and Drexel and Company in the 1920s. He was so widely respected as an intellectual that he was elected president of the American Philosophical Society, and in 1930 he resigned his corporate positions to become president of the University of Pennsylvania. Another pioneer was John A. Stevenson, who became president of the Penn Mutual Life Insurance Company in 1939 and was a director of ten other companies, a trustee of five universities, a director of four professional associations and a member or director of eight public institutions or foundations. He had once been a professor of education at the Carnegie Institute of Technology and was the author of several books on teaching. A third intellectual in management was Walter Sherman Gifford, president of the American Telephone & Telegraph Company from 1925 to 1948. He was a trustee of the General Education Board, of the Rockefeller Foundation, of Johns Hopkins

University and of Cooper Union, honorary chancellor of Union College, president of the Harvard Alumni Association, and the author of "Does Business Want Scholars?" More recently, J. Irwin Miller, chairman of the board of Cummins Engine Company, was described in a *Fortune* article as the "Egghead in the Diesel Industry"; he owned and played a Stradivarius, read Greek, and was the author of an article in *Fortune* on "The Dilemma of the Corporation Man." According to John S. Tomajan, president of the Washburn Company, the two guiding influences in his life were Donne and Spenser. Raymond Courtright, president of the New York subsidiary of Bowser, Inc., knew fifty languages, including Egyptian hieroglyphics.

In the arts, Charles Ives was the senior member of one of the largest insurance brokerage firms in the U.S. from 1916 to 1930; it was during his business career that he became an eminent composer. In 1947 he won the Pulitzer Prize (for a piece written decades earlier, while he was active in business). Wallace Stevens, a vice-president of the Hartford Accident and Indemnity Company from 1934 to 1955, was recognized as one of the country's outstanding poets, and was a Pulitzer Prize winner in 1954. Hyman J. Sobiloff, chairman of the board of Biederman Furniture Company and a director of other corporations, published several volumes of poetry.

Among the more famous oligarchs who have shown creative abilities is Du Pont board chairman Crawford H. Greenewalt. An outstanding photographer of birds, he wrote an article for *National Geographic* telling how he went to Brazil to photograph the extraordinary *Loddigesia mirabilis,* the "marvelous hummingbird." In the text of the article Greenewalt wrote:

> While I am no anatomist, I was once an engineer, and I find it remarkable that the muscles controlling the outer tail feathers are powerful enough to cause the extraordinary movement pictured. Ruschi (the Brazilian hummingbird expert) says the male *Loddigesia* uses his tail feathers to make himself especially attrac-

tive to his lady. He has seen the nuptial flight, in which the male hovers in front of the presumably dazzled female, raising one tail feather after the other high above his head, somewhat like a living semaphore. She seems to find these acrobatics irresistible. I should love to photograph the process, but I regret to admit that I have not yet figured out how to induce this romance to take place before the camera. Perhaps in time my wits will prove equal to the challenge. If so, I shall be off again to Brazil, or Peru, or wherever I must go to take the picture.

There is reason to believe that men with such intellectual and creative resources are equal to the challenge of reexamining the basic assumptions of current management policies and formulating the concepts which can transform the corporation from an archaic instrument of self-interest into a constructive force in society. Greenewalt's statements on management subjects did not display the same freshness and originality as his brief comments on South American wildlife, and this has been true of many other intellectuals in management positions. But presumably this is because their entire adult lives have been spent in an environment which encourages stereotyped thinking about what constitutes corporate success. It may be that the current atmosphere of social responsibility in top-management circles will encourage the intellectually minded executives now appearing on the scene to retain their youthful ambition to dedicate their lives to great causes; to free themselves of the standard clichés of the business world; and to apply creative and disciplined thought to the problem of discovering and articulating new purposes for corporate power.

11

The Prospects
for a
New Outlook

WHEN I WAS A BOY THE LAST THING IN THE WORLD I WANTED TO
be was a businessman. In junior high school my ambition was to
be a writer and a painter. In college I wrote an essay expressing
the hope that I wouldn't be caught up in the blind struggle for
money and status characteristic of the world of business, and that
I would be able to retain my ideals and fulfill my ambition to be
an artist or a writer. When I was twenty-three I married and took
a job as a Christmas-card salesman in order to earn a living, and a
year later I went into the public-relations business with a childhood friend, Bill Ruder, in order to earn money and status. As I
write this I am forty-seven; we have built one of the largest public-
relations companies in the world, have made an excellent living
and have become advisers to what I have called the corporate
oligarchy. Have I sacrificed my youthful ideals to achieve this
worldly success, or have I been able to use my creative resources

in my business career for purposes as worthy as those I had when I was young?

All men have a tendency to measure their adult life against some inner scale of values formed out of childhood aspirations. A major function of maturity is to be able to recognize this vague inner feeling for what it is and not mistake it for a message from on high. I do not think now that I cheated myself by not devoting myself exclusively to painting and writing. I suspect I became a businessman because my personality flourished in the job I was doing, and I found a way to achieve some creative satisfactions by working in a corporate environment. But I recognize that, unlike the painters and writers I know today, I cannot define or understand my work in terms that justify an intelligent and passionate dedication. When I try to formulate concrete goals for my corporate life that are overwhelmingly worth working toward, I feel that I am unable to find answers that are truly satisfying.

Have the heads of large corporations also experienced this difficulty? Did they dream when they were young of becoming artists, doctors, scientists or philosophers, and do they now feel there is something missing in their lives because they have become successful businessmen? I believe the answer is yes for many of them. I believe that even when an oligarch achieves another childhood dream and becomes rich, powerful and important in the world, there is something deep within him that is frustrated. He feels that profit and power alone do not satisfy his desire to devote himself to some worthy calling.

Considerable evidence has piled up during the last one hundred and fifty years to support this belief. The businessman has tried repeatedly to find ways to make his corporate life meaningful. Yet he has made painfully slow progress toward the development of an outlook which might enable him eventually to become an integrated human being or a dedicated man.

When he has tried to develop a dynasty, more often than not he has destroyed his sons and their sons in the process. When he has not destroyed them, he has too often imprisoned them in a life for which they were personally unsuited. When he has tried to renounce the dynastic ambition of earlier generations, he has failed to provide his family with a sense of values which would enable his children to fulfill themselves in their own ways.

The oligarch has not even been able to make a continuing impact on the future of his own corporation, and his achievements have not seemed to earn an important place in the history of his time. He has tried to believe that the expansion of corporate power is synonymous with progress, and that the success of his company is a triumph for society as well as for himself. Yet he has continually been attacked as an enemy of progress and a detractor from the true needs of society. He has fought a losing battle against government control and its implication that the public needs protection from his aggressive, irresponsible and often destructive ambitions.

Recently he has tried to achieve self-respect by actively seeking to improve his image, but he has made a ridiculous spectacle of himself whenever he has claimed to be something he is not or worried more about his appearance than about his substance. He has sometimes tried to give credence to his claims by converting a traditional interest in philanthropy into image-oriented public-service projects, and, while he has accomplished some good in these activities, the results are so small that it is foolish to claim that they fulfill the corporation's obligation to society. And when he has tried to become himself a public servant and to use his prestige as a corporate oligarch and his ability as a manager to further public causes, his lack of experience and judgment has made him more of a burden than an asset. When he has tried to think of himself as a leader of men, he has shown himself too often to be a man without vision and without a sense of history, one whose only claim to fame is the money and the status which do not satisfy even himself.

There are signs that some oligarchs are at least coming close to breaking through the profit barrier and making something more of their corporate lives than the mere accumulation of power and wealth. A hundred years ago this would have seemed the remotest of possibilities, but in the last two decades top executives appear to have been subjected to an inexorable pull toward community involvement. Their movement in that direction has been accelerated in the 1960s by outbursts of riots and violence that have awakened the country as a whole to the realities of the urban crisis and the unconscionable deprivation of blacks in a society dominated by whites. Seeking an improved image, expanding the original notion of public service, recognizing that the fate of the corporation depends on the fate of the nation, and developing genuinely creative interests which could help him become articulate, the oligarch is showing unmistakable signs of being ready to change his official position on what he is in business for. Indeed, the corporation has already begun to assume some of the characteristics of a social institution in American life rather than simply an economic instrument for producing wealth.

This change in his behavior has not, however, been accompanied by the necessary reorientation of priorities. Everything he does is still for the good of the company first and for the good of mankind last. The old profit motive as he formulates it in his outmoded ideology has continued to dominate the oligarch's mind.

Recently some corporate oligarchs have become worried that emphasis on profit making in corporate life is causing young people to choose nonbusiness careers. In 1967 a survey commissioned by *Newsweek* in cooperation with the National Industrial Conference Board revealed that only twelve per cent of college students interviewed considered business their first choice as a career. There has been talk in management circles about the education job which needs to be done to make a business career more attractive to thoughtful university students, as if this were the heart of the problem. It is not. The heart of the problem is that sensitive, questioning young Americans identify the desire for corporate profit with the appetite for personal wealth. And no matter how many socially beneficial activities corporations engage in, a young idealist in an affluent society does not want to make the accumulation of riches his primary purpose in life.

2

It is true that in the 1950s, when the corporate oligarch first became seriously concerned about the difficulty of attracting bright college graduates into management careers, young men were having trouble finding any ideal of greatness to which they could enthusiastically dedicate their lives. The corporation was not the only segment of contemporary life that lacked appeal for many Americans.

In 1960 *Life* published a series of essays on "The National Purpose" to force Americans "to re-examine themselves and their aspirations." It was intended to be a call to greatness for whoever would become the nation's next President. The keynote for the series was a statement by Walter Lippmann expressing the mood of the times. "The critical weakness of our society," he wrote, "is that for the time being our people do not have great purposes which they are united in wanting to achieve. The public mood of the country is defensive, to hold on and to conserve, not to push forward and to create. We talk about ourselves these days as if we were a completed society, one which has achieved its purposes, and has no further great business to transact . . ."

The unique contribution made by John F. Kennedy, who won that election campaign, was that for many he supplied precisely what the *Life* series called for, a renewed sense of purpose to which young people could feel profoundly dedicated. And the great tragedy of our time was that his assassination and the assassination of his brother Robert, who five years later seemed on the verge of renewing his great spirit, destroyed the sense of nobility which had been almost miraculously reintroduced into the American personality. For a brief moment America had been uplifted by a leader in "whose radiance," to use Carlyle's phrase, "all souls [could] feel that it is well with them."

But the lack of an inspired national purpose has not prevented the arts or the sciences from arousing the missionary zeal of young men. When James Agee was in high school he wrote about his ambitions to become a writer, "The general verdict is that I can do a lot if I don't give up and write advertisements. . . . I'll croak before I write ads or sell bonds—or do anything except write." And when he was in college he wrote, "I'm from now on committed to writing with a horrible definiteness . . . I'd do anything on earth to become a really great writer." If he had "given up" and become a successful advertising copywriter or, what he probably would have considered worse, a corporate oligarch, what would he have thought of his earlier dream? How does the onetime scientist who has become president of a company producing scientific products (and there are an increasing number of such former scientists among the new oligarchs) feel when his former associates accuse him of wasting his talents by being an executive? How do I feel when a visitor to my office admires my paintings and thinks he is paying me a compliment by asking why I don't "chuck all this business nonsense" and devote my life to art?

Why indeed? This question has haunted businessmen for generations, and it haunts them today. Even oligarchs who do not have special creative interests like painting have thought seriously about this. Having made their fortune, they sometimes wonder why they shouldn't leave their business and devote their energies to some more useful enterprise.

This is particularly true among entrepreneurs who started their own businesses and built them into substantial corporations, men who became captains of industry like those of the nineteenth century and then, as their companies went public or were merged into larger corporations, became twentieth-century oligarchs. Because they could see themselves crossing the threshold of security, they knew they had an opportunity to stop and pick another career if they wanted to. Why not search for the sense of destiny outside their business that they couldn't find within it? One young president I know had made millions before he was forty; I remember his taking me on a tour of his impressive new plant, stopping before a remarkable new piece of machinery he had just installed and saying to me, "What do I want it for? Where am I going? Should I quit, take my money and do something else? The only reason I can find to stay and continue to build the company is to help produce a way of making a living for all the people who work for me. But I have no idea if that makes any sense." Another founder-president, who today is the chief executive officer of a large public company, told me that he gets up in the early hours of the morning after a sleepless night and walks the street wondering what he should do with his life now that he has become successful and has no reason to continue to be a slave to his company. Still another told me that he hates his business; it has just been a way of making money for him; now that he has made millions he sees no reason why he shouldn't quit and do something with his life that would give him real satisfaction.

Such men usually do not quit, but it is not because they have found compelling reasons to stay. The one company president I know who seriously tried to retire in his early forties because he had made enough money to satisfy his needs insisted that he found the regimen of sleeping late, reading, watching television and socializing completely satisfying, but no one believed him, least of all his wife and children. Many others who left their businesses admitted that they became restless and subsequently resumed their management careers to make more money, work harder than ever, build bigger companies. The business world is filled with stories of men who retired in their thirties, after making their first million, and then after a couple of years of traveling or idling plunged back into business as the only way of life they enjoyed. One of the longest periods of retirement was spent by A. J. Cassatt, who retired as first vice-president of the Pennsylvania Railroad at the age of forty-two and for seventeen years devoted himself to horsebreeding. When he was fifty-nine he was called back to assume the presidency of the company. Almost always the return to corporate life is considered a return to sanity by men who find it harder to find meaning in leisure than in work. They return to their desks in the hope that a second go-round will somehow turn up a worthier purpose than the first.

A few who have succeeded in escaping what they consider to be a purposeless corporate career have left business to go into politics, hoping thereby to accomplish something useful in the world. This was a standard pattern for many nineteenth-century businessmen who graduated from their corporate responsibilities and bought their way into the Senate, which until 1913 was nominally appointed by state legislatures but was actually chosen at party caucuses, held behind closed doors, where pecuniary bargains were frequently consummated. Many others won municipal, state or national elective offices. Still others were appointed to administrative posts, where, since the days of Andrew Mellon, it had been thought that "efficiency" and the "business approach" were ideals toward which government should aspire. So popular has this latter trend become in recent years that the highest echelon of the Eisenhower Administration was said to have consisted of "seventeen millionaires and one plumber."

The satisfaction which a few men do get from retirement or from public careers makes it all the harder for the confirmed corporate oligarchs to give an adequate explanation of why they stay in business life longer than is necessary to achieve security. Sometimes an explanation is sought in the part-time public service which attracts many businessmen. But can public-service projects ever succeed in elevating the corporate function above the mere making of money? After all, these are tangential to the essential nature of business. In a sense, public-service activities are little more than an attempt to superimpose an ideal on an activity that heretofore has been essentially lacking in idealism.

Every other Thursday there is a luncheon meeting in an elegant New York club, attended by heads of corporations who enjoy Bible discussions on the theme "Man shall not live by bread alone, but by every word that proceeds out of the mouth of God." One of the top executives who participates regularly in these luncheon meetings recently said, "It reminds me of what the early Christians must have done, coming together for support and strength and fortification in a hostile environment." The present-day hostile environment is presumably the corporation, and the oligarchs who attend these luncheons seem to be trying to counter this hostility not by changing its essential nature, but by periodically retreating from it to nourish their souls.

Can such part-time idealism really help the oligarch to find meaning in his business life? Hardly. It is particularly unlikely for the executive who spends the rest of his time buried in work, and slavish devotion to business is the common pattern of executive behavior. Corporate oligarchs drive themselves so hard they have little time to think of purpose at all. Work itself becomes the purpose of their lives, and, because they are haunted by Max Weber's puritanical ghosts, their very exhaustion makes them feel virtuous. "Thinking men know," Henry Ford once said, "that work is the salvation of the race, morally, physically, socially. Work does more than get us our living; it gets us our life."

The oligarch who may secretly envy those who have retired from business and moved on to more worthy pursuits outwardly scorns them for their retreat from hard work. This has always been so in the business world. Some five hundred years ago Jakob Fugger told an associate who had retired and wanted him to do the same that to stop making money was cowardly; he vowed that he would continue working for money as long as he could. Peter Drucker once noted that executives generally work harder as they grow older, contradicting the notion that success gives more time for leisure. A *Newsweek* survey made in 1952 found some executives who claimed to work as much as one hundred and twelve hours a week, which is sixteen hours a day, seven days a week. One executive I know says he works eighteen hours a day, and he admits that he is like a dope addict who would like to free himself of his compulsion to work but cannot. Not surprisingly, such men are often those who concern themselves least with the search for human values and meaningful goals in their corporations. The deeper questions are buried under their mountain of work.

The contention that the corporate oligarch wants anything more out of life than the practical rewards of hard work has been disputed by many levelheaded and practical-minded judges of executive motivations. They believe that the job of making a living does not have to be an inspired undertaking. It is part of life to have to devote a good part of one's energies to doing work for which society is willing to pay a price, and it is natural that those who are in charge of the system enjoy both the power they wield and the high price their jobs command.

Among the practical rewards of hard work are the goods a corporation produces and the jobs it provides. Some consider the search for other ideals unnecessary and irrelevant. In 1929, when the social aspects of corporate life were just beginning to be explored, James Truslow Adams wrote that "the new American gospel of service" was covering over the "bare facts of business," which are that "the businessman performs a highly useful function in society [by seeing to it] that the public gets its full money's worth." Almost four decades later, profit was replacing production as the chief goal of business. "The modern corporation is not and cannot be expected to be a 'responsible' institution in our society," Andrew Hacker wrote in 1966. "For all the self-congratulatory handouts depicting the large firm as a 'good citizen,' the fact remains that a business enterprise exists purely and simply to make more profits—a large proportion of which it proceeds to pour back into itself." Hacker was confident that if Eli Lilly or Searle and the other drug companies discovered that they could chalk up larger profits by discontinuing the production of vaccines and taking up the manufacture of frozen orange juice instead, they would have no qualms or hesitation about the wisdom of such a step. He concluded:

A corporation, then, cannot be expected to shoulder the aristocratic mantle. No one should be surprised that in the areas of civil rights and civil liberties our large companies have failed to take any significant initiative. The men who preside over them are not philosopher-kings, and no expectation should be held out that they may become so. At best, they can be counted on to give some well-publicized dollars to local community chests and university scholarships. But after those checks are written (and the handing over of them has been photographed) it is time to get back to business.

Thus, if the oligarch needs an ideal, such pragmatic observers believe, it should be profit. They think there is no need to look beyond profits for some other public good which other institutions can perform. This fits in with management's official ideology. An advertisement by Du Pont states that corporate profits serve the investor, the government employee, the union leader, the newspaperman, the mayor, the professor, the consumer, the plant worker, the family and the baby—the last because "rising population demands vigorous economic growth, which in a free society can be powered only by profit incentives." Another advertisement, by the Union Oil Company of California, states that "you simply can't have economic growth or material progress without profits."

But such a point of view leaves the corporate oligarch precisely where he has stood too long, as a man who tries to justify his position of power in terms of the economic benefits he prizes so highly, but who ignores those values to which the rest of the nation gives a higher priority, the health, education and welfare of its citizens.

3

The trouble with all attempts to limit the concern of the corporate oligarch to profit is that they deny him the opportunity to be a creative individual, capable of developing his own vision of human progress and of choosing a course of action which expresses that vision. He is reduced to a cog in the economic wheels of the nation. His job is to make a profit, improve production, create jobs, even exult in his own power; but he is not entitled to behave like a philosopher king or concern himself about how to use his business power wisely.

C. Wright Mills refused to feel sorry for the oligarch: he was the man who had everything. But according to nearly all conventional business theory, he has everything except a frame of reference in which he can work toward the betterment of man.

Why must the oligarch accept this stunted humanity? Is there something about the free-enterprise system which requires its major producer in the economic sphere to be isolated from the higher functions of the community? Why should the oligarch be that rare character in a democratic society who is thought to serve the cause of progress only as he attempts to satisfy his own self-interest? No one expects a doctor to prescribe a remedy which produces profit for him—or anybody else—at the expense of the patient. Nobody expects the lawyer to advise his client to take a course of action which will produce the highest fee rather than that which is in accord with the law. An architect will not win the respect of his peers—or of anyone else—if he designs a building that will produce the greatest income to himself at the expense of the integrity of the design or the usefulness of the building to the occupant. An artist or a scientist is not considered great because he gives a higher priority to making money than to expressing the universal truths he senses in his mind or heart.

In these fields, nobility of purpose is taken for granted. And making money or even achieving worldly success is nearly always taken as a warning signal that important values are being sacrificed. Gertrude Stein once quoted Picasso as saying, "You know, your family, everybody, if you are a genius and unsuccessful, everybody treats you as if you were a genius, but when you come to be successful, when you commence to earn money, when you are really successful, then your family and everybody no longer treats you like a genius, they treat you like a man who has become successful." Roy Lichtenstein once explained that Pop Art in America was invented by young painters who felt that abstract-expressionist painting—which they greatly admired—had been too widely accepted by the public: if they were to paint in the same style and thereby appeal to this ready market, their creativity and originality would be stifled by what was sure to be a premature financial success. The oligarch, who is, after all, also a human being—sometimes an intelligent, sensitive, articulate human being—is just as likely to be stifled, or at least condemned to mediocrity, by catering to the market and by exalting worldly success over what the sages have always considered worthier achievements.

The wrong question was asked by *Fortune* in an article called "Do Corporations Have a Higher Duty Than Profits?" It is man who has the higher duty, and, as Chester I. Barnard pointed out, the corporation is an organization created to accomplish the purposes of man. The corporate oligarch has a responsibility to himself as a human being to be concerned about society.

In other articles, *Fortune* has discovered what happens to oligarchs when they avoid this responsibility. At some point they recognize that they are a success. They have accomplished what they set out to accomplish in life. But their triumph is an empty one. They want to continue to feel a yearning to work toward something greater, but they can't find the incentive, "since the accumulation of money, their habitual yardstick, has lost much of its meaning." They discover that "they have spent a lifetime struggling up the wrong mountain." And if they do persuade themselves to go on toward greater success, working harder and harder toward meaningless goals, their preoccupation with activity becomes "simply the burying of unresolved problems—an insatiable anxiety, not an insatiable appetite for self-expression or achievement."

The oligarch who permits himself to concentrate his energies on such an unfulfilling enterprise is a slave to the system, not its leader. He seeks only "to fulfill the expectation of others," as Eugene E. Jennings put it, "and to live within the established imperatives of the organization." But if he is a man of vision, why cannot he try to make more of the corporation than an instrument of economic growth and avoid being trapped by the notion that building a bigger and more profitable business is the only virtue of which he is capable? Why cannot he, as a leader, make for himself—and perhaps for all those who work and follow him—an opportunity to develop as far as possible, all the important attributes of human nature which can provide enduring satisfactions?

This does not mean that the oligarch should be given the right to usurp the powers of government. It is a premise of democracy that no seat of power which is not responsible directly to the electorate should be permitted to control the destiny of the citizenry. The danger of any attempt by management to shape the social and cultural life of the community is clear. This was demonstrated by the paternalistic corporations of the late nineteenth and early twentieth centuries, such as the Colorado mining companies which produced the tragic Ludlow massacre. The contemporary oligarch cannot deceive himself into believing that what is good for the community will ultimately produce more business for him. Even when a company owns a town, business is only one element in the community. But if it is dangerous for an industrial leader to have too much power over the social and the intellectual as well as the economic lives of people, it is equally reprehensible for him to isolate himself from these interests. For unless the corporate oligarch can conduct himself as a member of the human race, dedicated to the higher values of society, the enormous power he wields must ultimately be taken over by a government which is directly responsible to the electorate. Unless executives develop a sense of mission to use whatever power they gain for the purpose of making a better world, the vitality of the capitalist system will soon vanish. A new form of society better able to inspire leaders with an integrated view of themselves and the community will take its place.

How can the corporate oligarch introduce a sense of purpose

into his business life, where profit must, after all, play a central role, and where there are often conflicts between profit and the higher values of society? How can he broaden what is basically an economic function so that it can be simultaneously aimed at making a better world?

The answer certainly cannot be found simply by using increasing amounts of shareholders' money in philanthropic enterprises that catch the fancy of top management. "The real challenge," said Eli Goldston, president of Eastern Gas and Fuel Associates, in a talk to a graduating class of the Harvard Business School Management Development Program, "is to do good for society while doing well for your business. This takes a little time and effort," he said. "In today's growing national economy, a company really has to be pretty badly managed not to be able to increase its earnings modestly at least each year. . . . If you really want to, you and your companies can pretty much coast together on the growing Gross National Product of America. You can build plants in relatively remote suburban areas inaccessible from the Negro ghetto and manufacture hardware to be propelled into outer space; you can live in a prosperous white suburb; and thereby you can divorce yourself from a chance to help your country in a time of grave crisis and, indeed, from a chance to participate in a rare business venture. Justice Oliver Wendell Holmes, Jr., put the issue accurately when he said, 'Life is action and passion. I think it is required of a man that he should share the action and passion of his time at peril of being judged not to have lived.' "

The writers who scorn any higher purpose for the corporation believe that an executive who tries to develop ideals in his business life will inevitably be forced to acknowledge that profit must take the higher priority. Unless an entirely new frame of reference for corporation decision making can be developed, such an executive will eventually find it necessary to compromise his ideals or delude himself into thinking that expediency is another name for justice.

It is certainly true that a new frame of reference has not been adequately articulated by even the most visionary oligarchs. There has been much fumbling in the shadows to find workable guidelines. But the profit defenders are deceiving themselves by not recognizing the undeniable concern expressed by many oligarchs about the public interest, and their efforts to relate corporate activity to community welfare, as the beginning of a new outlook that is capable of transforming the corporation into a broader institution.

Such a development does not imply the eventual overthrow of the profit system. It may well, however, introduce a new variation of the eighteenth-century notion that the investment function of the corporation can be satisfied with reasonably limited profits. Some excess revenues of the Society for the Establishment of Useful Manufactures would have been obliged by law to be turned over to the state for cultural purposes. The corporation of tomorrow may well adopt the principle that its excess revenues must also be used for worthy purposes, not to improve the corporate image but to realize the determination of corporate leaders to achieve meaningful social benefits for the community. Increased profits will be sought not for the purpose of producing a bonanza for stockholders or building unlimited power for the corporate oligarchy, but for public purposes clearly acknowledged by top management. And, perhaps most importantly, the oligarch will not direct the corporation to engage in any commercial activity, no matter how profitable, that will be inconsistent with the corporation's ultimate public goal. The making of profit will not justify a conflict with public interests, for the serving of those interests will be the object of the profit.

How realistic is it to imagine that this remarkable state of affairs is likely to come to pass? More so than most are willing to admit. A psychologist, David C. McClelland, made an analysis of this high impulse to achievement among corporate oligarchs and concluded that there has been a confusion in the minds of both Marxist and classical economists between the so-called profit motive and the achievement motive. After nearly fifteen years of research into the human motive that appears to be largely responsible for economic growth, he pointed out that the entrepreneurial spirit is likely to be as high among government officials as it is among top corporate executives, and that it can be as high, or higher, among managers of industrial enterprises in Communist countries like Poland and Russia as it is in the United States. In capitalist countries, the keen interest which executives have in profit is "merely a symptom of a strong achievement concern." Executives are no more interested in money for its own sake, McClelland believed, than the government official or the Communist manager. The supposed devotion to profit, therefore, is an illusion that has been confusing corporate thinkers for generations. What the oligarchs have been working for in the name of profit has been the solution of what they consider to be important problems. It is a mistake to believe that their psychological motive is simply to operate the moneymaking machine their predecessors invented.

It is difficult for the oligarch to see himself as he really is, his naked self as it were, beneath his traditional profit-colored uniform. But in the privacy of his own thoughts he has often sensed the truth of what McClelland dared to suggest. "I don't know what kept me going," said Thomas F. Bolack, looking back on his early career as an oil man, "but I figure it was a desire to show up geologists and oil men who ridiculed me, rather than an urge to make money." Henry Ford was a problem solver: when he was a child he liked to repair watches, when he was a young husband and father he set up engines in his kitchen to experiment with them, and when he was a mature man he dreamed of "democratizing the automobile." George M. Bunker, chairman of the board of Martin Marietta, was proud of the boldness, imagination and resourcefulness which had enabled his company to build in record time the largest missile plant in the Western world at a time when the United States suddenly found itself badly outdistanced in the space race.

The ability of these men to accomplish difficult tasks was aided by their skill at handling costly operations in a financially responsible manner, but the earning of profit was a means of facilitating their efforts, not the goal toward which their ambitions were aimed.

4

If the oligarch is to become a leader of society, he must relate his desires for achievement to purposes worth working for, but how is he to decide what really is in the public interest? This has been the stumbling block in the past when oligarchs have insisted, even in the sale of worthless patent medicines, that they were giving the public what it wanted. They have never been reliable judges of what is good for society, particularly when profits or even problem solving are at stake. So long as management is not responsible to an electorate, can there be any real guarantee that public interests will in fact be served?

There can be such a guarantee only if the corporate manager proclaims his dedication to those values most highly respected by other educated men of society, and asks to be judged in terms of how well the corporation enhances those values. Public elections are not required to assure dedication to public interests on the part of university presidents, hospital directors, museum curators. But an accepted code of performance is; and it is the responsibility of a board of trustees to see to it that the public interest is served. The commitments stated by the corporate oligarch and his board of directors are so vague and platitudinous that the public has every reason to be skeptical.

A survey published by the American Management Association in 1958 revealed the uselessness of most company creeds and philosophies. Clark Brothers Company, for instance, stated that it was dedicated to making the company "a better place to work in, a better place to buy from, a better place to sell to, a better place to invest in, and, a better neighbor." Cluett, Peabody and Company, Inc., was determined to "satisfy, to the highest possible degree, the interests of four major groups: our stockholders, our employees, our customers, the public." A statement signed by Harlow H. Curtice of General Motors stated that the company wished to produce "More and Better Things for More People," and that to accomplish this objective, as well as "to assure the continued success of General Motors and to maintain our competitive position," the company would strive to "(1) Put the Right People in the Right Places; (2) Train Everyone for the Job to Be Done; (3) Make the Organization a Coordinated Team; (4) Supply the Right Tools and the Right Conditions; (5) Give Security with Opportunity, Incentive, Recognition; (6) Look Ahead, Plan Ahead . . . for More and Bigger Things."

Some oligarchs have done better. Robert Wood Johnson of Johnson & Johnson once wrote a credo which began: "We believe that our first responsibility is to the doctors, nurses, hospitals, mothers, and all others who use our products. Our products must always be of the highest quality. We must constantly strive to reduce the cost of these products. Our orders must be promptly and accurately filled. Our dealers must make a fair profit."

This still falls short as an inspiring declaration of principles capable of providing a meaningful incentive for a thoughtful executive. But is there more to be said about the mission of producing a Band-Aid, or an automobile, or a bar of soap, or a cigarette, or a die-casting for a vending machine, or a plastic container for a hair shampoo? Is it foolish to imagine that these can fulfill the higher purposes of man? A polio vaccine will save lives and a Horowitz recording will produce profound aesthetic experiences; but the same cannot be said about an aspirin or a bottle of beer. Some of the worst improprieties of the commercial world are the result of making ridiculous claims for the properties of mundane products. Yet there is a certain drama in the most commonplace object. Hairpins from ancient civilizations can evoke feelings of wonder because they say something about the universality of human nature. A corporate executive responsible for making hairpins in our time can, if he has the vision, feel something of the same wonder in his product and can help others see it, too. Indeed, even the great oil, steel and railroad magnates of the nineteenth century who have been so highly criticized as robber barons felt this sense of pride in their industrial accomplishments. Contemporary executives who worry about their corporate images are actually searching for a way to relate their products and their business to vital human experiences. Frederick R. Kappel, chairman of American Telephone & Telegraph, alluded to this search when he said, "Our job in industry is to provide increasing public value—that is, an increasing abundance of commodities, structures, systems and services that minister to human needs and support human aspirations."

Even this, however, is what Henry H. Hunter, a vice-president of the Olin Mathieson Chemical Corporation, has described as a "deceptively simple proposition." Unless the possibility of conflict between corporate profits and public interest is recognized, and the primacy of human values over profits is acknowledged, management's concern about the welfare of society will be an empty piety.

The great corporate leader of tomorrow, if he is to be great, can succeed only if he substitutes value centers for profit centers in his management lexicon. "Profit" and "growth" will still be the language of business as "votes" and "party" are in politics. But profits, like votes, must be taken as a means to accomplish greater ends. The Machiavellian rule that ideals should be conceived only as devices to achieve power must be reversed. Power must be seen as a means of realizing ideals. And the corporate oligarch must become an integrated human being whose personal values and creative ambitions are as important to the fulfillment of his business obligations as to his private aspirations.

When he was chairman of Xerox, Sol Linowitz once said, "You can't separate me as a businessman from me as a human being," and he made it clear that all his personal ideals for the betterment of man must be as operative in his business life as they are in his private life. One felt this spirit throughout the company's operations. The product responsible for the most spectacular big-business success of the 1960s was revolutionary, and it was introduced to the public with great marketing acumen and a record-breaking profit margin. The value of the Xerox stock rose to sixty-six times the initial investment from 1959 to 1966. But one could always sense a presence at Xerox of a management that really cared about its product. When the 813 copier was introduced in 1963, Joseph Wilson, the then president of the company and the man who in the 1950s committed about twice the amount of his family company's earnings to product research, made the following statement:

Think about the exploding mass of information in the laboratories and libraries of the world—and the need to make it available more readily to people, more cheaply, more rapidly. Think of the data erupting from a whole army of computers—and the difficulty of handling them. Think of new technologies like space exploration, creating needs for information at a pace almost incomprehensible . . . Think about the billions of people in the Southern Hemisphere, who are anxious to learn from us how to enrich their lives a bit. . . .

The need for new forms of graphic communications, it seems to us, is as important as any need man has. It is a field that potentially, through innovation, through creative products and services, will serve men well indeed.

People need food, energy and shelter. But they also need to communicate with each other, else much work is wasted. We must know about the ideas of the past. We need to exchange ideas with people of the present. We want to leave values for people to come.

We do not communicate very well by touching, or tasting, or smelling—a little better by hearing, perhaps, but usually the sense of sight is the one through which comprehension comes.

The point is that things have to be written to be known. This is the field of Xerox.

The subtle, but vital, interrelationship between a sensitivity to the social consequences of a product and the extracurricular activities of the corporation was manifested six months later when Xerox announced at its annual stockholders' meeting that it would spend $4 million for a special television series on the United Nations in which there would be no product commercials. Some shareholders objected. Then the popular entertainer Mitch Miller, who, as an owner of five thousand shares, was in the audience, grabbed a microphone and said, "All we see on television these days is detectives gouging people in the gut, idiotic Westerns and mysteries, and fathers being made fools of. I say to get the U. N. on television for Xerox is one helluva buy!" The audience applauded and the stockholder controversy was over. Subsequently the company received almost fifteen thousand letters objecting to the U.N. broadcasts, but management refused to be intimidated and the series appeared on the American Broadcasting Company network in 1965. Later Joseph Wilson told John Brooks of *The New Yorker* that "the attacks only served to call attention to the very point we were trying to make—that world cooperation is our business because without it there would be no world and therefore no business." Then, speculating as to whether the campaign was good business or good citizenship, he said that so far the company had not "found a conflict between what we consider our responsibility and good business. . . . [We] may have to stand in the firing line yet. . . . You can't honestly predict what you'd do in a case like that. I *think* I know what we'd do."

There are those who are unimpressed by Joseph Wilson's talk about good citizenship while he holds company stock worth many millions of dollars. I think they are wrong. Wilson showed in the 1950s, when the Xerox process was being developed, that he was a man who would risk financial security for something he believed in. One feels that success would not prevent him from doing so again. He doesn't have to make the sacrifice in order to prove that he would do so if put to the test, any more than a politician must lose an election campaign in order to prove that he is a man of principle who has the courage to support unpopular positions. But if an elected official isn't prepared to do so he isn't worthy of public trust. Neither is the corporate oligarch.

I believe that many top executives of major corporations are groping for a way to make such a commitment to principle which stockholders, employees and customers would respect. The few who have succeeded in doing so are men of vision who have made the business of business an inspiring cause. When the publisher Philip Graham died, Alfred Frankfurter wrote this in an *Art News* editorial:

> . . . nobody who knew him would ever say that economic success alone had been his primary objective. His ideals, one came to know in working around him, were of the kind formed by men as the result of profound studies in the law from which they emerge not merely as lawyers, but as jurists. Philip Graham's profoundly and courageously expressed convictions about justice on a world as well as local scale was the basic quality of the man as it emerged out of the heat of mutual working contacts. When the undersigned asked him why he wanted to purchase *Art News* and the corporation owning it, Philip Graham replied: "Because I believe the Washington Post Company ought to own and publish the best art magazine in America."

It is no doubt simpler for an executive whose company produces a "glamour" product to be eloquent about his commitment to quality than it is for other corporate oligarchs. But it is foolish to imagine that the establishment of a meaningful goal is restricted in any way by the nature of one's product. The structure of most large corporations today encompasses the production and distribution of a great variety of products and services. The search for purpose ultimately must take place within the mind and character of the corporate oligarch, not in the mechanics of his business.

How can one conduct such a search, how can one articulate the fruits of discovery, if there are any, how can one apply a carefully formulated ideal to business practices, how can one test out the validity of one's ideal by subjecting company policies to public scrutiny? I know of no one who has found a simple prescription. Every day, management responsibilities require the top executive to keep track of the financial aspects of his company. This may not be the favorite part of his job, but he enjoys seeing the numbers come out right and worries when they don't. He is conscious of the implications of his growth to his own ego satisfaction, to his pocketbook, to his family, to his status and possibly to his children's careers. He wonders if he will ever reach the stage where he will be able to concentrate on his work without asking, What's in it for me? Much of his conversations with others in his company, therefore, revolves around what they are getting out of their jobs in terms of ego satisfaction and monetary reward rather than as human beings concerned about doing something useful in society. He asks himself, Is this the way to find a profound goal in one's work? He may spend time trying to define the important functions which he thinks his business can perform in society. But this often seems to be an extracurricular pastime rather than an integral part of the everyday conduct of his business. Periodically he and his associates may make an effort to speak out in public about those things they do of which they are most proud as human beings—the philanthropy, the public-service promotions, the projects they undertake to help solve community problems. He may feel that much of this improves his corporate image and adds status to his company's position in society; but even this consideration seems to take second place to that which contributes directly to the company's profit. He wonders, Is it possible I will ever be able to reverse the forces which make the causes of humanity and my own conscience subordinate to the balance sheet?

This is the struggle in which the corporate oligarch is engaged. It is an effort with which I, along with a vast number of American executives, strongly identify, and which I hope will in time help me arrive at a new point of view toward my business career. The absence of guidelines makes the struggle extraordinarily difficult.

But it does not mean that an answer cannot and will not be found. Of this I am sure: if the corporate oligarch does not, in the years ahead, create a new sense of purpose in his business, he will not be able to commit the full resources of his organization to the betterment of man. If, on the other hand, he realizes the promise shown by a few pioneers, he will succeed one day in transforming the corporation into a vital public institution worthy of the dedicated efforts of the nation's ablest citizens. No leader of men could ask for a greater opportunity.

Index

Index

302

Index

Index

Noblesse oblige, 95–96
North Carolina, 90
Northern Securities Company, 163
Northern Pacific Railroad, 37
Northwestern University (Evanston, Ill.), 58
Norton Company, 99–100
Nunlist, Frank J., 134–35

Octopus, The (Norris), 192
Ogden Corporation, 63
Oil Industry Information Committee report, 194–96
Oligarchy, defined, 22–24
Olin Mathieson Chemical Corporation, 229, 295
Opinion Research Corporation, 199, 205, 209
"Opportunity Line" (television program), 236–37
Organizational outlook, 15–16
    new, see Corporate purpose
Owen, Robert, 216
Owner-managers, 111–12
Ownership (shareholders, stockholders), 23–24, 142, 268, 291, 294, 297
    of colonial corporations, 27, 30
    of conglomerates, 149–50, 152–153
    in corporate hierarchy, 16
    corporate ideology of, 137–38, 144–46
    executive, 19, 74–75, 79
    executive responsibility toward, 45–47, 52–53, 58–59, 62–63, 247
    family, 120
    by foundations, 242
    government, 50
    management vs., 13–14
    public, 23, 110–13, 145–46
    of railroads, 36–37
    responds to corporate scandal, 202
    by trust companies, 39–40, 41–42
"Ownership complex," 138

Packers, the Private Car Lines and the People, The (Armour), 265
Paepke, Walter P., 232

Paine, Thomas, 29, 188
Palm, C. Harry, 173
Palmer, Potter, 67
Panic of 1873, 37, 164
Parker, Theodore, 264
Parker Pen Company, 228
Parsons College (Fairfield, Iowa), 106
Partners in Plunder, 165
Patent Medicine Association, 170–171
Paterson, N. J., 30
Patman, Wright, 242
Patterson, John H., 218, 227
Patterson, Tom, 209
Pemberton, Israel, 220
"Penfriend" program, 228
Penn, William, 30
Penney, J. C., 217, 257
Pennsylvania, 82, 204, 207, 219, 236–37
    state constitution of, 90
Pennsylvania Railroad, 38, 160, 282
Perkins, Charles Elliott, 70
Philadelphia, 219, 236
Philadelphia General Advertiser, 157
Philanthropy, 107, 145, 218–27, 233, 255, 278, 299
    corporate, 223–27, 241
    as outlet for personal wealth, 73, 84, 219–21
Philip Morris, Inc., 117, 187, 231
Phillippe, Gerald L., 235
Picasso, Pablo, 287–88
Pittsburgh, 82, 207, 237
Plato, 23
Poland, 292
Political extremism, 203–4, 241–42
Politics, 15, 50, 271, 293, 295, 297–298
    of capitalism, 13
    early corporate influence on, 32, 34, 38, 42
    international, 99–100
    political action, 161–62
    See also Government; Government service
Poor Richard's Almanac (Franklin), 70, 131–32
Pop Art, 288
Populist movement (1890s), 164

Index

Stevens and Company, Inc., J. P., 141
Stevenson, Adlai E., 209
Stevenson, John A., 273
Stigler, George J., 126
Stillman, James, 40
Stockholders, *see* Investment; Ownership
"Stop Worrying About Your Image" (Finn), 210
Store image, 199–200
Storm King Mountain plant, 168
Storrow, James J., 43
"Story of a Great Monopoly, The" (Lloyd), 158
Super Market Institute, 199–200
Supreme Court of Michigan, 176
Supreme Court rulings, 234
    antitrust, 40
    on integration, 219
Swearingen, John E., 75
Swedish West India Company, 28
Swope, Gerard, 200

Taj Mahal (Agra, India), 66
Taplinger Associates, Inc., Robert S., 209–10
Tarbell, Ida M., 68, 159
Taubman, Howard, 243
Taussig, F. W., 120
Taylor, Frederick Winslow, 16
Technocracy, 15
Teledyne, 148
"Telemobility" (essay), 270
"Television and the World of Politics" (Kintner), 266
Tender offers, 152
Texaco, Inc., 201, 230
Texas School Book Depository (Dallas), 204
Textile Products Identification Act of 1958, 166
Textron, 147, 148
Theory of the Leisure Class, The (Veblen), 81
Think (house organ), 269
Thomas, E. J., 105
Thomson, J. Edgar, 38
Thorndike, Israel, 29
Time (magazine), 116–17, 230
Tocqueville, Alexis de, 31, 254

Tomajan, John S., 274
Top management, 17–18, 271–72
    community involvement of, 233–236
    contribution of, 22
    definition of, 20–21
    position of, 15, 17
    "visibility" of, 262–63
Torch Drive (1966), 224
Tour Through My Library and Other Papers, A (Comegys), 255
Townsend, Lynn A., 110, 235
Trade associations, 169–71
Trademarks, registered, 199
Trans World Airlines, 76
Transportation Acts (1920, 1940, 1958), 165
Transportation Center of Northwestern University, 58
Travelers Insurance Company, 254
Travelers Record, The (company record), 254
Triumphant Democracy (Carnegie), 70
Trollope, Anthony, 31
Trusts, 39–40, 41–42, 163
    family, 83–84
    management, 79
    philanthropic, 219, 223
    See also Antitrust measures
"Truth in Lending" act (1968), 166
"Truth in Packaging" act (1966), 166
Tugwell, Rexford G., 164–65
"Tycoon Is Dead, The" (article), 43

Union Carbide Corporation, 142
Union Oil Company of California, 286
Union Pacific Railroad, 37, 255
Union Pacific Railroad Act (1862), 36
Union Wharf Company (New Haven), 30
United Foundation of Metropolitan Detroit, 235
United Fund, 235, 241
United Nations, 297
United States Steel Corporation, 82, 105, 199, 261

About the Author

David Finn is Chairman of the Board and a co-founder of Ruder & Finn, Inc., which has grown since its beginning in 1948 to be one of the largest public relations firms in the world. It has offices in New York, London, Paris, Milan, Jerusalem, Toronto, and major cities of the United States.

Mr. Finn is also Chairman of the Board of the Jewish Museum, Treasurer of the MacDowell Colony, a trustee of the Jewish Theological Seminary of America. He is a painter and sculptor whose work has been shown in several one-man exhibitions. He lives with his wife and four children in New Rochelle, New York.